DISASTER
ON THE DEE

Robert Stephenson's Nemesis of 1847

DISASTER ON THE DEE

Robert Stephenson's Nemesis of 1847

PETER R. LEWIS

TEMPUS

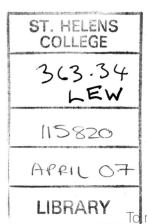
To my father, Rhys Thomas Lewis, in his 103rd year.

First published 2007

Tempus Publishing Limited
The Mill, Brimscombe Port,
Stroud, Gloucestershire, GL5 2QG
www.tempus-publishing.com

British Library Cataloguing in Publication Data.
A catalogue record for this book is available from the British Library.

ISBN 978 0 7524 4266 2

Typesetting and origination by Tempus Publishing Limited
Printed in Great Britain

Contents

Acknowledgements

First and foremost, I would like to thank my students on the post-graduate course, *Forensic Engineering*, for listening to my ideas during several lectures on the topic at weekend schools for the Open University. They provided a strong stimulus to persevere with this book. The author would also like to thank his many colleagues in the Materials Engineering Department at the Open University, for the interesting discussions and support they have provided, especially Colin Gagg, who co-authored a paper on the Dee bridge we published in *Interdisciplinary Science Reviews* (see Bibliography). Both he and Rehana Malik kindly provided photographs of the Stephenson bridge at Wolverton, and the cast-iron trough at Calverton. Colin also performed the polaroscopy mentioned in Chapter 6, and commented on various drafts of this book. Other colleagues expressed interest and comment, including Ken Reynolds, Ian Norman, Gordon Imlach, Richard Hearne, Dr Salih Gungor and Dr Martin Rist, Roger Dobson, Clive Fetter, Dr Mike Fitzpatrick, Mark Endean, Stan Hiller and Debbie Derbyshire. Dr Mike Edwards of Cranfield Unversity (Department of Materials and Medical Products) and Dr Sarah Hainsworth of the Mechanical Engineering Department at Leicester University all performed a similar role. Professor Rod Smith of Imperial College Department of Mechanical Engineering (Railway Studies), and Dr DRH Jones, editor of *Engineering Failure Analysis*, the primary and pre-eminent journal for the study of failure of engineered products, stimulated my interest in the subject. I have had many discussions with Professor Henry Petroski (Civil Engineering, Duke University) and John Rapley, author of *The Britannia and other Tubular Bridges* (Tempus 2003) on the Dee disaster, and thank them for their constructive criticism. He also supplied many detailed engineering drawings of the bridge, and several papers on the topic. While not always agreeing, Keith Horne played a similar role. I have liaised extensively with Bob Burt of Lockheed Martin (Structural Integrity Group), especially in his building a finite element model of the Dee bridge, and hope he continues this very worthwhile project.

My thanks are extended to the Institution of Structural Engineers, particularly Lawrence Hurst for inviting me to give a lecture to the History Study Group on the Tay bridge disaster in December 2003, after which there followed a vigorous discussion on the causes of both the Tay and Dee accidents. I was treated to an excellent meal which continued the discussion, one member identifying the cavetto moulding on the Dee girder. The Open University Library was very helpful in accessing the Parliamentary Archive, held on microfiche, and now available online. The files are not always of the highest quality, however, and help was needed in manipulating the images to achieve the best possible reproduction. The archivist and librarian of the Institution of Civil Engineers supplied excellent copies of original reports of the Dee disaster. Chester County Record Office kindly supplied copies of contemporary prints, and *The Railway Magazine* gave permission to use photographic copies of the Norwood bridge accident. The webmaster of the Warwickshire Railways archive kindly gave permission to use the pictures of the Wooton bridge failure, having been unable to locate the originals. I would like to thank Wikipedia and the Railways archive for accepting several submissions regarding historic failures, not least for their establishment of a permanent archive of important events in the history of engineering, open to all to research and inspect. The Ironbridge Gorge Trust Library kindly supplied detailed papers of the analysis of the Ironbridge fractures.

Last, but by no means least, I would like to thank my father and children, my brother, John Lewis, and his extended family, for their interest in the project, and tolerance of my frequent absences on photographic expeditions.

Dr Peter R. Lewis
Dept of Materials Engineering
Faculty of Technology
The Open University
Walton Hall
MILTON KEYNES MK7 6AA
p.r.lewis@open.ac.uk

Foreword

Most people are surprised to learn that we kill as many on our roads in the UK in a single year as the total number of passengers killed throughout the long history of our railways. Despite this statistically small mortality rate, the huge volume of existing literature concerning railway accidents is an indication of the great interest and fascination we have with disasters on our railways. This book is the most interesting and useful addition to this extensive library.

The collapse of the Dee bridge at Chester in 1847, around which much of this book is centered, is not, to the casual layman, one of the best known accidents in railway history; perhaps because the death toll was relatively small compared with, for example, the lamentable number killed by the much later collapse of the Tay bridge in 1879. (The Tay disaster is described in the author's earlier book, *Beautiful Railway Bridge of the Silvery Tay*, 2004.) However, the aftermath of the failure was very significant. As is explained in this book, it nearly led to the downfall of the famous engineer, Robert Stephenson. Indeed, he was somewhat fortunate to escape with little more than mild censure. It led to a Royal Commission on the use of iron in railway structures, the report of which is a key source of our knowledge of the state of engineering at that time. Experiments on a heroic scale elucidated some empirical facts about the fatigue of large structural members made from iron and lay the foundations of many of the existing testing techniques for the measurement of fatigue resistance. I have always marveled at the reliance on practical, empirical and qualitative knowledge over quantitative theory of our early railway engineers. This state of affairs has to a certain extent continued up to the present and is one of the reasons for the technically weak performance of our railways in comparison to developments elsewhere. This theme is perhaps one which may be worthy of development in the future.

Peter Lewis has done us a great service by unearthing and reinterpreting the contemporary reports of these early railway accidents. A theme which clearly emerges is the pervasive influence of fatigue on critical components. It is, therefore, perhaps surprising that during the last few years accidents at Hatfield (broken rail), Sandy (fractured wheel), Eschede (fatigued wheel rim) and Southall junction (fractured fish-plate) have all been caused by fatigue. It is clear that just because the problem has been studied for a long period of time, it does not absolve new generations from having to re-learn the hard lessons of the past. This is one of the most valuable aspects of the present study. There is much more, however. No reader will be failed to be moved by the age-old themes of human weakness, the interplay of cost, safety and the desire to progress new technology. It is also true that these same themes reoccur in our deliberations of the railway of today.

Roderick A Smith
Imperial College London, 17 December 2006

Preface

When the bridge over the river Dee collapsed in 1847, the public were scandalised. Engineers in Britain were leading a revolution in mass transportation, and yet they were fallible. The public were not acclimatised to mass casualties from the new technology of the railways. They might be used to mass killings in riots, as had occurred regularly in the 1820s and 30s, but the railways offered something different. They offered a route out of poverty or enslavement to the land, the lot of so many of the rural population. The agricultural labourer could travel to the new industrial towns, perhaps for a better life working in a factory. They also offered the chance of travel to meet relations, or friends; to see, probably for the first time, surrounding countryside and townscapes from an angle never seen before by anyone. The railways gave hope. Much more hope than the canals had delivered – they were primarily for transporting goods, not people.

There had been terrible accidents on the railways not long before: everyone had heard of the miserable death of Mr Huskisson, the reforming MP for Liverpool, who was crushed on the opening day of the Liverpool & Manchester Railway. But who had heard of Versailles in 1842, when over fifty had died by fire, locked in their carriages after the locomotive lost an axle? On the other hand, many knew about Sonning, in 1841, when seven workmen were crushed in a collision with a landslip on the GWR. Although the 'carriages' were simply open goods wagons with planks for seats, the railways themselves seemed blameless.

But the fall of the Dee bridge was different. It was one of the first major river crossings on the Chester & Holyhead Railway, and it was shorter than the river Conwy or the Menai Straits. So it seemed an easy gap for Robert Stephenson to bridge. He used a method he had developed over the years, but this would be the longest for this particular design. He used cast-iron girders laid straight over the space, with the track laid on wood between the girders. But it suddenly fell only a few months after being opened, when a passenger train was crossing. The great engineer had seemed invincible, and had been lauded for his railway linking London to Birmingham. He was friends with many other famous engineers of the day, Brunel, Locke, Vignoles, and entrepreneurs like George Hudson (who had nominated him for the seat of Whitby in Yorkshire). He could argue with authority and nous when railway bills came to Parliament, unlike his father, who had difficulty in responding to artful questions by clever lawyers.

And the Chester Railway was an important link with Ireland: it offered hope to the long-suffering Irish, people who were suffering a famine like no other in their history. The link offered the chance of food convoys, comfort and assistance from the many benevolent aristocrats in England. On the other hand, it could also allow more rapid transport of British troops to quell the frequent riots stimulated by the potato blight, and their yearning for independence from the mainland.

This then, is the story of that accident, as told by the eye witnesses at the subsequent inquest, and by the experts called to give their opinion as to why it fell. It is also the story of the rise of the new railway inspectorate, military engineers who investigated accidents fearlessly, and were resistant to outside interference. They were still learning on the job about the new technology, pointing out the divergences of practice between the different railway companies, and encouraging the application of safer methods of working the system. They would have much to do as the country developed the system to form a national network, with some problems proving stubbornly intractable. Boiler explosions, axle and wheel breaks were common then, and bridge failures were to continue, especially from the widespread use of the treacherous cast iron used in so many girder bridges. For cast iron lay at the very heart of the industrial revolution which had been pioneered in Britain. It had been the first synthetic mass-produced material, won using the country's rich coal resources, and was applied to many different jobs as manufacturers searched for better ways of making things. It was used extensively in buildings, to support floors, create balconies, balustrades and fences, so easy was it to cast the fluid metal to shape. Bridges and aqueducts seemed to be an excellent way to use the metal to best effect, replacing the increasingly scarce resource of timber. And it reached an apogee at the Crystal Palace, the vast structure created to house the Great Exhibition of 1851.

However, the Dee bridge accident had far-reaching effects on all these new uses, and engineers would be more careful after its properties had been more thoroughly explored. The accident led to a Royal Commission on its use, specifically for its application in railway bridges, but ultimately for its use in any seriously loaded structure. The experiments they designed for the Commission would also change engineering practice, forcing engineers to test prototypes and models much more rigorously than had been the case till that point in time. This then, is the story of how cast iron came to be the new material of the industrial revolution, and why its use suddenly became questioned when a bridge of simple design fell, and what happened afterwards. Cast iron continued to cause problems for many years, and its untutored use ultimately led to the worst railway disaster ever, the fall of the Tay bridge in 1879, when over seventy-five souls were lost when another new bridge, the marvel of its time, collapsed in a storm.

1

Bridging the Gap

Closure is comforting in every sense of the word. A bridge represents closure of a physical gap in a line of communication, the crossing of a valley, gorge or chasm. Metaphorically, use of the word is very wide, but it is the physical bridge which comes to mind first, and the bridge has a long and interesting history. For bridges link communities together and increase interaction between people, usually to the benefit of all. Bridge construction makes best use of whatever materials are available, and it is during the industrial revolution in Britain that many materials were developed into new forms, and came to be used in bridges. Cast iron became an alternative new material for structures.

The iconic example is the Ironbridge at Coalbrookdale in Shropshire, England *(1.1)*. Its construction represents a landmark in the industrial revolution, when Britain led the world in creating new products through design and innovation. The Ironbridge crosses the river Severn at a point where the banks are high and steep, linking two industrial communities on either side. It was built in 1779 by a group of local ironmasters and businessmen from cast iron, the production of which had recently been increased by a blast furnace nearby *(1.2)*.

Its construction came at a time of upheaval across Europe and America; the French Revolution and the American War of Independence were both fresh in the memory and were destined to change the world forever. And the construction of the bridge marked another step in the revolution of the industrial manufacture of goods, a revolution led by Britain.

Cast Iron

Cast iron was a well-known form of iron and had been used in firebacks and other heat-resistant products for many centuries. It had become an important material for weaponry in the form of cannons, as well as cannon balls. With the increased importance of the Royal Navy, from Henry VIII onwards, more cast iron was required than could be met by traditional sources like the wooded areas of the Forest of Dean and the Sussex Weald, where charcoal had been made from wood burnt slowly in a restricted supply of air (by heaping a stack of logs, igniting and covering with earth). The charcoal, a pure form of carbon, was then smelted in small furnaces with local iron ore to produce the cast iron needed.

There were many problems with this form of manufacture. Not least was the kind of iron ore used, relatively low in its iron content and containing many impurities, some of which found their way into the final product. The problem of impurities was to last a very long time, and was only really tackled and solved towards the end of the Victorian period when better analytical tools and methods of manufacture became available.

But the whole process was very slow since the manufacture of charcoal was the rate-limiting step. There was a longer-term restriction in the supply of trees to provide the timber: hardwoods are slow-growing and good timber was much in demand for structural purposes, such as building, and those ever larger ships of the Navy (as well as commercial shipping). Hardwood was the universal material for most tools, and was of course also widely used as fuel. Such small-scale manufacture could not meet the voracious demands of an expanding economy in the eighteenth century. And there was no way new forests could be created immediately to provide the extra resources. To realise the scale of the crisis one only has to look at a map of the country (then or now), and appreciate that Britain is one of the least forested countries in Europe.

Only one potential solution could be conceived. Coal had been mined on a small scale in coalfields in the Midlands and the North for many years to supply local needs, especially for heating and cooking. Some of these coalfields were extensive, especially those in Northumberland and Durham, South Wales and Scotland, but others were limited in size, such as that at Coalbrookdale. However, it was there that Abraham Darby I invented a way of smelting local iron ore with a new form of coal: coke. There are few kinds of coal which will yield a porous yet strong fuel when heated in the absence of air, but the local coal fulfilled that role, and it was to be a turning point in finding an alternative to charcoal. The point is this: the coke must be strong enough to support the burden of iron ore at the base of the blast furnace, especially if the blast furnace is large and the burden correspondingly heavy. The coke was made just like the charcoal before it: by piling into heaps and restricting the supply of air. The sulphurous and noxious gases given off must have made local life unpleasant, giving rise to the term 'bedlam' after one of the local sites used for such production.

He built his original furnace at Coalbrookdale in 1707, using the foundations of an earlier furnace, and used the iron for casting into pots and pans, firebacks and other hardware for hearths. The range of products would widen as the years went by, and as people developed

Opposite: (1.1)
The Ironbridge at
Coalbrookdale.

Right: (1.2)
The blast furnace at
Coalbrookdale.

new applications. The remains of the 'Old Furnace' are shown in *(1.2)*, with successive enlargements by the iron beams built into the structure. The final phase shown here is 1777. The blocked hole below is where the pig iron was tapped, and run via the channel in the floor into the mould. Simple 'pigs' would be the staple product, although shaped castings could be made. The burden would consist of a mixture of coke, limestone and iron ore, all of which were available locally. The limestone is needed to combine with impurites in the mixture such as silica sand, and so form a slag. The air needed to oxidise the coke in the burden of the furnace was provided via holes part-way up the furnace, and would be pressurised by bellows to increase the heat and raise it enough to start the reduction reactions. The tap could have been used for casting some of the members required for the new bridge, although the manufacturing phase probably involved other furnaces in the industrial complex.

Bridge Materials

It was his grandson, Abraham Darby III, who was the owner by 1777, and he was a prime mover in building the new bridge. A local architect, Thomas Pritchard, who had some knowledge of the properties of cast iron, designed the structure. The main problem with cast iron is its brittleness when pulled apart or bent. In other words, it behaves like glass when bent or tensioned. Unlike wrought iron or steel, it cannot absorb much energy when tensioned, and will not yield without breaking. It is strong, however, when loaded in compression. Both steel and wrought iron will yield to high tension loads without breaking into pieces, which is why they are such valuable structural materials. But neither were available at the time in the quantity needed for such a large bridge as that planned in Coalbrookdale, with a projected length of 100ft from bank to bank.

But Pritchard would have been aware that cast iron is very strong when compressed, so the structure was designed to put every member into compression, just like a conventional masonry bridge (of which he had built a number locally). The arch is the structural element which puts the constituent parts into compression, for stone or brick is also weak in tension.

A cast-iron bridge would have to be built as an arch, but could be made much lighter because its compressive strength is so much greater than masonry. The parts could also be made much larger thanks to casting methods, which allowed liquid metal to flow into a sand mould with ease. Stone can be cut into large blocks (think of the large blocks for the Great Pyramid), but it is a slow and labour-intensive activity. Bricks are inherently small structural units, so can be handled easily, but again demand many hours of labour for their use in construction.

Bridge Design

So Pritchard would have developed the idea of using long curved beams cast in one piece, but which could be easily assembled together to make a much larger framework, a single arch. This problem would be solved using carpentry methods, such as dovetails and slotted joints. Several such arches would be needed to create a roadway of sufficient width. Remembering the problem of its weakness in tension (or bending, which puts the lower side in tension), he would also have been aware of the need to support those long thin beams laterally. That needed straight members to be fitted between the arches at regular points, and connected together in the same way with 'woodwork' joints. The final designs of every component part must have been drawn up for the patternmaker to create the wooden replica. They would be needed for casting the final parts. Such patterns would also have been useful in checking that the parts would fit together correctly by erecting a wooden mock-up of the final structure. Whether this was done or not is not known from contemporary records, but it is the most likely way in which a designer would have checked his paper ideas. Manhandling wooden facsimiles is much easier than their cast-iron copies. In fact, Pritchard made at least one model of the bridge at a scale of 1/24, which survives to this day in the National Museum of Scotland. However, that model may well have been for display rather than use. Another model was probably used to see how the many components fitted together, to explore the best way to put the parts together, and judge the final shape. Model making, then and now, is part-and-parcel of the way architects work. And it would not necessarily be very small scale, but maybe 1/10, so the model would be substantial and large. They would also serve another purpose: to show the project's many shareholders the progress that had been made at various stages.

    Pritchard and Darby will also have been aware that models are one thing, but the real thing is something quite different. Cast iron is nearly *eight times* heavier than wood (volume for volume), so manhandling cast-iron parts would involve considerable effort. But presumably their experience of manipulating models gave them the answer to how to assemble the final parts after casting. What tests were done to ensure that the parts would support expected loads; and if done at all or even contemplated, remains unknown. If casting was expensive, then deliberately loading a beam only to break it would be an extra cost to bear. And in any case, what would it show? Structural design then was still a matter of empiricism, with little or no knowledge of theory to guide the designer. If a component survived the loads imposed upon it, then it was successful and more could be made. They had cast girders before, as witnessed by the small girders built into and supporting the Old Furnace *(1.2)*, although these members will not have been as highly loaded as free girders in a bridge. On the other hand they were loaded by bricks above, and some of that load was supported by the beam, albeit spread to the layer of bricks below.

Casting to Shape

Only when there was a clear way of bringing the parts together across the river would the go-ahead be given to start the casting. The amount of iron needed would be known fairly precisely from the drawings (by calculation) and confirmed by the models (by measurement). The weight of iron is given in contemporary documents as 378 tons 15 cwt, cast into more than 800 different items, although of only twelve basic types. Now, the output of blast furnaces of the type shown in *(1.2)* was only about 20 tons per week, with an individual tap of about 2 tons, so not only will the whole manufacturing period have been rather slow, but some of the larger items must have needed several taps to complete. It would lower the quality of any large casting, such as the main ribs, which weighed 5 tons 5 cwt, and were 70ft long. The first tap would solidify before the next iron could be added, a problem which could produce cracks in the original part, and a very weak interface between the two layers of iron.

Alternatively, a different type of furnace, an air furnace, may have been used instead. It would have produced a greater quantity of molten metal, not by reduction of the iron ore, but by re-melting iron that had already been made. As long as the capacity was greater than about 6 tons, then a large rib could be made in one operation (some extra allowance is needed for spillage and other losses). It is likely that the various parts were cast into open moulds created in the sand by the furnace, as recorded by contemporary documents.

Each wooden pattern would be laid in loose casting sand, and the sand tamped into the outer surface of the wood so as to reproduce the exact design required. The wooden pattern would then be removed, taking care that all of the sand pattern was unaffected. So, on one part of the casting, the surface would be free, the metal forming a level plane where it finally came to rest. No doubt this required the foundryman to ensure that only the exact amount of molten iron was allowed to flow into the mould. An ever-present problem with cast iron is the formation of blowholes, usually by gases producing bubbles which are frozen into the structure when the metal solidifies. Bubbles would naturally tend to rise to the surface, so the upper free surface was often far from smooth, but was level. The gases arise from various sources, at least one being carbon oxidising to carbon dioxide. Cast iron contains about 4 per cent carbon, and will oxidise readily with any oxygen it contacts (especially at a free surface). Water present in the casting sand will instantly vapourise if any touches the molten metal, which would be about 1,600°C.

But that is not the end of a casting process. Such structures as the ribs will have needed extra care just for the sheer size of the component, the larger the size, the greater the chance of making a mistake, or the sand collapsing at a point in the mould. How many were rejected and recycled is not known, but they will have added to the complexity of the job. On the other hand, observation of the final structure *(1.1)* shows many of the components exhibiting serious defects.

A foundry has reconstructed the ribs experimentally and revealed the problems in making large castings. Cooling rates, for example, will have varied through the length, creating shrinkage cavities. The optimum pouring point will have been at the centre, so minimising the distance liquid would travel before reaching the end of the mould. Being very fluid, waves would run along the exposed upper surface, requiring slow pouring to minimise defects the waves could produce, such as erosion of the mould sides.

The purity of the iron would also have been important in quality control. Slag and other deleterious impurities would float to the top, where they could be skimmed off. But other inclusions might fail to float before solidification, and remain hidden within the bulk metal. Like blowholes, they represent defects which weaken the final structure. Blowholes represent the most serious kind of defect, because when the component is stressed in the final structure, the stress will be greater there than elsewhere. The problem of stress raisers is a problem which remains with cast-iron products (and most other cast or moulded products) to this day. Such hidden defects created many problems in later cast iron structures, such as buildings and bridges, causing sudden and mysterious failures. Many cast-iron components remain in historic structures, often hidden from view (such as cast-iron girders supporting floors).

Erection of Parts

Wooden patterns may have been used as a full-scale model to establish the best way of assembling the parts. They will certainly have been much lighter than the castings, and were a good way of exploring component manipulation over the river. It will, of course, have been much easier on dry land first, and will have given the erectors some experience of the problems of moving large parts like the ribs.

It was previously thought that large wooden towers were built either side of the river to erect the cast-iron parts in the summer of 1779. A much simpler route was probably chosen, the clue to which was shown in a contemporary watercolour discovered in Sweden in 1997 by a Finnish engineer. Two large vertical poles were raised each side of the river, and stabilised by a cross-piece. The framework could then be used to lift the half-ribs with block and tackle, ropes and pulleys. The bottom of each rib would be anchored initially in a base plate. The very first arch will, of course, have been the most difficult to erect, especially the critical junction between the two ribs at the crown. Micromanipulation of the tips of the ribs was necessary so that a bolt could be inserted through corresponding holes in each rib to fix them in place. Once that had been achieved, the other four arches would have been easier to erect since the scaffold will have been that much more stable. In addition, the completed ribs would have been stabilised against lateral movement by horizontal tie bars, the same bars that can be seen on the present structure *(1.1)*. The sequence was demonstrated by the BBC Timewatch team when a half-scale reproduction was built across a canal, so proving that the method was viable.

Once the five ribs were in place and stabilised, then the outer ribs could be added, an operation still needing care so as not to put too much load on the castings. For example, the long ribs would be at risk of bending failure if they fell from a height. The outer ribs would also need careful manipulation to be threaded through the large slotted columns *(1.1)* and wedged into position. At what stage the roadway itself was added is not known for certain, but it will probably have been added at an early stage in the erection of the outer ribs, simply to stabilise the superstructure. The integrity of a spaceframe like the Ironbridge relies on tying the members together so that the loads are more evenly distributed and not concentrated at any one point. During erection, however, there must be some flexibility of movement to allow fitment of parts. This is where the joints are important because they are larger than needed, and would only be finally fixed by knocking chocks and wedges into the spaces at the joint. Before that operation, temporary fixing could be done by using wooden rather than wrought-iron wedges. Both are tough materials which can withstand hammering without cracking, but nevertheless care would have been taken in final fixing owing to the chance of brittle cracking of the cast-iron members.

Final State of Bridge

There were many other features of the bridge which had to be built from conventional materials following the erection of the main cast-iron framework. It included the approaches and abutments, parts of which could have been built beforehand. However, most authorities, such as Neil Cossens and Arthur Raistrick, agree that the approach bridges were built after the iron framework. If constructed before, it would have been easier to erect the ironwork, but this appears not to have been the case. But the masonry base must have been built first, which, together with their cast-iron base plates, would anchor the ribs in place. Two further, much smaller cast-iron bridges on the approach from the south (at left in *(1.1)*) were built in 1821–23 to replace the original masonry arches. It is surprising that they were not made of iron in the first place if the principle of using an iron structure for the main crossing had already been decided. The necessary extra work was carried out in the summer of 1780.

Tourist Spectacle

The bridge was finally opened for traffic, both by foot and carriage, on New Year's Day 1781. It must have been a great day to celebrate, if not for Abraham Darby, considering his debt on the project, at least everyone else who could now cross the river with ease and alacrity. Cracks were seen in the abutments after opening and they clearly needed repair, but apparently no serious cracks had been seen in the bridge itself, or, if any had been seen, they did not cause serious concern. The tolls taken paid off the debt only very slowly, and certainly not fast enough to relieve Darby of his financial burden. In the long term, however, it paid off handsomely. Darby and the trustees publicised the bridge very widely, by commissioning paintings and etchings of its appearance, which made it a talking point in drawing rooms everywhere. It became a tourist spectacle, at least for those who could afford to visit from a distance, an icon of the growing industrial revolution.

It was at about this time that James Watt and Mathew Boulton in Birmingham were putting the final touches to their new 'fire engine', an improved steam engine. They used cast iron for their cylinders, and a new way of boring the piston space to much higher tolerance than was then in use for the existing Newcomen engines used widely in coal and metal mines. This new engine would further stimulate production not just in the mines, but also by application to mechanised production of metal artefacts. And it would power the bellows feeding air to the numerous blast furnaces in Coalbrookdale and the surrounding area. The bellows were originally powered by a waterwheel, then a Newcomen engine was installed to refresh the reservoir when water was scarce.

The Current State of the Bridge

The observant visitor to the Ironbridge will, after an initial phase of admiration, notice the many defects exhibited openly on the cast-iron framework. There are many brittle cracks present in various parts, especially on the north side which is easily accessible from the marketplace in the town. And some of these brittle cracks have run to completion, allowing complete separation of the formerly connected parts. The various attempts to reinforce the most serious defects are also very visible, as well as the casting defects present on most of the component parts. Having seen such defects, the observer will then wonder why the structure still stands.

Firstly, the visible defects on the north side of the framework can be examined. The ornate pillars which connect the innermost ribs and the first concentric set of ribs have cracked in numerous places and become separated. Those seen from the west side of the structure are especially evident *(1.3)*. Although an oblique photograph, the pillar on the left appears to show both vertical separation and movement from north to south. The far pillar appears to show just vertical separation, both showing a similar separation distance. It is most interesting that both have fractured in the same place, just above a dovetail joint into the inner rib below, although the shape of the cracks is slightly different. There could be an intrinsic weakness here, possibly at a lateral inner corner to the dovetail projection.

Some of the pillars on the east side of the bridge show a similar problem in a position corresponding to the west side *(1.4)*. But here the crack is across the top of the pillar rather than the base. However, there is a clear section revealed in the lower dovetail joint which confirms the problem of stress concentration. There are two sharp inner corners to the dovetail, intact here but cracked elsewhere. The formation of the crack at the top will have relieved the strain on the pillar. The relative position of the corresponding crack surfaces also shows lateral as well as vertical movement, just like its mate on the west side of the bridge. The same picture shows the surrounding pillars, apparently crack free, at least of major separation cracks, and also shows how the dovetail was pinned by a bolt through holes in the socket and pillar base.

A lower part of the northern superstructure shows an intact pillar, but with pitting in the outer surface from blowholes in the original molten metal at casting *(1.7)*. The pillar just behind shows similar pitting, and indeed, many of the main ribs show a roughening from smaller scale blowholes in their surfaces. Such defects would not have been tolerated even just a few years later, because they lower the ultimate strength of the component, as well as having a bad appearance. Recycling of poorly cast parts was probably minimal,

(1.3) Fractured pillars
on the Ironbridge.

and only practised if the part was so badly defective as to be impossible to use at all (such as a completely cracked rib). Like the previous example, there is a lateral wrought-iron reinforcing strap which is attached to two ribs and straddles others. Such reinforcing measures have been used elsewhere in the structure, presumably arising from the visible distress to such members as the pillars.

There is different damage visible in the north support structure *(1.6)*. The first to immediately catch the eye is the large plate fitted to one of the large vertical members (centre right in the picture). It encompasses the whole joint and is bolted to an identical plate on the rear of the joint, so nothing is visible to indicate the damage. To the left however, is a large crack from the corner of a slot in one of the inner ribs. It has started at the corner of the slot, probably under pressure from the bar inserted to close and fix the joint with a horizontal bar running across the middle of the picture. The crack is shown in detail in *(1.6)*, and there is a significant gap which has been formed as a result of the failure. Although the details of the reinforced joint are invisible, a similar joint on the east side of the structure indicates a possible explanation. It shows a lateral crack in one of the main support columns, perhaps running into the corner of the adjacent slot for a lower main rib.

So what is the cause of such cracks? It is unlikely that the corner cracks from slots represent anything other than local stresses produced by assembly. That implies that they were formed by hammering in the chocks just after the structure had been raised and fixed into its final position. They are unlikely to have been formed by incumbent loads such as traffic passing over the bridge, or by strain from movement in the abutments. However, the separated cracks in the pillars represent something more serious, and probably that very problem which worried the builders after cracks had been found in the masonry abutments. There has been a shift in the relative positions of the connecting ribs, showing that they could well have been caused by movement at the base of the ribs on the north bank. All the cracks appear old and painted over, so may be of a similar age to the bridge itself. On the other hand, fresh cracks in cast iron are much more difficult to spot, especially if there has been no separation of the fracture surfaces.

(1.4) Broken pillars and casting flaws on Ironbridge.

(1.5) Visible blowholes in pillars.

(1.6) Fracture from corner, and brace on column.

They are the hairline cracks dreaded by structural experts, whether in aircraft, buildings or bridges (among many other products) because they are so difficult to see by the naked eye alone. Perhaps the most notorious were those which were found during the Comet disaster investigation, when several new aircraft disappeared over the Mediterranean during the early 1950s. Other methods must be used to expose them to open view, before they grow too far and threaten the structure involved.

But any concern over the cracks in the Ironbridge is misplaced. This is clearly a structure which has been overdesigned. In other words, more cast iron has been used for the structure than was really needed for it to support itself, any imposed loads, and even unexpected events such as floods and scour, or abutment movement. For example, severe floods of the Severn occurred in February 1795, and destroyed or damaged numerous bridges, including a wooden bridge at nearby Coalport. Yet the Ironbridge escaped serious damage. There could not have been a better advertisement for its design, although the abutments may have given cause for concern, with their solid walls being subjected to immense pressure from the raging waters. At least an iron bridge did not present such a large surface area to water pressure, and probably encouraged the construction of the small iron bridges on the south abutment to replace the masonry arches.

Conservation

The need for appropriate conservation of the structure, now the centre of a World Heritage Site, has been addressed several times in the past century, most notably in the 1950s when major works were carried out to stabilise the abutments. It included a ferro-concrete counter-arch built across and under the river to balance the slippage of the banks.

A survey in 1970 counted fifty-three visible fractures in the cast iron of the bridge, forty-two being concentrated on the north side. Of that total, no less than twenty-three were located on the hidden dovetail joints of the pillars, some examples of which have already been discussed. A more alarming event occurred in 1967, when a cantilever strut fell from the bridge. These components came to rest on the sides, near the roadway, and well away from the crown, so there was no danger of the bridge's imminent collapse. However, it did give the opportunity to analyse the material in some detail. Three samples cut for tensile testing showed a tensile strength of 8.5tpsi (tons per square inch), substantially lower than the compressive strength of 13.5tpsi. In addition, sections cut and polished from the strut revealed much porosity and some large blowholes near the centre of the casting. The carbon content was relatively low at 3.25 per cent (compared with a content of 2.65 per cent in an arch sample), with just over 1 per cent silicon and smaller quantities of manganese, phosphorous and sulphur. The strut had failed and fallen because of a brittle fracture at a square bolt hole used to attach the strut to the main structure, another example of the stress-concentrating effects of sharp corners. The authors of the report on the metallurgy of the strut, Morton and Moseley, explained the fractures as being caused by a geological slip of the bank on the north side. They calculated that a load of about 100 tons would have been needed to fracture one of the dovetail pillars, but this calculation was based on the simple cross section and the known tensile strength.

However, they did not locate the source of the critical crack from the fracture surface, and so made no allowance for the stress-concentration effect of, for example, a sharp corner. Spherical blowholes will generally double the applied stress, but corners can aggravate the problem by a factor of up to ten, so the actual load needed to break the pillar was probably much lower, perhaps as little as 10 tons, and even less if a crack existed at the origin from the original casting. Stress raisers in the same zone act not in addition but as multipliers of one another. So a crack in a blowhole at a corner may concentrate the load to extremely high levels, and probably in excess of a factor of ten.

More recently, starting in 1999, the bridge has been surveyed in detail prior to painting, with yet more information emerging about the way it was designed and built. Close inspection of the main ribs shows that wooden patterns were probably not used, because there are size variations from rib to rib. The centre arch of the five seems to have been erected first, followed by the surrounding arches, and they differ slightly in dimensions. In addition, trowel marks have been found on the metal surfaces, indicating that the moulds were prepared by hand rather than by pattern. Presumably this needed some care in drawing the shape in the sand to an accuracy which could be repeated. The survey revealed details of the design of the crown joint and bearer where the road deck meets the top of the arches.

Coalport Bridge

The construction of the bridge did not just give locals an easier route across the river, but, much more importantly, it inspired others to repeat the success. That is a characteristic of original and novel design, it leads the way to further success. It was never patented, perhaps because Pritchard died before the bridge was completed and Darby was deeply in debt, because the bridge soaked up more resources than expected. Patenting then was even more expensive than it is now, involving expensive lawyers, and with no apparent prospect of revenues from imitators. But copiers there were when the success of the bridge became evident to all. It was built faster and using less material than a conventional masonry bridge, but could the method or design be improved? If the structure could be designed to use less of the expensive cast iron then great savings could be made and so lower the total cost. Using less material would also have the benefit of shortening casting time, construction and assembly at site.

The proof lies in another local bridge two miles downstream at Coalport, a slightly longer bridge than Ironbridge at 104ft, and with a shallower arch *(1.7)*. The original bridge here (Preen's Eddy bridge) was made of wood with brick abutments and a single masonry pier in the centre of the river. It was completed in 1780 but damaged so badly in the floods of 1795 that substantial repairs were carried out. The central pier was removed, and the wooden roadway supported on three cast-iron ribs spanning the river in one throw. It was a low-cost repair, involving minimal use of cast iron, and one of the ribs cracked in 1817. The owners replaced the cracked arch and added another two, so giving five to support the roadway, which was also replaced with cast-ironwork. The main arches were braced laterally and vertically, but with minimal use of cast iron, and it has survived from the completion date of 1818 to this day. The bridge is still taking vehicular traffic, albeit with a weight limit of 3 tons and a speed limit of 10mph. The roadway is flatter than the humped Ironbridge, making for easier use by motorised traffic.

Closer inspection of the cast-iron components shows just how they were able to save material *(1.8)*. The ribs are designed to resist the downward load of the road, by having a thinner, rectangular section rather than the massive, nearly square section of the ribs of the Ironbridge. This is akin to the use of floor beams with their thin section facing upwards to resist the pressure from the floor and occupants. They make efficient use of the material by giving the greatest stiffness in the vertical direction. This makes the arches more flexible to lateral movement, and some degree of curvature can be seen by looking along the ribs *(1.9)*. It is resisted by simple wrought-iron cross bars supported on the ribs by chocks, and attached by bolts to vertical members. The overall quality of the iron is much improved, with no surface roughness visible, and with far fewer components than at Ironbridge. It must have proved easier to erect, especially with abutments already in place, so that the main ribs could be lifted without the use of vertical poles, although a cross bar would have been needed for the initial connection of the ribs at the crown.

Stress concentrations are few, and corners which do occur, such as corners on the chocks are rounded, so remain uncracked. It is a totally utilitarian bridge, with none of the ornate decoration used on the Ironbridge, resulting in substantial savings on material. The weight of material was less than half that used on the Ironbridge (389 tons), yet it is elegant and supremely functional. Decoration is reserved for the balustrade, yielding yet further savings of the costly raw material. The cost is unknown, but must have been considerably less than the Ironbridge, and the project thus was more profitable.

The bridge was renovated in 2004 by Shropshire County Council, and involved replacing the cast-iron plates under the road with steel plates bonded with epoxy resin to the framework. Unlike Ironbridge, it continues to carry vehicles.

Inspiration

The Ironbridge was an inspiration to architects and engineers towards the close of the eighteenth century, especially Thomas Telford, then a rising engineer employed locally. The development of new bridges was slower than might have been expected, perhaps because potential clients were deterred by the high costs of the original project. But improved communications were needed in most parts of the country, and not least across the Severn. The Ironbridge was well publicised, with renowned artists such as Michael Angelo Rooker and others producing paintings of the structure which were distributed widely. But local influence must have been greater, simply because the bridge could be seen more easily, with the company facilities nearby for inspection and staff on hand for consultation. Direct examination of new products is always more impressive than documentation, however well executed.

Several small versions of the Ironbridge were built for parks and country house estates, as well as possibly within the Coalbrookdale works itself. A small-scale version of the bridge was even supplied to a chateau outside Paris. No doubt the original wooden patterns could be easily reused, and the design modified to suit particular customers. The landed gentry

Left: (1.7) The cast-iron bridge at Coalport.

Above: (1.8) Main ribs at Coalport with vertical pillars.

Left: (1.9) The support structure at Coalport.

could afford the high cost of such a bridge, although the development costs had already been paid for, and thus the costs of any new replica would be lower than the original. Whether the concept of a kit-of-parts which could be shipped anywhere started here with the Ironbridge or not, it certainly grew with time as the company extended the uses of cast iron. The project engineers will have put their inventive minds to the task of working out the best way to design products for ease of assembly and transport, a concept which could exploit the growing communication network, especially the canals. The idea was applied to many other products, ranging from whole buildings (and even churches) to the common kitchen range, a development which has outlasted all of the other products, and is still with us today in the form of the cast-iron range produced by Aga and Rayburn. And they are still made at Coalbrookdale, by a company which has continued to innovate.

Buildwas

A crossing above Coalbrookdale at Buildwas became urgent after the 1795 floods. The original bridge was made of masonry, and had been partly wrecked by the surging river. Thomas Telford designed the entirely new bridge of cast iron to be erected in its place. It was finished in 1796, using cast-iron arches made in Coalbrookdale, to create a single span of 130ft over the river. But it used only 170 tons of cast iron, a remarkable reduction over the Ironbridge weight of about 379 tons. This alone must have meant a large saving in material costs, with additional savings possible by using a smaller number of parts. The design was based on a wooden bridge over the Rhine at Schaffhausen, Switzerland. Nevertheless, the total cost was greater than expected, and the masonry contractors went bust. Less labour will have been needed for moving the heavy components from Coalbrookdale, and then into their final position. The bridge was used until 1905, when it was demolished and replaced. Part of this bridge was then replaced in 1992. An early drawing of the bridge shows flat arch cast-iron ribs, with the roadway lower than the crown, which was supported on the lower parts of the arches. This gave a flatter road, so overcoming the humpbacked effect prominent on the Ironbridge.

Telford went on to design and build many other cast-iron bridges elsewhere in the country, especially road bridges such as the famous 'Waterloo' bridge at Betwys-y-Coed on the A5 at the entrance to Snowdonia in North Wales. He was the engineer for the new road passing through the region to the Menai Straits, and the creator of the suspension bridge across the Straits, which completed the road to Anglesey and Holyhead.

Sunderland Bridge

That the Ironbridge had caught the imagination of influential people is evident by the construction of a much larger cast-iron bridge at Sunderland, Co. Durham. It was the brainchild of Rowland Burdon, architect and Tory MP for the county (1790–1806). The port of Sunderland was a major outlet for the growing coal industry of the region, this was in addition to the other ports in the north-east such as Newcastle. Thomas Wilson managed the project for Burdon, who was the major investor in the project. It was a great advance on the Ironbridge in its design, using a substantially smaller amount of cast iron (260 tons) for a much longer span over the river Wear of 236ft. At over twice the span of Ironbridge, it used nearly half the weight of cast iron. It also introduced wrought-iron tie bars as major structural elements, a material much more capable of resisting brittle cracks than cast iron.

The design principle this time was patented by Burdon, and Wilson went on to build similar bridges elsewhere in the country (some of which failed). The Sunderland cast-iron bridge was restored in 1859 by Robert Stephenson, and eventually replaced by a steel bridge in 1929.

Tom Paine

It was a time of revolutions not just in engineering, but in the political life of nations. The war of independence had broken out in 1775 at Concord, Massachusetts, with the rebellious colonist militia attacking British soldiers (according to the British) or defending themselves against brutal occupying forces (from the American viewpoint). The British government of George III had ruled the colony without recognising their rights, or, more importantly, granting them democratic representation, despite taxing them heavily to pay for warfare on other fronts. The conflict had built up over many years. The despotic rule by most European monarchs produced many radical thinkers, among them Tom Paine. He had a rich and varied career, but his claim to fame rests with a pamphlet he wrote espousing the colonists' cause. It attacked the British government for their tyranny. He was a great friend of Benjamin Franklin, one of the founding fathers of the American Revolution. Like many colonists, he supported the French Revolution for removing the French monarchy in 1789, although he might have regretted visiting the country, because, when he attempted to save some of its unfortunate victims from the guillotine he was promptly arrested himself and incarcerated. He was eventually rescued by the American ambassador.

He also aspired to be an inventor, and patented an interesting design for an iron bridge in 1789. He proposed a bridge over the Schuykill River in Pennsylvania, and other bridges. Some of them nearly came to fruition, but were never ultimately fulfilled. Nevertheless, his enthusiasm for the new technology is indicative of the new ideas sweeping through the western world.

He is remembered not for his bridges but for his political stance in opposing arbitrary and tyrannical rule by monarchs. In his pamphlet *Rights of Man* he developed his ideas and publicised them widely, and was persecuted by the British government for his efforts. Like Voltaire, most of his ideas have become reality, including the right to elect governments and the right to express one's beliefs freely.

Sunderland and Tickford Bridges

The work of Wilson and Telford established that cast-iron bridges could be economical when designed efficiently. The cast-iron arched bridge became very common in the early Victorian period, and many remain. Thomas Wilson, for example, built many cast-iron bridges after his valuable experience on the Sunderland bridge. And one of these was a failure, the 180ft span

(1.10) Cast-iron bridge at Newton Pagnell, reinforced by carbon-fibre in the spandrels.

bridge over the river Yarm in Co. Durham. It weighed about 250 tons, but collapsed suddenly in 1806 into the river within months of completion. The reasons for the failure remain obscure, although abutment resistance to the lateral pressures exerted by the structure may have been insufficient. An earlier bridge at Staines sank slowly into the river owing to similar problems. That did not stop this enterprising man: far from it, because he went on to build many more cast-iron bridges, many of which have stood the test of time. A particularly good example is the earliest known cast-iron bridge to still be in use as a public road today, even earlier than that at Coalport. This remarkable survivor is the bridge at Newport Pagnell, Bucks. The Tickford bridge was finished in 1810, and so it well pre-dates the Coalport bridge *(1.10)*. Like many early cast-iron arch bridges, it is elegant yet highly functional. There are six arched ribs in two layers with the spandrels filled with hoops, and it resembles Ironbridge more closely than the Coalport bridge. The ribs are supported laterally by clasps wrapped around the members, a safe form of attachment not involving the integrity of the parts so joined together.

Cast-iron bridges are very common over much of the country, and were widely used during the Victorian period for canals, roads and railways. The designs which have generally survived involve arches so that the material is only compressed. Examples where it was put into tension either failed or were replaced as a precaution, especially on the railways. Some are still in use, normally renovated by extra support where needed, and others have been bypassed by more recent structures. A listing can be found in the Institute of Civil Engineers' Heritage guides (see bibliography).

Testing

One intriguing aspect of the design of the early cast-iron bridges is the role played by the testing of structural elements. No information seems to have survived about tests on the Ironbridge, whether the entire finished structure or the individual cast components. Testing would later become an important aspect of bridge construction, mainly because it was a way of designing closer to the needs of any bridge. Why use more material than is necessary to span a given width, and carry a given load? The question arises of whether Telford tested components for his Buildwas bridge, or the trough aqueducts. It appears that in fact he did test several components, not only to destruction to determine their intrinsic strength by hanging successively greater weights from the centre of a component, but also to gain an idea of the degree of deflection under various loads.

When the abutments were removed in tests, failure occurred, emphasising the importance of resisting the lateral thrust by a loaded bridge. But how could that information best be used to estimate the stiffness or strength of the final product? It would enable him to estimate the total load the bridge would support when loaded, and he would be able to compare that load with the typical loads expected from traffic over the bridge. With a wide margin of safety, he would be able to assure his clients of the integrity of the structure. Another critical issue is movement at joints, because they will probably be not only the weakest part of the assembled structure, but also the most flexible, especially if they are a free fit, using mortice and tenon joints.

While prototype testing is now a normal and vital part of product development, it was not so readily accepted then, especially for large projects like building a bridge. In a sense, it was even more important than people realised at the time. Harrison tested his famous clocks rigorously so that he could improve their time-keeping, but it was more difficult with bridge components of the size first created at the Ironbridge. Whether or not they did in fact test the individual parts such as the ribs is unknown. They probably relied instead on their own experience with previous experience of the integrity of smaller castings, such as those used in the blast furnace. But in order to improve the design of iron bridges to use less material (and so cut costs), testing of individual components would be an important part of the development leading to the final product. The ultimate test would of course be loading by users, and the test of time.

2
Canals in the Sky

But it was not only simple bridges where the larger castings from Coalbrookdale and the many other local foundries could be used. This was an era famous for its canals, another vital feature of the growing revolution in industrial methods. Although rivers such as the Wey in Surrey had been canalised as early as 1653, a starting point for continuous artificial waterways is the construction of the Bridgewater Canal in Manchester in 1761, which allowed coal to be brought directly into the city by barge from the collieries of Worsley, about ten miles east of the city centre. It was built as a contour canal by James Brindley. The canal lowered the price of coal substantially, so stimulating the growth of industry in Manchester, this growth meant the outlay could be paid back very quickly, within a few years in fact. Much larger cargoes of coal could be carried by barge than was then possible by pack animals using roads or paths. The economies of scale using the new technology were impressive.

Many other canals followed, despite the problems in raising capital and applying for an Act of Parliament, quite apart from the many engineering obstacles. Many of the first canals imitated the design of the Bridgewater, but contour canals (such as the Oxford Canal, linking the Midlands and London via Oxford) could be very expensive owing to their great length. One way around the problem was to build locks to overcome gradients, locks were a new technology being developed to aid the design and construction of canals. It would shorten the route if the cost-benefit analysis showed a saving, bringing goods carried that much faster from source to market.

It started with coal, but other goods could easily be transported the same way, such as agricultural produce, raw materials like timber, iron castings, bricks and slates, building stone, and the increasing output of textile mills. In this way, raw materials could be shipped to the new factories or building sites, while carrying the finished products of the factories back to the urban markets.

It started a trend which peaked after the Ironbridge had been built in 1793, a time known as 'canal mania', when everyone wanted a share of the action. The profits could be good, provided the canals were well planned to link the new factories with the largest markets. And they could also act as a stimulant to further growth, because new developments would be sited to exploit the new canals, often on their banks.

Canal Network

A major objective of engineers like Brindley was to produce a trunk system which would allow transport over much greater distances, linking the growing industrial centres with ports, and other sources of raw materials. It would aim to connect navigable rivers like the Severn, Trent and Thames with the canals. Just like major bridges, such projects needed (and still need) an Act of Parliament to proceed, such an Act had to take into account many different property rights in addition to surveyor's reports and engineering estimates of the works necessary for completion. The legal costs could be substantial, especially if there was opposition to the project from landed gentry, or MPs with an interest, whether for or against a project.

But there were many obstacles to longer canals than the Bridgewater, especially rivers, which could be crossed at a high level only by aqueducts, usually approached by massive embankments. Deep cuttings were also needed to keep to the level.

The canal itself was formed by creating a trough in the ground and then lining it with clay, a process known as 'puddling'. It was not an easy task because of the weak mechanical properties of clay, especially when wet. It has a high degree of plasticity, and low stresses will cause the material to deform easily. Even its own weight might be enough to cause the sides of a puddled trough to collapse, thus allowing water to seep through. Small leaks could grow rapidly, and under an increasing flow the banks could easily be breached. There was considerable variability in the clays used for 'puddling', and the breaching of canal walls was a not infrequent event on the growing canal system. Not only could the breach cause serious damage to property, but the function of the canal would be lost, so affecting revenue. But impermeable materials had been available for many years in the form of cast iron, the only objection being its very high cost. After the Ironbridge, engineers were clearly looking for other applications where its properties could be exploited to the greatest advantage. And since canal building was at its height in the late 1700s, why not use the material for sealing canals, especially in those parts which were critical, such as aqueducts?

Longdon-on-Tern

A few aqueducts were made of cast-iron troughs, with short sections bolted together and sealed to provide a complete structure. One of the most interesting survivors (and one of the earliest to be built) lies just outside Shrewsbury, on the now defunct Shrewsbury Canal. The canal linked Coalbrookdale to Shrewsbury, and was intended to provide the county's market town with metal goods and coal, with agricultural produce to be sent in return.

Although the rest of the canal has disappeared under the plough, a length of the cast-iron trough has been left at Longdon-on-Tern, where the aqueduct crosses the eponymous local river *(2.1)*. It was built in 1796 after the February floods of 1795 damaged the initial brick and masonry structures (some of which remain at the site), and the proprietors called in Thomas Telford to build a more robust aqueduct which would offer less resistance to floodwater. With the example of Ironbridge, a cast-iron alternative seemed to be a better, faster, and cheaper solution to the problem.

About 186ft long, 9ft wide and 4ft deep, the aqueduct crosses the river and its small flood plain, supported by cruciform cast-iron girders set in stone bases. The structure is composed of cast sheet about 1in thick, fitted with edges which are bolted together

(2.1) Longdon-on-Tern cast-iron aqueduct.

to maintain a watertight seal *(2.1)*. The joints are set at an angle, a design feature which reduces the possibility of brittle cracking because the inner hydrostatic pressure acts to produce vertical cracks growing from the weakest part, the joint. If angled, the possibility of cracking is much reduced. The angle varies in a regular way, but the individual pieces must have needed great care to cast. Distortion caused by differential shrinkage of the molten iron in the mould was one of the problems faced by the foundry, and most of the plates are gently curved outwards. It is not the effect of the water pressure during its life, but rather an artefact of the manufacture. The art of casting had developed greatly since the Ironbridge was made, but there were still details to be improved.

The details of the construction of the supports are also interesting *(2.2)*. The bases of the cast-iron girders are set into a cast-iron block, into recesses which match the shape of the cruciform girder section. The large block is cracked at the centre, and the fracture looks very old. It may have occurred just after casting from thermal stresses induced during cooling. There is no effective stress acting here, so no driving force to open the crack further. There are generous radii on the many internal corners in the casting, probably reflecting a growing awareness of the importance of minimising stress raisers through detailed design. Further lateral support is given by diagonal tie bars bolted at their centres. Apart from a little rusting in the pockets where the girders are set, the structure has survived remarkably intact. The structure is now empty, and looks rather forlorn without its accompanying canal completely ploughed out.

At about this time, Telford had been involved in the first known tests of cast-iron components, as already discussed in the last chapter. They involved loading a rib or arch to failure, simply by adding weights to the centre of the component until the part fractured. Notes of some of his experiments have survived, and they show that tests were being made at the Ketley iron foundry in Coalbrookdale in April 1795, the foundry that was owned and operated by William Reynolds. Some of the experiments may have been designed to test the strength of the ribs of his bridge at Buildwas, but the notes also show that he was interested in the compressive strength of cast-iron columns and struts. The results would have been of direct relevance to the struts supporting the Longdon

Left: (2.2) The supports for the aqueduct.

Opposite: (2.3) The Chirk aqueduct.

aqueduct, and they clearly demonstrated the high compressive strength of the material. He reported that a 3ft bar of cast iron had a breaking load of 5 tons, and since the actual load on the Longdon struts was only about 1 ton, there would have been a safety factor of about five when the aqueduct carried water to standard depth.

Pont-y-Cafnau

The idea of using a cast-iron trough had occurred to other engineers working at the time, especially at Pont-y-Cafnau in south Wales. A much shorter structure than the Longdon aqueduct, it was designed by George Watkin to carry a water supply and railway track, and bears a distant similarity to the latter, especially in its use of cast-iron girders in the form of an A-frame to support the structure. It fed water to the Cyrfarthfa ironworks in the Taff Valley near Merthyr Tydfil, but the trough was much smaller than that built by Telford. That it was an important step in design can be judged by the sketch made by William Reynolds in his notebook (1794), the same Reynolds who was a partner with Darby in the Coalbrookdale works. One wonders whether the idea was passed on to Telford. It may have been irrelevant anyway, because L.T.C. Rolt states that Telford had clearly developed the idea of a cast-iron trough before the Longdon aqueduct was built in early 1794. But the Longdon aqueduct is a much more substantial design, different in form and construction, and was designed for a canal and not a small water supply. Telford probably knew about Pont-y-Cafnau from Reynolds, but it was hardly a prototype for Longdon, which is designed in quite a different way, a way appropriate for a much longer structure.

A short (44ft) cast-iron trough aqueduct was built by Benjamin Outram taking the Derby Canal over the Markeaton Brook near Holmes, and finished a few weeks before the Longdon structure. It was probably built by the Butterley Co., ironmasters in the Midlands. But, like the Pont-y-Cafnau aqueduct, it does not compare in scale with Longdon. On the other hand, it does illustrate the point that many engineers were thinking along the same lines, in making greater use of cast iron. It was a material which gave them much

greater freedom in design, and lowered costs substantially over equivalent masonry or brick structures. As far as is known, no patent was issued for the cast-iron trough for canal aqueducts, and if one were issued, there would clearly be competing claims for priority.

Chirk Aqueduct

Longdon-on-Tern was a stepping stone for Thomas Telford, and there were to be much larger projects which attracted even greater public attention. Two in particular stand out for their dramatic effect in a landscape, the masonry aqueduct at Chirk, and the much larger Pontcysyllte structure. The first made use of cast iron for the base of the canal, so saving masonry in the structure, but, more importantly, assuring an impermeable base *(2.3)*. The iron plates tied the outside walls of the canal together. The piers were constructed very carefully and the top parts are hollow, but they were provided with internal cross walls to strengthen the external façade. It was started by Telford in the same year he finished the Longdon aqueduct, 1796, and was opened for traffic in 1801. The only weakness in its design was the side wall, which leaked, and was therefore a cause for concern. To remedy this, the sides were retrofitted with cast-iron plates in 1869, retaining the outer wall, so that the external view maintains the impression of an all-masonry structure.

The canal itself was planned to connect the Severn and Dee, but instead it was always just a branch which ended up at the Horseshoe falls above Llangollen. No doubt the local slate quarries provided much business for the canal, as well as coal from small local collieries, and the feeder canal is also an important source of water lower down in its course. The larger viaduct by its side is the railway viaduct built for the Shrewsbury–Chester line. Nowadays the canal is a popular venue for pleasure boats, together with its larger cousin, the resplendent Pontcysyllte aqueduct.

Pontcysyllte

Anyone who has visited Pontcysyllte must admire the skill of Telford in its design and creation *(2.4)*. The aqueduct would take about ten years to build, starting in 1795 and finishing in 1805. It exploited the idea of the iron trough developed and proved at Longdon but would need masonry towers to support the trough. The towers would take the greatest time in construction, with much smaller structural units than the aqueduct itself. As at the Chirk aqueduct, the piers would be hollow, requiring a high standard of masonry work. Assembly of the iron trough would not take much time at all, using his prior experience at Longdon, but the trough was to be redesigned to move the towpath from below so that it rose above the canal. It would be more convenient for the horses, and would also give users a greater sense of safety. The modification would demand a wider aqueduct, from 9ft to 11ft 10in to accommodate the extra width, and the cantilever towpath would be supported by posts set into the base of the trough. It would be 5ft 3in deep. The plates for the trough were redesigned and the angled joints were also changed *(2.5)*; the flanges, however, were still joined by bolts. Each span (nineteen in all, on eighteen piers) is supported by four cast-iron arched ribs, braced laterally and externally by large plates attached by bolts to the outer ribs. This support structure is quite different to that at Longdon, and reflects the greater mass of water held in the trough. One interesting feature of all canal aqueducts is that the static load is constant and dynamic loads are almost completely absent. Even when a barge moves over a span, the load is the same as when empty, a direct consequence of Archimedes principle. Any floating object displaces a mass of water equal to that of the object, so has no effect on the downward load at any point. In effect the load of the barge is distributed through the water. So cast-iron canal walls are not subjected to cyclical or dynamic loads, a vital factor in helping to conserve them to the present day.

At 1,007ft long, the aqueduct is unique and is by far the largest in Britain, or anywhere for that matter. It was renovated in 2003–04, and some ribs were found to be cracked. They were braced laterally and pinned, and in addition masonry repairs were performed. There was, however, considerable corrosion of many of the wrought-iron bolts holding the components together; they were replaced by exactly equivalent hand-forged replicas.

The aqueduct is even more spectacular when crossed by foot or by boat *(2.6)*. One is at least protected by the handrail on the towpath if travelling on foot, but boat owners have no such protection on the far side of the canal. Vertigo is sometimes an acceptable accompaniment to the pleasure of exposure to great heights. Although the canal is a dead end, it remains a well-visited spot for boaters, who can travel further to Llangollen. However, the canal is also an important source of drinking water for Shrewsbury and other towns in Shropshire.

Cosgrove Aqueduct

Telford's aqueducts were justly famous in his time and were a grand success while the cast-iron trough became widely used elsewhere on the canal network. Although never

Above: (2.4) The
Pontcysyllte aqueduct.

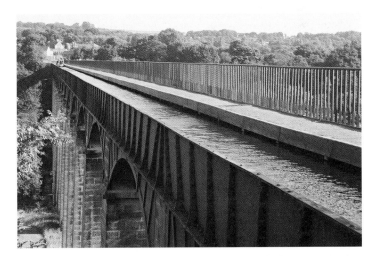

Right: (2.5) Cast-iron
trough at Pontcysyllte.

(2.6) The supports at
Pontcysyllte.

so large, they were used where aqueducts over roads or other obstacles were needed, or where another structure had failed. A good example is the Cosgrove aqueduct on the Grand Junction Canal near the new town of Milton Keynes.

The valley of the river Ouse was a serious problem for the builders of the Grand Junction. In the absence of a viaduct over the river itself, a temporary solution involved a series of eight locks on the banks of the river, built in 1800, so that at least the canal could be used for through traffic. However, it could only be a stop-gap, because the river flooded frequently in the winter months. A massive embankment was needed to carry the canal over the flood plain, together with an aqueduct over the river itself. The gigantic embankment, which even today is very impressive, is about 36ft high above the valley floor and 150ft wide, extending about half a mile from side to side of the valley. The pioneer canal builder William Jessop suggested a brick aqueduct over the river, with three arches to be supported by two brick piers, this impressive construction was duly opened on 26 August 1805. The piers were built on dry land to one side of the river, which was then diverted.

A section of the canal embankment collapsed in January 1806, probably over the old course of the river, and was then repaired. However, the aqueduct itself collapsed in February 1808. The situation was very serious, as can be judged by a local news report from the *Northampton Mercury*:

Stony Stratford, Feb 22. On Friday morning last, the inhabitants of this town were thrown into the utmost consternation, by information which arrived from Wolverton, that the large aqueduct arches under the immensely high embankment for carrying the new line of the Grand Junction Canal across our valley, about a mile below the town, had fallen in; and that the river Ouse was so dammed up thereby, that this town must surely be inundated to a great depth. On repairing to the spot, however, it was found, that one of the arches, which had been propped up underneath with timber, soon after the centres were removed, was still standing; and that this one arch, owing to there being no flood in the river, was able to carry off the water of the river as fast as it came down … the ends of each of the broken arches were found standing in a crippled state…

The reasons for the failure are not apparent from this report, but perhaps the piers were undermined by river action, a common problem with piers in the middle of rivers. The river was not in flood, however, and at this point it was not an especially large stream. It flows sluggishly across the flood plain, and any scouring action would have been low.

Fortunately the old locks were still in working order, and were reopened to keep traffic moving. A more reliable structure for the river crossing was needed, and what better solution than a cast-iron trough? The concept was well tried and tested by Telford, although a larger section was needed than that which he used at Longton-on-Tern. Scaling up a trough was not difficult, because the pressure from the water is only determined by its depth. On the other hand, the total weight needed greater support from the extra dead load, both of the casting itself and the enclosed water. Patterns for the castings could be readily made, and the castings, once made, could easily be sent to the spot by the canal itself. The parts of the kit were relatively easy to assemble, bolt together, and erect to form the final structure *(2.7)*.

The parts were cast at the Ketley foundry of Coalbrookdale (who had already been involved with Telford on the Longdon aqueduct) to a design by Benjamin Bevan, a local engineer (from Leighton Buzzard) with the canal company, and the structure was

Above: (2.7) Cosgrove aqueduct on the Grand Junction Canal.

Right: (2.8) The Cosgrove aqueduct showing the support arches under the trough.

completed by January 1811. It included a single masonry pier, so the bridge itself has just two spans, and the trough is 15ft wide, 6ft 6in deep, extending to a length of 101ft. The towpath is cantilevered from one side, as at Pontcysyllte, and is supported by diagonal struts. It remains in active use, a tribute to its design and construction. The design is, as the dimensions show, larger in section than Telford's troughs at Chirk and Pontcysyllte. There was extra support for the basin from curved joints built into the sides of the trough, and the floor shows an arched design for maximising the resistance to the downward load from the water *(2.8)*. In addition, extra support for the side plates is provided by curved ribs, cunningly keyed into cast iron. It is a very impressive piece of engineering, especially as it is so high above the river, at about 60ft. The design also includes two 'cattle creeps', narrow tunnels either side of the aqueduct to allow easy access across the canal for farm animals.

The problem with the first aqueduct led to a legal dispute with the original contractor, and the issue went to trial, with damages eventually being awarded to the Grand Junction Co. for loss of trade while the canal was out of action, as well as the cost of the replacement aqueduct.

Other Trough Aqueducts

It was not the only rapid application of Telford's idea. There are many such examples of trough aqueducts still in use on the nationwide network of canals. Indeed, one of the longest troughs is on the Stratford-upon-Avon Canal at Bearley. It was opened in 1816, and is nearly 480ft long, just under half the length of Pontcysyllte itself (1,007ft). Like the Longdon-on-Tern aqueduct, the towpath is set at the level of the base rather than the top of the canal.

There are other examples locally, such as Wooton Wawen (1813) and the concept was being used as late as 1851, as shown by the trough aqueduct on the Leamington Canal between Warwick and Leamington Spa in the Midlands. In that year, a new railway was being built between the two towns as part of the Birmingham and Oxford Junction Railway, and was subsequently leased by the Great Western Railway (GWR). Since the railway was lower than the canal, an aqueduct was needed. It is 18ft wide and comprises four equal spans of 21ft at a skew angle. The outward appearance is of a brick-arched structure, but it conceals six cast-iron ribs which support the waterway itself. They are double cantilevers which mate with lugs cast on the bottom side of the base of the trough.

Telford also applied the idea widely in local, North Midlands canals, including the Engine Arm aqueduct in Smethwick. It carries one canal over another, and the cast-iron trough is hidden by a unique ecclesiastical design, an arcade of arches and columns supported by a single cast-iron arch 52ft wide. There are five ribs in the arch, and the arcades support the towpaths either side of the canal itself.

The idea worked well, since although some of the material is in tension (the lower walls are under a hoop stress acting at right angles to the vertical sides, and parallel with axis of the canal), the tension is low, and constant. There can still be impact damage from passing boats, but loads must be small since only glancing blows are possible. Indeed, many cast-iron troughs are further protected by a wooden boom along the upper inside edges. There was (and is) always the danger of hidden defects within the castings, especially blow holes, cracks or inclusions of slag. However, the external quality of most of the visible metal is good, suggesting that casting methods had improved drastically since 1779, when the Ironbridge was built.

3

Birth of the Railways

It was not meant to be like this. The opening of the first passenger railway between Liverpool and Manchester in 1830 was an unmitigated disaster. It should have been a triumph with plaudits to all those who made it possible, not least to George Stephenson, the engineer who pioneered its construction and the machines which were to run upon the line. It should have been a tribute to those officers of the company who had the foresight to invest and direct the railway, such as Henry Booth, its Treasurer and guiding light. The reforming politicians who stood up for change in the way the country was governed should also have recouped their hard labours in promoting the cause of improved communications. But the official opening was nothing like this. The Prime Minister, the Duke of Wellington, was greeted by a mob as the train entered the new Manchester station, the mob hurling brickbats and clods of earth at what they saw as a tyrant who ignored the needs and aspirations of the people. In fear for his life, he stayed in the train and ordered a rapid retreat, quite unlike his previous military stance as the victor of Waterloo and the many other triumphs over Napoleon. The incident followed a tragic fatality near the centre of the line, when William Huskisson was run down by the locomotive *Rocket*. He had been attempting a rapprochement with the 'Iron Duke', having fallen out with the great man over the problem of reform. As a distinguished politician and cabinet minister (he had been president of the Board of Trade), he had been a vociferous proponent of the new railway. It was ironic that he, of all people, should have been struck down by the very technology he had supported so strongly. Although not killed immediately (as is the norm now when struck by a moving train), he was terribly injured and had been carried to the house of a local clergyman. He expired there many hours later in great pain. Although the whole day had been soured by such incidents, the event had also attracted supportive crowds, at least at the Liverpool end, eager to see the new technology prove itself in public.

But how did such a grand venture come to be in the first place, and what problems had been solved to bring it into being?

Coming of the Railways: Coal Mining

To understand how the Liverpool & Manchester Railway Co. was established involves a retrospective of the industrial changes wrought in the previous decades. In the first place, Britain had developed machines to an extraordinary state, more so than any other country. And they were created through necessity: the country had an extensive mining industry from Elizabethan times onward, both for the coal present everywhere in the north and west, and for metal ores in the older rocks of the north, west and south-west. The tin and copper mines of Cornwall and Devon were especially rich, but once exhausted at the surface, had been followed by progressively deeper mines.

Once underground, the miners faced the problem of water flooding the workings and preventing further progress. In some cases, the problem could be solved by driving a tunnel below the workings from a hillside nearby. It was only possible where mines had been driven into exposed hills or mountains, but such mines were actually very common in Wales and Yorkshire. But their ores were mainly lead and copper in abundance, and small-scale mining underground was often unencumbered by water. The ores were also of relatively low value owing to their abundance, but tin ore was much more valuable, and was an essential element present in valuable alloys like bronze and pewter. Indeed, tin was a rare element internationally, and Cornwall had large reserves which had been exploited from Bronze Age times, several millennia earlier. By contrast, coal was present in many separate and distinct coalfields in the country (but not Cornwall or Devon). It had also been exploited from early times, most notably by the Romans, who needed fuel for their heated bath-houses, their extensive smithing industries and for general domestic use. Coal seams were exposed in many parts of the country and could be exploited easily, then followed underground by drifts or vertical shafts. Although no Roman coal mines are known, they used the method of driving drainage tunnels, and went further when such methods were no longer feasible. To de-water shafts they developed sophisticated methods using treadmills or reverse waterwheels, and Archimedean screws also worked by manual labour.

Harnessing Coal

However, such methods were labour intensive and of limited capacity, despite being widely used with the revival of deep mining during the Renaissance. If coal was a potent source of energy, could not some form of mechanical motion be produced with an appropriate engine? Experimental work by Boyle and Hooke had shown that heat was produced when compressing a gas, and that a vacuum could raise water by about 30ft in a tube. Even the Greeks had known that a steam jet could produce rotary movement. And so Mr Savery invented his pump (1670s), an engine for raising water from a mine. Once an idea has been born, other inventors can then develop the idea, and Newcomen did just that with his more efficient beam engine (1767), a machine designed to work by using steam to power a beam which could lift water from a mine shaft. It enabled mine owners to develop underground coal seams which otherwise would have been inaccessible owing to flooding. The coal needed to fuel the boilers of the Newcomen engines was readily available and cheap at the minehead, and led to a big expansion of the coal mining industry. The engine worked by raising steam from a boiler, the steam being fed by pipe to a condenser, a giant cylinder fitted with a piston attached to the end of the beam. When a spray of cold water was injected into the steam, it cooled the steam and it condensed back to water, the large change in volume creating a vacuum. The piston then

(3.1) Newcomen
steam engine.

reacted by being pressed down by the atmosphere into the cylinder, so moving the end
of the beam down *(3.1)*.

The spread in use of such an engine at coal mines everywhere in the country meant
a big increase in the coal output, stimulating wider use of the fuel for domestic heating
and for industry. And the engines could also be used for dewatering metal mines, such as
the lead mines of North Yorkshire and mid-Wales, and the tin and copper mines of the
south-west. All such metals were in demand for the extensive new buildings being erected,
particularly in the Georgian period. Both lead and copper were used widely as roofing
materials, being soft and malleable. They could be rolled into thin sheets, and easily bent
into the complex shapes needed for roof details.

Developing the Steam Engine

But the Newcomen beam engine was rather inefficient in converting heat energy into
mechanical motion. It was a problem when metal mines were distant from the coal mines,
largely because the cost of transport was high. Cornwall is especially far from coal mining
regions, South Wales being the nearest source. One possible solution was for the coal to
be carried across the Bristol Channel by freighter direct to Cornwall, especially if the
mines were close to the sea, such as at Bottallack. Inevitably, however, the costs of transport
would be reflected in the price charged at the minehead.

So, how could the steam engine be improved? It was James Watt who made the crucial breakthrough with his rather ingenious solution to the problem. He was the first to recognise that the Newcomen engine was inefficient because the cycle involved reheating the cylinder at each stroke from cold to hot, a process which was then repeated endlessly. The cylinder was made from cast iron, so a lot of heat was absorbed without any useful output (apart from heating the local environment). Why not use a subsidiary and much smaller cylinder to condense the steam, and save the waste? With his training as an instrument maker, he built models to demonstrate the improvement which resulted, and his point was made. When he found a sponsor in Mathew Boulton, a Birmingham manufacturer, his career was made. The patent followed, but with an equally ingenious condition for potential licensees: he would take a third of the savings by using his machine as a licence fee.

The new, improved engine was slowly adopted by mine owners, especially those metal mine owners who were far from the sources of the fuel. Cornish users however, were continually trying to circumvent Watt's patent so as to make yet greater savings. The extension of Watt's patent in 1775 must have been a very bitter pill for the Cornishmen, because it would only expire in 1800.

Locomotives

Richard Trevithick, for example, was one such mine captain who was in perpetual trouble with Watt, but he responded in a rather innovative way. He realised that if safe and reliable boilers could be made, then steam at a higher than atmospheric pressure could give much greater efficiency in a steam engine than the Watt engine working at atmospheric pressure only. The entire device could be made physically smaller as well, since energy would be concentrated in a smaller volume of space. Trevithick went further than just using the new engines in mine dewatering, however; he eventually produced engines small enough to drive carriages in road vehicles. Fault for the failure of his attempts in the early 1800s lay not so much in his highly innovative designs, but rather in the poor state of the roads. Without effective ways of absorbing the vibrations caused by the many potholes, his machines would be doomed to early mechanical failure. It would not be till 1837 that rubber would be developed for shock-absorbing tyres for carriages, and even then, forgotten until Dunlop's pioneering invention of the bicycle tyre.

Trevithick also developed the first true locomotive to run on a trackway. He was asked to develop such a machine for a mine owner in South Wales, to save the costs of man or pony haulage. Such tramways had been developed over many years to improve transport of the coal (or mineral) from the pithead to storage or distribution to users. It was known as *Pen-y-Darren*, and its development marks a turning point in the use of steam power. But, despite much publicity, the idea failed to take off, one problem being the low strength of the cast-iron rails then used for tramways. They were easily cracked by the weight of the engine or the coal tubs it was hauling. It was not until about a decade later that his ideas were rejuvenated by coal owners, and their engineers, in the north-east of the country. It was one of the fastest growing coal fields in the country, with a range of pits in the counties of Durham and Northumberland.

George Stephenson

As an engineer, George Stephenson had considerable experience in maintaining pit beam engines at several different coal mines. His skills as an artificer were much in demand following a job he performed in 1811 on an underperforming Newcomen pumping engine. It was attempting to dewater flooded coal workings at High Pit near Newcastle. The machine did not have enough power to raise the water, and Stephenson was called upon to try to fix the engine. He observed that the critical part of the cycle, when a jet of water is injected into the cylinder to condense the steam, was not achieving the desired effect *(3.1)*. The reasons were that the water jet was insufficient to produce efficient cooling because the water pressure was too low, and the tubing size too small. The result was a poor vacuum, which could not lift the water from the pit.

The solution to the problem was two-fold: raise the water tank so as to give a greater pressure, and increase the size of the water tube. In the event he raised the tank by no less than 10ft, and replaced the tube feeding the jet. The changes were successful in creating a better vacuum, increasing the power of the engine, and eventually in opening the workings for coal extraction. As a result he was appointed to look after all the engines worked at the pits owned by the Grand Allies, the pit owners.

During this period, he was able to build thirty-nine engines, and develop underground haulage for collieries which had expanded greatly as a result of intensive working. For example, he installed tramways underground and three haulage engines at Killingworth colliery, as well as pithead haulage machinery. Both systems improved movement of the coal, and made extension of the workings much easier. But they came at some increase in risk, simply because steam engines underground needed boilers, and the furnaces needed to raise steam. Especial care was needed to enclose the furnaces and prevent firedamp reaching them, for the danger of gas explosions was ever-present in the gassy seams in this area of the coalfield. With the growth in extent of the workings underground, fires were already used to create ventilation throughout the galleries and coalface. They were situated at the base of a separate shaft, so that the hot flue gases would rise and pull in air from the workings. The flow of air needed careful control to ensure that all the galleries were ventilated, and so prevent the accumulation of methane (firedamp) pockets. Firedamp explosions were the cause of many explosions throughout the British coalfields, and great loss of life.

The Safety Lamp

One such explosion at Felling colliery near Gateshead south of the river Tyne in 1812 was to have national repercussions. It occurred on 25 May of that year in a newly opened part of the mine which was to work the Low seam. The firedamp explosion ripped through the galleries and emerged from the downcast shaft (the John pit, over 600ft deep), but further explosions followed, as one witness described:

The subterranean fire broke forth with two heavy discharges from the John pit, which was almost instantaneously followed by one from the William pit. A slight trembling, as from an earthquake, was felt for about half a mile around the workings; and the noise of the explosion … was heard to three or four miles distant … Immense quantities of dust and small coal accompanied these blasts, and rose high into the air…

So there were two explosions, the first quickly setting off another. Several survivors were found from the John pit about half an hour later, but it was realised that casualties would be high since the explosions had occurred during a shift change. Would-be rescuers who descended the shaft were defeated by afterdamp, the toxic gases left after an explosion, and hastily retreated to the surface. Just as they were ascending, another smaller blast rocked the mine, hastening their departure. A fire had started in the workings, and both shafts were sealed to extinguish it. It was only a month and a half later that the workings could be explored to reclaim the bodies of the victims. The disaster had claimed ninety-two miners, and was the worst yet to affect the British coalfields.

In the aftermath, there was a national furore. Pressure was exerted through the local, and eventually, the national press, to investigate the causes of such a terrible calamity in order to prevent future occurrences. Both Humphrey Davy, an eminent chemist working at the Royal Institution in London, and George Stephenson attempted to address a central problem in such disasters: the lack of a safe miners' lamp. Up till then, illumination in coalpits was by candle, which was an obvious way in which firedamp could be ignited. Miners knew of the dangers, and would evacuate when firedamp levels were high, for example, when a blow-out of gas occurred in a seam. But the danger remained ever-present, because methane is odourless, and effectively invisible. Only low amounts mixed with air are needed to cause an explosion (approximately 7–9 per cent). A protected flame lamp was needed urgently to forestall the possibility of igniting such mixtures.

Davy attacked the problem by guarding the flame with fine iron gauze, the cover allowing firedamp to enter, but preventing the flame propagating outside the lamp. It was a simple but apparently effective solution. Stephenson tackled it by restricting the air flow to the flame by fine tubes, and provided a glass chimney to direct the exhaust upwards in a controlled fashion. Both lamps were tested in gassy atmospheres and showed that the gas would ignite inside the lamp, but not penetrate through to the outer atmosphere. Neither patented their device, but a vicious dispute arose over priority. The facts show that they were entirely independent inventions, and both were used subsequently in many pits. Davy was rewarded by grateful coal owners with a prize of £2,000, while supporters of Stephenson rewarded him with the sum of nearly £1,000 (all of which was invested in Stephenson's new locomotive factory).

Endless subsequent discussion of the controversy has deflected attention away from a vital point: neither lamp was intrinsically safe, and would need much further improvement to be secure underground. Because of the enclosures, the light was reduced, and both were very poor sources of illumination. They could be damaged very easily in the severe working environment of a coal mine, the gauze by rusting or physical damage, the glass simply by being so fragile.

Explosions in collieries continued with ever greater casualties, despite the use of such 'safe' lamps. It is possible to argue that their introduction led to a false sense of security, and so actually increased the dangers to which miners were exposed. The ongoing problem led to several Royal Commissions on colliery lighting, and many improvements on the basic designs, such as multiple gauzes. Explosions could also be caused by many other sources of ignition, such as incendiary sparking from iron tools when struck a hard blow by rock or another implement, and uncontrolled use of explosives to drive tunnels. With the introduction of electric lamps towards the end of the Victorian period came the first great benefit of improved illumination, but also another danger, which came in the form of electric sparking between unprotected contacts.

The problem of flammable gas was also the source of another problem: coal dust explosions, which, because coal dust was present everywhere in the workings, could be ignited by a methane explosion, and so consume the entire pit. The suggestion, however, was not to be made until much later, when scientists like Michael Faraday (Davy's assistant at the Royal Institution) began to investigate pit disasters in great detail.

Improved Locomotives

But Stephenson's main effort in this period came to focus on developing means of hauling coal tubs by steam-driven locomotives. Trevithick had left a rich heritage in his machines, with much room for further improvement. But the priority disputes would increase in both number and bitterness as better locomotives were gradually developed. Trevithick had made several important discoveries when harnessing high-pressure steam to haulage, the ferocity of the fire being increased by exhausting the steam into the fire chimney, so that steam was raised that much more quickly. He had also proved that traction of iron wheels on iron rails was high, enabling heavy loads to be drawn. His original engine had the piston and cylinder working horizontally, making for an awkward connection to the wheels. A very similar locomotive was built on Tyneside in 1805, but the rails were even more fragile than in Wales, being built of wood and not surviving heavy use by iron wheels. Like *Pen-y-Darren*, it was reduced to working as a static engine.

However, the initial success of Trevithick's locomotives sowed a seed which sprang to life when conditions were ripe. The Napoleonic Wars created a shortage of fodder for horses (among many other shortages), and since coal was cheap at collieries, several engineers attempted to revive the idea. Blenkinsop redesigned the layout of the locomotive in 1812 and paid a royalty to Trevithick under his patent. He used two cylinders rather than one, and made them both vertical, so that connecting rods from the end of the piston rose above the engine. He also used a gear to drive the locomotive along a cast-iron rack fixed to the track. The engines he built were known as *Prince Regent* and *Salamanca*. Other engineers were equally active, including William Brunton of the famous Butterley ironworks near Derby. His engine was to explode, killing the driver and fireman in one of the first rail disasters. Boiler explosions were to be a recurring problem as the railways expanded.

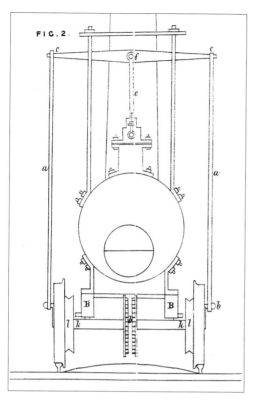

FIG. 2.

(3.2) Stephenson's Locomotive Patent.

George Stephenson similarly built a locomotive in 1814 at Killingworth colliery, and called it *Blucher*, after the Prussian general with whom Wellington was allied in the war against the French. The rails were crucial to the 5-ton-plus locomotives, so he developed cast-iron rails, rather than cast-iron plates or wooden beams on which the loco would run. They were pot-bellied (deep in the middle and narrowing to the sides) to resist the maximum load in the centre. And he also used a flanged wheel for the loco so that its travel would be positively guided. Stephenson simplified the transmission by coupling the crank rods directly to the wheels, and moved the cylinders directly over them to improve the drive. He also used a chain drive between the wheels and tender, patenting his improvements in February 1815 (Patent No.3887), a few months before the Battle of Waterloo *(3.2)*. One other innovation came from his hands: steam suspension ('steam springs') to improve the ride of the locomotive on the rails, an ever-present concern given the problem of brittle fracture of the cast iron. His development of the cast-iron rail was included in the same patent (No.4067 of 1816) for his steam springs. The Killingworth colliery wagon way was completely relaid using the new design of rail.

Stockton & Darlington Railway

Stephenson's success with his first locomotive led to many other developments, including commissions for more engines, sixteen being built for clients by the time he left Killingworth colliery. He also laid his patent rails at several other local collieries, effectively proving the integrity of his design. But bigger things were afoot. Tramways were widely used at collieries in all the coalfields of Britain, but they were relatively short, and were mainly powered by horses pulling the coal tubs (apart from the many collieries in Tyneside now powered by locomotives). Some were much longer, such as the Surrey tramway, some were twenty-five miles long, and there were several in South Wales of similar length, all worked by horses. For example, the Swansea to Mumbles tramway can claim to be one of the first to offer public transportation along the seafront.

With the expansion of colliery size, and the opening up of remote fields, there was increasing demand for longer tramways. The West Auckland coalfield, near Durham city, was a case in point. Proposals had been made in the 1810s for such a tramway to link the coalfield with Stockton to make the coal more readily saleable in the larger towns. A canal had also been suggested, but the new technology seemed to offer greater speed of delivery. The sponsors took the bold step of hiring George Stephenson as their surveyor and engineer to plan such a railway, which he did in 1822.

It was a single track line which exploited the latest technical improvements. John Birkinshaw had developed a way of rolling wrought-iron rails, and patented the idea in 1821. They could be made in 15ft lengths, longer than their cast-iron equivalent, and were much tougher when resisting imposed loads from locomotives. Stephenson recommended they be adopted for the new railway, despite his own interest in cast-iron rails. Once again, the brittle nature of cast iron had proved to be an obstacle to its structural use, especially when heavily stressed, so as to produce a tension under the loaded part of the component concerned. The line exploited both locomotives and fixed haulage engines, the latter being widely used in collieries to haul wagons up the inclined planes of drift mines, and cages up the shafts leading to the coal faces.

The line opened officially in 1825, to much local rejoicing, because not only did it prove a great boon for coal-carrying, but people could use the new form of transport too. And it possessed a very early cast-iron bridge designed by George Stephenson himself. A small bridge, it crossed the river Gaunless, on the line, and was quite different to Pont-y-Cafnau in design. The track was supported by ten cast-iron pillars braced diagonally with wrought iron, with semi-circular bracing under the rails. So cast iron could be used successfully, so long as it was only put in compression. It was a design which would be modified and adapted for the much larger structures which would be needed for wider spans as the railway network expanded.

Industrial Development

But it is Stephenson's next project which has come to symbolise the start of the great railway revolution, the Liverpool & Manchester Railway. Following the end of the Napoleonic Wars with France, the industrial revolution had gathered pace. Above all else, it was led by the textile industry, in which machines which replaced the human hand were developed by Arkwright and many others. By organising the nascent industry into factories, many machines could be arranged together to maximise the efficiency of manufacture. It was natural that those factories should be situated close to a supply of running water because the machines demanded energy for their running, and the watermill was the age-old solution to the problem of motive power. The greater the fall of water, the more energy was available, so the new textile industries were found in hilly regions of the country, where the fall was naturally greater than elsewhere.

The first industries were thus found in Derbyshire, in Lancashire and in Yorkshire where the Pennines, the backbone of England, created the height of land and the ready supply of precipitation for water power. But there were many other locations in Britain where mills and factories grew, such as in Flintshire and the Cotswolds. The engineering of watermills improved dramatically with the development of new mechanisms using both wrought and cast iron. The wheel itself could be made from iron hoops with the vanes of metal too, making it lighter and hence more responsive to the flow of water from the leet. Large dams for storing the water were built to supply the industry all year round with the precious commodity, enabling continuity of manufacture. The way in which the rotary power was transmitted to the factory improved too, with large belt drives working numerous shafts. Individual machines could be worked from a master shaft by slave drives, all of course now in metal rather than heavy and cumbersome wooden equipment. The belts themselves were formed from heavy duty textile fabrics, the precursors of modern conveyor belting, and made from strong flaxen fabrics.

As time went by, different regions tended to specialise in different fibres and textile forms, Gloucestershire and Yorkshire in wool, Lancashire in cotton, according to local supplies of the raw materials and historic ties. But Lancashire was different in that it needed large supplies of cotton, which could only be imported. The main source of supply was the cotton plantations of the southern states of the USA, so a large import trade built up between the nearest port, Liverpool and the largest manufacturing centre, Manchester, and its hinterland. The only routes between the two growing industrial towns were the turnpike and several canals, linked tortuously together to provide a poor transportation network. It was no way to supply a growing industry.

Liverpool & Manchester Railway

Thus arose the desperate need for better communications between the two towns, and the success of the Stockton & Darlington project had captured the imagination of local entrepreneurs and businessmen in the cotton trade. So began the fight to establish a new railway, but this time it would be a railway planned in detail and dedicated to carrying goods and people between two manufacturing centres.

The battle to start the railway was very expensive, partly because the technology needed was still developing, and many engineering problems would need solving 'on the hoof'. But those were not the only problems. Possible routes would need surveying, and if the plan was then approved by Parliament, much land would need to be bought over which both the rails would run, as well as for the depots and warehouses needed at either terminus. It was all a very risky undertaking, given the opposition of canal companies, who would suffer from the competition, and many landowners between the two towns who resisted sale. The Bridgewater Canal and the Mersey & Irwell Navigation would vehemently oppose the venture.

However, the project had some very powerful backers, amongst them were the leading businessmen of the towns (who had the greatest to gain) as well as some reformist and radical politicians, such as William Huskisson, a former cabinet minister in the Tory government of the day. And it was a reactionary government, led by the 'Iron Duke', the hero of Waterloo, but unequal to the task of reforming the British Parliament, and much else besides. It was a government formed from the aristocracy, with MPs selected by patronage and corruption. Indeed, many members represented small towns with small populations, such as the 'rotten boroughs'. There were also seats owned by aristocrats, with a tiny number of voters (often aldermen from the local council), that could be readily bought for cash. The government had failed lamentably to address key issues such as the price of food, the rise of industry, as well as issues such as slavery and basic human rights. It was a brutal government too, regularly using troops to suppress peaceful political meetings, such as the justly infamous Peterloo massacre that shook Manchester in 1817. There had been many riots protesting about the loss of jobs occasioned by the use of improved machines, especially in the textile and lace industries. The protesters were named Luddites after their mythical hero, Nedd Ludd. Gangs would roam the countryside smashing the new machines from 1811 onwards.

George Stephenson was the obvious choice to engineer the scheme, fresh with vital experience from the Stockton & Darlington Railway in the north-east. It was far from being a clean run, especially when it emerged (during Parliamentary enquiry) that his surveying results were deeply flawed. The plans were revised, and resubmitted to Parliament, eventually receiving approval in 1826. But there were still many practical decisions needed, especially the form of motive power. Fixed engines could haul carriages, and were in use on the Stockton & Darlington line, especially on severe gradients. The line was relatively level however, the only harsh gradients being at the Liverpool end, and either side of the Rainhill level, so locomotives seemed the obvious choice for running trains along the line. It was decided to hold a competition to test the many different designs of engine then either in use or development.

Rainhill Trials

The competition was held during October 1829 at Rainhill, about halfway along the route of the railway (by now nearing completion). Each competing locomotive had to haul a load of three times its own weight at a speed of at least 10mph. The locomotives had to run twenty times up and down the track at Rainhill, which made the distance roughly equal to a return trip between the two towns. Afraid that heavy locomotives would break the rails, only machines that weighed less than 6 tons could compete in the competition. Ten locomotives were originally entered for the trials, but only five turned up, and two of these were withdrawn because of mechanical problems. *Sans Pareil* and *Novelty* performed well initially, but mechanical breakdowns forced their exit. In the case of *Novelty*, the leather bellows which forced the draught through the furnace had caught fire.

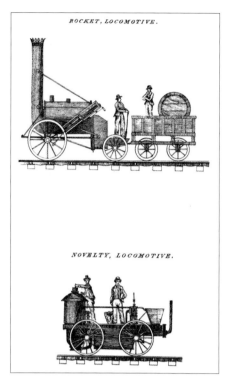

ROCKET, LOCOMOTIVE.

NOVELTY, LOCOMOTIVE.

(3.3) Rocket and Novelty.

It was a totally different design to *Rocket*, and underpowered by comparison, with a smaller boiler *(3.3)*. The clear winner was the *Rocket*, produced by George and his son, Robert, an engine quite different in design *(3.3)* to the earlier engines in use at Stockton, such as *Locomotion*.

Rocket was innovative in several ways compared with previous engines. For a start it was much more efficient in converting heat to motion. Robert Stephenson had replaced the single boiler tube (where the hot flames from the fire heated the water), by multiple tubes. It increased the surface area enormously, so heating the water much faster to boiling point. The piston was placed outside the boiler and worked directly on the wheels. It was the prototype of a long line of locomotives designed by Robert Stephenson, and served as a model for other engineers.

Completing the Line

Building the line itself was a superhuman task. Not only were there many rivers to cross, but the bridges would often need to be inclined at an angle to the banks (the so-called 'skew' bridges). The longest crossing at Sankey Brook (and Canal) needed a multi-arch brick and masonry viaduct of no less than nine arches, each of 50ft span. Experience in building such large structures had already been well established in canal aqueducts, such as the Barton aqueduct over the river Irwell, as well as the more recent Pontcysyllte and Chirk, where the cast-iron troughs carrying the canal rested on large masonry piers.

A quite different problem was faced crossing Chat Moss, a bleak moor roughly midway between the two towns. There were no stable foundations to be found there, so brushwood was piled into the bog until a firm footing was established. At the Liverpool end, a deep cutting through bare rock was necessary in order to maintain a steady gradient, and there were other cuttings needed to keep the gradient as shallow as possible. The final connection at the Liverpool end also needed a tunnel connection to the docks, and the gradient fell steeply, so a stationary engine was used for haulage.

Where the land fell away, embankments were needed to keep the gradients low. The works needed careful planning with the overburden from the cuttings supplying the mass of material needed for the banks. The bridges were also expensive, requiring skill, planning and good design. They were also the most highly stressed parts of the track, needing care in ensuring their integrity and longevity.

Water Street Bridge

In his description of the project published shortly after the opening, Henry Booth presented a table of all the sixty-three bridges and viaducts needed for the line, except one. While all were brick or masonry-built, the Water Street bridge was quite different. It was a cast-iron girder bridge, the girders were made locally by engineer William Fairbairn, operating from new premises in an industrial estate in Ancoats, half a mile from Water Street. Indeed, it was perhaps one of the first estates specifically dedicated to new industry, with mills, workshops and foundries grouped together and providing mutual support. Wear and tear of machinery would need constant maintenance and parts would have to be replaced to keep manufacture smooth and continuous. Improved designs of components could be prototyped and tested more easily if the machine shop was close by, enabling a fast turn-around. Likewise, large cast-iron girders required laborious transport from foundry to site, so the closer the two, the greater the saving in time and effort. William Fairbairn's company had been on the site since 1817 and he had developed and made a wide range of equipment over the years, including some of the first iron hulls for ships using riveted wrought-iron plate, iron watermill parts, and steam engines.

Cast-iron Girders

The Water Street bridge would have been well within his capabilities as a designer and the foremost engineer of the town. Some of his first work had been in draughting plans for large cast-iron beams for an arch bridge (including the wooden patterns), and in renewing textile drive machinery in cotton mills. In one project, for example, he had replaced cumbersome wooden drive shafts and drums with lighter cast- and wrought-iron devices. His skills were applied to many projects both in Britain and on continental Europe, and included building two 50ft diameter waterwheels for mills at Catrine in Scotland. He developed a new design for a wrought-iron bucket which allowed air to be vented easily, and so improved their effectiveness as they filled with water from the mill leat. He had also used cast-iron girders in mill construction, along with other architects and engineers. As the factory system had grown in the eighteenth century, buildings dedicated to storage both of raw materials and finished products became essential. Wood was used at first, but all wooden construction made them susceptible to fire, with total loss the usual result. As confidence in cast iron grew, designs for so-called 'fire-proof' warehouses were developed. They used cast-iron beams and brick to create the floors, supported by cast-iron columns. Engineers had by this time appreciated that further weight savings on the rectangular slab (as in the ribs of the Coalport bridge) could be made by removing metal from either side of the slab to produce an I-section.

The cast-iron beams were designed not just to support the floor above, but were also used to create the floor from their lower flanges. Arches were then built across the flanges with bricks so as to fill the gap between the girders (so-called 'jack' arches). In section they comprised a vertical web with two large lower flanges at right angles to the web, and often smaller flanges at the top of the web. When top-loaded, the girder would bend into an arc. The degree of deformation was resisted by the flanges, especially the lower pair since these were put into tension. Systematic tests on different forms of the flanges by workers such as Tredgold (later followed by Hodgkinson, who worked with Fairbairn in Manchester in the late 1820s) showed that larger lower flanges were more effective in supporting the overhead load. These workers tested different section girders to destruction, a simpler test than measuring the deflection at different loads, but potentially misleading since strength is much more sensitive to defects in the iron. Nevertheless, they inferred that large lower flanges and smaller upper flanges were the way forward. In effect, they had discovered that cast iron is much stronger in compression than tension, by about a factor of six. Indeed, the upper flanges in such floor beams could be omitted altogether, saving weight and placing more of the load where it was best supported.

So a design for cast-iron girders in buildings led directly to a possible design of horizontal girders for the Water Street bridge. Hodgkinson and Fairbairn refined their design further by curving the lower flanges so that they were of greatest width towards the centre of the giant main beams. The flanges were then used to support smaller cross girders, whose flanges could be used to construct the jack arches to plug the gaps in the floor of the bridge. The final design of the bridge thus consisted of five massive girders 29ft 9in long to span the roadway below, supported by cast-iron columns moulded in classical fashion. At nearly 54ft the skew bridge was wide enough to support four railway lines. The balustrade was moulded in cast iron to match the Greek columns, and the two footways either side were also covered.

The bridge functioned well for much of the life of the railway itself, until a crisis of confidence in all cast-iron under-bridges arose as a result of the failure of a bridge at Norwood in London at the end of the century. It was demolished in 1902, and replaced by the present structure, next to the restored station, now part of the Manchester Science Museum *(3.4)*. It retains some of the features of the original in the panelling of the balustrade, while a Greek column can just be seen on the bridge behind. Pictures of the original bridge show similar decoration of the facades, in keeping with the aesthetics of the time.

(3.4) Water Street bridge next to the stationmaster's house at Manchester.

(3.5) Manchester terminus on the L&MR.

Sneak Preview

Before the formal opening there were opportunities for a select few to experience the thrill of travelling by steam loco. One such visitor was Fanny Kemble, then acting on stage in Liverpool. Aged twenty-one, she had made her debut the previous year in *Romeo and Juliet* at Covent Garden, and was invited by no less a person than George Stephenson to a trial run a month before the official start. She was in a party of sixteen, and gives a quaint description of the locomotive:

> *We were introduced to the little engine that was to drag us along the rails. She (for they make these curious little fire engines all mares) consisted of a boiler, a stove, a small platform, a bench, and behind it a barrel containing enough water to prevent her being thirsty for fifteen miles. She goes upon wheels, which are her feet and are moved by bright steel legs called pistons; these are propelled by steam, and in proportion as more steam is applied to the upper extremities (the hip-joints, I*

suppose) of these pistons, the faster they move the wheels; and when it is desirable to diminish the
speed, the steam, which unless suffered to escape would burst the boiler, evaporates through a safety
valve into the air.

She goes on to describe the controls:

The reins, bit and bridle of this wonderful beast is a small steel handle, which applies or withdraws the
steam from its legs or pistons, so that a child could manage it. The coals, which are its oats, are under
the bench. This snorting little animal, which I felt rather inclined to pat, was then harnessed to our
carriage, and Mr Stephenson having taken me on the bench of the engine with him, we started at about
10mph.

And then the start of the journey at Liverpool:

The steam horse being ill adapted for going up and down hill, the road was kept at a certain level …
Almost at starting it was cut through the solid rock which formed a wall on either side of it, about
sixty feet high. You can't imagine how strange it felt to be journeying thus without any visible cause of
progress other than the magical machine, with its flying white breath, and rhythmical, unvarying pace.
After proceeding through this rocky defile, we presently found ourselves raised upon embankments ten
or twelve feet high; we than came to a moss … on which no foot could tread without sinking, and yet
it bore the road which bore us.

They were about halfway along the line, and were approaching the Sankey viaduct:

We had now come fifteen miles and stopped where the road traversed a wide and deep valley. Stephenson
made me alight and led me down to the bottom of this ravine, over which he has thrown a magnificent
viaduct of nine arches, the middle one of which is seventy feet high. It was lovely and beautiful beyond
words. He explained to me the whole construction of the steam-engine, and said he could soon make
a famous engineer of me, which, considering the wonderful things he has achieved, I dare say is not
impossible.

She was clearly entranced by the whole experience, and especially by George Stephenson
himself, despite the gulf in their ages. Such a romantic introduction to the new railway
deserved an equally romantic opening, but the reality was quite different.

The Grand Opening

The Liverpool & Manchester Railway was opened on 15 September 1830 to great
acclaim. The prime minister, the 'Iron Duke' himself, and a large number of politicians,
including Sir Robert Peel, William Huskisson (a former President of the Board of Trade,
MP for Liverpool, and a promoter of the railway) business people and other celebrities
attended the opening ceremony held initially at the Liverpool end of the line. Fanny
Kemble left a vivid description of the events that day:

The most intense curiosity and excitement prevailed, and though the weather was uncertain, enormous masses of densely packed people lined the road, shouting and waving hats and handkerchiefs as we flew by them. We travelled at 35 miles an hour (swifter than a bird flies). When I closed my eyes this sensation of flying was quite delightful. I had been unluckily separated from my mother in the first distribution of places, but by an exchange of seats which she was enabled to make she rejoined me when I was at the height of my ecstasy, which was considerably dampened by finding that she was frightened to death, and intent upon nothing but devising means of escaping from a situation which appeared to her to threaten with instant annihilation herself and all her travelling companions.

She was right about the dangers of fast locomotives, because the opening was marred by the death of one of its promoters, no less a person than William Huskisson. Several trains had started along the track, but the train carrying Wellington had halted when *Rocket* was seen approaching at speed. The events were witnessed by many there, including one of Wellington's companions, Lady Wilton:

The engine had stopped to take a supply of water, and several of the gentlemen in the directors' carriage had jumped out to look about them. Lord Wilton, Count Batthyany, Count Matuscenitz and Mr. Huskisson among the rest were standing talking in the middle of the road, when an engine on the other line, which was parading up and down merely to show its speed, was seen coming down upon them like lightening. The most active of those in peril sprang back into their seats; Lord Wilton saved his life only by rushing behind the Duke's carriage, and Count Matuscenitz had but just leaped into it, with the engine all but touching his heels as he did so; while poor Mr. Huskisson, less active from the effects of age and ill-health, bewildered, too, by the frantic cries of 'Stop the engine! Clear the track!' that resounded on all sides, completely lost his head, looked helplessly to the right and left, and was instantaneously prostrated by the fatal machine, which dashed down like a thunderbolt upon him, and passed over his leg, smashing and mangling it in the most horrible way.

Although not killed, Huskisson was badly injured, and was carried by train to a local vicarage to be tended there. He died later in the day. And he was not the only one to die during the early life of the railway. Ten masons were drowned, for example, when their boat overturned during the building of the bridge over the Irwell at the Manchester end. After these traumatic events, Fanny Kemble resumed her journal:

When we neared Manchester the sky grew cloudy and dark, and it began to rain. The vast concourse of people who had assembled to witness the triumphant arrival of the successful travellers was of the lowest orders of mechanics and artisans, among whom great distress and a dangerous spirit of discontent with the government at that time prevailed. Groans and hisses greeted the carriage, full of influential personages, in which the Duke of Wellington sat. High above the grim and grimy crowd of scowling faces a loom had been erected, at which sat a tattered, starved-looking weaver, evidently set there as a representative man, to protest against the triumph of machinery and the gain and glory which the wealthy Liverpool and Manchester men were likely to derive from it.

A reception had been planned at the Manchester station with refreshments for the distinguished guests. The sour treatment from the crowds of protesters, however, could not induce Wellington to leave his carriage, so the celebration was muted. It must have come as a shock to the premier to realise the depth of opposition to his reactionary policies, especially on reform of the Parliamentary system. Growing industrial towns were poorly represented in the House of Commons, if at all. Fanny Kemble continued her successful stage career, but then a few years later, left for the USA, never to return to Britain.

The party was due to return to Liverpool for a grand banquet, but in the driving rain, couplings failed and the party arrived far too late for the celebration. Wellington had, in any case, left the train three miles before Liverpool to visit a friend, so the banquet was suspended. He refused to travel by train for many years to come, a reflection of his conservative attitudes, especially political reform, the issue on which Huskisson had resigned from his cabinet a few years before.

L&MR in Operation

Expectations of the new railway were high, and were completely realised, and indeed exceeded. Travel at speed was very novel, and the L&MR attracted many passengers simply for the experience. It also opened up new and unusual views of the surrounding town and country-scapes. Everyone, or at least those who could afford the fare, could now share Fanny Kemble's thrill of riding a train. Whenever new railways were opened a similar effect occurred, bridges and viaducts being especially exciting for their exposure to great heights. The first train (and many of the subsequent) to cross the Tay bridge in 1878 attracted sightseers for just the same reason.

Passenger and goods services were run, with three trains a day leaving each terminus to meet demand from the public and merchants. The journey took nearly two hours with stops at intermediate stations, as well as picking up water. Second-class coaches were soon introduced with a single fare of 4 shillings (compared to a stage coach fare of 10 shillings inside, or 5 shillings outside). Special excursion trains were organised to view the Sankey viaduct. The competition between road and rail was unequal, however; the coach journey took over twice as long, and was much less comfortable on the unmade roads of the day than the smooth ride on the level rails. By the year end, fourteen of the twenty-four stage-coaches working between the two towns had been withdrawn. Returns on the L&MR were good, the first five months of 1831 showed a profit of £30,000, providing a dividend of 4.5 per cent to the lucky shareholders. Freight carriage also grew rapidly following the boom in passenger services.

The problems of running a regular service were numerous. For a start there was always the risk of accidents from the moving trains, as highlighted by Huskisson's death at the opening ceremony. Most at risk simply by proximity were railway staff themselves. The loco *Patentee*, for example, exploded while hauling a goods train, and both driver and fireman were immediately killed. In another accident, workmen had put a plank over the rails to provide a seat for a meal break. *Phoenix* hit the plank at speed, the fireman was thrown from the engine and killed under the wheels. The fireman on *Mercury* was crushed when uncoupling a wagon, by being caught between the vehicles.

Signals to warn engines of other trains on the line, or other obstacles to progress were needed, especially when visibility was poor. Fog, rain and night-time operations would need care during driving, for example. Speed was difficult to judge, and drivers frequently ran into the stops, the problem being exacerbated by poor braking on the locos. In 1832, an engine ploughed into a standing train at Rainhill station, killing several people. And there was the ever-present problem of people or animals wandering onto the line. Three passengers were killed in 1833 when waiting for a train, having wandered along the line while waiting they were struck with little warning. By-laws would be enacted to prevent trespass on the rails, and (then as now) the press were always alert to the news value in railway accidents. Special policemen were stationed at regular intervals along the line, but were often too far apart (about a mile) to be able to prevent serious accidents. They also acted as signalmen in the early days before being replaced by mechanical devices.

As with the introduction of all new technology, improvements to machines and equipment were continuous, both to respond to passenger safety and comfort, and to extend the life of the investment. Henry Booth himself invented a new screw coupling to hold carriages closely together, and limit buffeting during train stop-start. Braking was very primitive on the first trains, and was improved by Stephenson with his self-acting brakes, although hand-operated screw-operated wheel rim brakes became the norm. They were not very efficient, and as train speeds increased over the years, searching for a solution would prove to be a problem. It would not be until the 1870s that pneumatic air brakes acting on all carriages simultaneously would be introduced.

Demand for locomotives to haul the increasing amount of traffic on the line was incessant. Within seven months, Stephenson's company in Newcastle had supplied no less than eighteen new engines (including *Rocket*). By 1834, there were twenty-seven Stephenson locomotives working the line. Weights had also increased from *Rocket* (4 tons) to *Goliath* and *Sampson* at 10 tons, and six wheels were introduced with later engines, spreading the weight more evenly on the rails. Speeds increased too with larger more efficient engines. *Planet* completed the distance between the two towns in just one hour in 1830 on a test run, averaging 30mph, but achieving up to 40mph on the straight *(3.6)*. However, speeds were initially limited for safety reasons to no more than 20mph, and engines were forced to slow down on bridges and high embankments. The improved performance of locomotives was achieved by increasing steam pressure, and making the pistons drive the wheels horizontally, rather than the inclined position, as on *Rocket*.

Mechanical wear and tear on the engines was high, with axle breakage and wheel fractures a particular problem (probably caused by fatigue, as would be shown by the terrible Versailles accident in France in 1842). As the number of trains working the line increased, both with goods and passenger services, the track itself suffered severely from the rolling contact, exacerbated by the increasing weight of the engines.

The rails were in a very poor condition within just two years, and the whole route was relaid with new wrought-iron rails during 1836. Such experiences were of great benefit to the other new lines then being built or planned, such as the London to Birmingham railway.

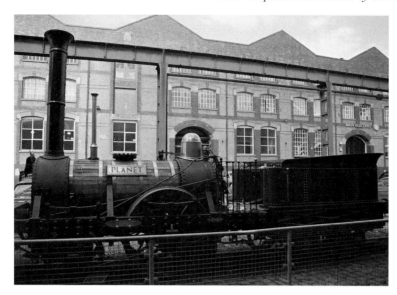

(3.6) Replica
locomotive at
Manchester
Science Museum.

That the condition of the track was vital to safe transport can be judged by an account of an accident shortly after the line was opened. It happened a week after the official opening and was investigated by intrepid reporters from the Mechanics Magazine. It had involved Braithwaite and Ericsson's engine, *William the Fourth*, and had occurred on 24 September, when the engine was returning to Manchester over the Sankey crossing:

> *We reached the scene of the accident about day-break … We have seldom witnessed anything more fearful. But that the embankment on the left hand consisted of soft earth and sand, in which the engine at once embedded itself, up to the nave of the off wheel, it must have inevitably gone over, and, with all the persons in attendance upon it, been dashed to pieces. Had the ground been hard, or had the sleepers on which the rails are laid only protruded a foot or two farther, nothing could have averted such a catastrophe. As it was, one person only was slightly wounded, and the engine not irreparably damaged.*

They then proceeded to investigate the causes of the incident:

> *The report of the engineer and other persons on the engine and accompanying tender was, that they believed the accident to have been occasioned by some obstruction thrown across the rails; but as it was dark at the time (about seven o'clock) they could not positively assert as much. Neither had they taken any pains to ascertain, on the instant, whether their suspicions were well-founded. Some men engaged in repairing this part of the railway had left off work shortly before, and it was supposed that some of their tools might have been left accidentally lying across one of the rails. On minutely surveying the ground, however, which it was admitted remained in status quo, we felt convinced there was no foundation for this supposition. The tools of the workmen were all laid out very carefully on the outside of the embankment, and there were no broken fragments or splinters to be seen anywhere within a hundred yards.*

What then had been the cause of the accident? Had it arisen from any deflection or irregularity in the rails? We took a bricklayers level, which we found among the tools, and applied it to the rails for the space of about ten yards in the rear of the spot where the engine was lying. At the distance of ten yards the outside or left-hand rail was a quarter of an inch higher than the opposite rail; at nine yards nearly level with it; at eight yards and onwards to the engine, an inch and a half lower.

This sudden deflection at once accounted for the whole affair. The flange of the off-wheel having lost its hold of the rail, the engine, as a matter of course, slipped off, the tendency to do which was probably increased by the circumstance of the wheels of the tender (which was in advance of the engine) not being fixed to the axles, as is the case with Mr. Stephenson's tenders, and ought, we think, to be the case with all carriages which have to travel on such unprotected embankments as those of the Liverpool and Manchester Railway.

Accidents such as this could have been much more serious if the locomotive had rolled away out of control down the embankment *(3.7)*. The company would maintain a record of near misses, as well as more serious incidents, not just to remind engineers of the importance of track safety for the paying public, but also to follow claims with the contractors. The fact that the incident was reported publicly would serve as a warning for the general public, and many future accidents would be widely reported in the popular press.

Great Reform Act

The push for reform reached a crisis in 1830, when a bill to replace the rotten boroughs with a fairer system of representation was put before the House. Moreover, it proposed a wider franchise. Instead of aldermen and placemen, the franchise would be extended to male ratepayers of a certain standing. Although much more limited than some of the proposals made by the reformers, it was a sea change in attitudes from the endemic corruption of the existing system, and thus was opposed bitterly by the aristocracy who controlled Parliament. So, how could an elite body of men be persuaded to relinquish their own power? How could a bunch of turkeys vote for Christmas?

Not all the ruling elite were reactionaries, for a start. Some of the nobility had actually led the way in developing the new technologies, like the Duke of Bridgewater, for example, who had pioneered the early canal system. The later Grand Junction Canal was supported by the likes of the Duke of Grafton, Earl Spencer and the Marquis of Buckingham. Many other peers had benefited from the development of the L&MR, when their land was purchased for the line, and would make more money as new schemes were developed. The new link between Manchester and Liverpool was proving highly popular with the general public for the better communications, and judging by the sheer number of proposals for new lines, it was clear that change was happening fast. Manufacturers approved the better links for fast transport of finished goods as well as the vital imports of cotton needed for the textile industry, for

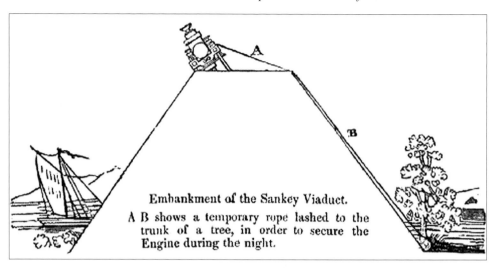

Embankment of the Sankey Viaduct.

A B shows a temporary rope lashed to the trunk of a tree, in order to secure the Engine during the night.

(3.7) A mishap on the Sankey viaduct on the L&MR.

example. Local people benefited from food transported by rail, giving farmers better access to the hungry towns, and fresher food for the populace.

Agitation for reform was widespread both in the towns and cities. It stemmed from rising food prices, itself encouraged by the Corn Laws, which guaranteed high prices to farmers by imposing tariffs on imported food. There was widespread disturbance in the countryside in 1830, as new threshing machines threatened the jobs of farm labourers, echoing the Luddite revolts of 1811, after the Napoleonic Wars had ended. Gangs of labourers roamed the countryside, especially in southern counties, adopting the name of their imaginary hero, Captain Swing. Letters signed by Swing would warn farmers of impending visits by the gangs, to smash machines and burn ricks. Machine wrecking even extended to new machines for papermaking, as at High Wycombe. Retribution was very harsh, and substantial bodies of troops and militia were deployed in those counties most seriously affected. Nearly 2,000 rioters were brought to trial at a special Assizes between November 1830 and March 1831. Of those convicted, nine were hung, 644 imprisoned and 481 transported for life to Australia, one of the largest contingents ever sent there.

In June 1830, King George IV had died, prompting a general election for the autumn. He was succeeded by his brother, William IV. Although most seats had already been bought or settled, there were a few seats with large electorates, such as the county seat of Yorkshire (another of the issues for reform was the highly variable qualification for voting). Henry Brougham, a rising lawyer and reformer, was one of the candidates. Both seats were won by the Whigs, including Brougham, who had travelled the county giving radical speeches. The election was a long drawn-out affair owing to variations in local practice, but Wellington's government were clearly losing votes, of those who were actually qualified to vote. He was wholly against any change in the Parliamentary system, despite the rising tide of opinion for reform.

Matters came to a head at the end of November 1830, when the government lost a vote on the civil list in the Commons. The list effectively paid government monies to royalty and hangers-on, much of it for sinecures, and other non-jobs. Earl Grey became the new Whig prime minister, supported by Lord John Russell, Lord Althorp (ancestor of the late Diana, Princess of Wales) and Brougham, so reform was on the cards. It was to be a long hard battle, however, with entrenched opposition from the bulk of the aristocracy, landed classes and others with all to lose from the introduction of something starting to resemble democracy. They introduced a reform bill during the 1831 session of Parliament, and although they won by one vote, a vote in the committee stage was lost. A constitutional crisis was in the offing. The King opposed reform, and so did the House of Lords. The bill went far to abolish rotten boroughs, but not far enough for the radicals. Another general election was called, in which the only real issue was reform. The Whigs increased their support, and effectively won the election. The nation supported reform, despite the electorate still representing only a very selective part of the total population. The reform bill was carried by a large majority in the Commons, but the game was far from over, because it was then summarily rejected in October 1831 by the House of Lords.

The people answered directly. There were riots across the country, a mob in Nottingham burnt the castle down, and the Duke of Wellington's famous House in London was attacked. Large meetings allowed the people to vent their anger at the behaviour of Parliament. That the future of the whole nation was at stake can be judged by the infamous Bristol riots at the end of October. A general meeting in the centre of the town was attacked by troops, and two men were killed. The rioting continued for over three days, many properties were destroyed by fire, and hundreds of people butchered by the troops. If the will of the people was for an insurrection, then this was the time. Unrest was widespread, with rick-burning commonplace. To add to the national misery, there was the first outbreak of cholera in London during the winter months.

Earl Grey proposed the creation of new peers to break the deadlock in the House of Lords, a proposal which has been repeated a number of times over the years during clashes between the Lords and Commons. A new bill was introduced before Christmas with minor changes, and this time passed both houses. But the Lords wanted further changes, leading Grey to resign. The King, by this time no doubt fearful for his own position, promised Grey the new peers he needed to force reform through, and the threat was strong enough for the bill to be passed into law. The nation had started to become democratic, and it is no accident that the new railways then coming into reality had coincided with the decision for change. They were a very visible reminder that change was vital for the country as a whole to benefit from the new technology. And it was not the only issue which would be raised in the coming years. Slavery, reform of the law, improvements to education, improving the lot of working people, repeal of the Corn Laws, and tackling the Irish problem would dominate future debates. The new railways would be a factor for change in all of those debates.

Henry Booth put it well when he wrote in his book on the building of the railway:

But perhaps the most striking result produced by the completion of this Railway, is the sudden and marvellous change which has been effected in our ideas of time and space. Notions which we have received from our ancestors, and verified by our own experiences, are overthrown in a day, and a new standard erected, by which to form our ideas for the future. Speed-despatch-distance are still relative terms, but their meaning has been changed within a few months; what was quick is now slow; what was distant is now near; and this change will not be limited to the environs of Liverpool and Manchester – it will pervade society at large.

A Manchester man, Archibald Prentice, went further in articulating the force for change exerted by the railway:

The opening of the Manchester and Liverpool Railway was one of the events of 1830, which was not without its influence, in future days, on the progress of public opinion. The anti-corn law agitation was wonderfully forwarded by quick railway travelling and the penny postage. Even in 1830 the railway promoted the cause of Reform. It was an innovation on the old ways of travelling, and a successful one; and people thought that something like this achievement in constructive and mechanical science might be affected in political science. It brought, besides, a little proprietary borough, which nobody had ever seen before, into full view. I recollect when passing over it for the first time, I said to a friend- 'Parliamentary Reform must follow' soon after the opening of this road. A million of persons will pass over it in the course of this year, and see that hitherto unseen village of Newton; and they must be convinced of the absurdity of its sending two members to Parliament, whilst Manchester sends none.

London & Birmingham Railway

The great success of the L&MR stimulated extension of railways to other parts of the country, most notably for the Grand Junction Railway linking Manchester and Birmingham, and a line to link Birmingham with London. The project to link the nation's capital and Birmingham, another industrial town which had grown fast during the preceding years was a premier challenge. With the experience of the L&MR to guide him, Robert Stephenson was appointed engineer-in-chief, and tackled the job with gusto.

It was to be a much longer railway, nearly 112 miles long from terminus to terminus compared with only thirty-one miles of the L&MR. The L&BR was formed as a company in 1833, and the line finally completed in 1838, although part had been open for some time before, this was the section between London Euston and Denbigh Hall, near Wolverton, about halfway along the line.

The survey of the proposed route would, like the Manchester line, aim to minimise the distance by taking as near a straight line as possible between the two cities and at as low a gradient as geography allowed. Stephenson wanted a gradient no greater than 1 in 330 for any given mile, and was helped in his survey by the existing route of the Grand Union Canal of 1803, which established levels through much of the route. And the line follows the canal through much of its more circuitous route, especially through the major obstacles, most notably the Chiltern Hills north of London and the Heights of Northampton. The former rose to nearly 1,000ft above sea level, comprising relatively soft chalk, but the latter (effectively a continuation of the Cotswolds) consisted of much harder limestones. The route would skirt the heights of these hills by exploiting gaps and valleys, but still had to negotiate lesser hills on the dip slopes. To keep a low gradient, the track would be laid in a deep cutting in the chalk, a massive undertaking owing to the depth of material which would have to be removed. The line was at its highest at Tring, 420ft above sea level. The Tring cutting was excavated entirely by navvies, labourers named after their employment in the not dissimilar work needed to cut canals. System was brought to bear on the job by organising them into squads to remove the overburden with nothing much more than spades and wheelbarrows. As the cutting grew deeper, the barrows were run up planks inclined on the sides of the pit, assisted by long ropes powered by horse gins. The Tring cutting was 2½ miles long and 60ft deep at its deepest, and is still impressive, like the Blisworth cutting further north. Not far away is the almost equally impressive cutting for the Grand Junction Canal, about 1½ miles long and 30ft deep.

The only exception to the gradient occurred at the London end of the line, where the terminus at Euston was below the level. A massive engine house was built about a mile from Euston to house the stationary steam engine needed to haul trains up the gradient. It was not dissimilar to the arrangements needed on the L&MR at Liverpool, where the Wapping tunnel was created to allow access to the waterfront, which also involved a high incline.

Wolverton

After traversing Aylesbury Vale, the railway reached the valley of the Ouse at Wolverton. Here the Grand Union Canal and the track were very close, and indeed crossed one another several times, as they had done in many places elsewhere on the line. Wolverton would be the centre of a locomotive and carriage works serving the whole line, and a large station was built here. Crewe and Swindon would play a similar role for the Grand Junction and Great Western Railways which were the next to be completed. Wolverton station was built at the edge of the Ouse Valley, one of the largest to be crossed, and very large embankments and a viaduct were needed here. J.C. Bourne, who produced many exceptional paintings of the line in a guide to the new railway published in 1839, records that:

> At this station the railway crosses the Grand Junction Canal, for the fourth time, by an iron bridge with horizontal main ribs, and then enters upon the great Wolverton Embankment, which extends across the valley of the Ouse to an extent of one mile and a half, being the longest on the line: it averages 48 feet in height, and is composed chiefly of clay, gravel, sand and lias limestone. In its course is a viaduct, consisting of six principal arches, of an elliptical form, having a span of 60 feet each, and rising 46 feet from the ground to the crown.

Bourne went on to describe some of the problems in the creation of this gigantic bank. One occurred just beyond the station, when part of the bank slipped away into the valley for a distance of 170ft. The gap created needed a wooden trestle bridge to carry the track across. The earth used in the bank posed the problem of spontaneous combustion from its iron sulphide content, which, in one case, burnt the wooden sleepers laid on the track. Some landslips can still be seen on the embankment just outside the modern Wolverton station.

The rail workshops grew into a very large concern, but all is now closed, and the modern rail track bypasses the old station (or what little is left of it). Despite the neglect

of the old Wolverton works, many of the massive works left by Stephenson are still visible *(3.8)*. The iron girder bridge mentioned by Bourne, for example, is well preserved and shows that the bridge was enlarged several times in its long life. As the track was widened, more girders were simply added alongside those already there. The original girders bear the name of Butterley, the foundry in Derby which supplied much cast iron to many projects here and elsewhere. The design of the girders is unsophisticated when compared with those at the Water Street bridge in Manchester. There is no curvature in the flanges, for example, to allow for greater resistance at the centre compared with the edges. There are no jack arches, but simple plates laid across at the top under the track.

It must have been relatively easy to transport the massive girders, probably by the canal over which the track runs. The returns from the Grand Junction Canal Co. show that 1836 was the busiest year in its history, and much of that business will have been carrying goods for the railway. Use of cast-iron girders will have kept costs low, just like the Water Street bridge in Manchester, certainly by comparison with the stone-built viaducts which were much more commonly used. Headroom was also saved, unlike the arched bridges. After the railway had been completed, tonnage carried on the canal dropped as goods were transferred to the new line, an inevitable result of faster carriage.

Stephenson's cast-iron girder bridge at Wolverton station is now a Grade I listed structure, like some of the other buildings, which should at least preserve them for posterity *(3.9)*. There were other cast-iron bridges which have been replaced because of the serious problems which arose from using such a brittle material, and the accidents which occurred when they broke under the weight of passing trains. But the magnificent brick arch viaduct survives almost totally intact (it too was enlarged for extra tracks), and is well used by the present Euston-Manchester line. There is a very similar brick viaduct

Opposite: (3.8) Deserted Wolverton works by the Grand Junction Canal, with cast-iron girder bridge at right.

Right: (3.9) Cast-iron girder bridge over Grand Junction Canal at Wolverton.

further north on the same line, at Wolston, where the railway crosses the river Avon and the Brandon to Wolston road.

Blisworth Cutting and Kilsby Tunnel

There was another deep cutting needed at Blisworth, where the line passed through the limestone, needing more effort on account of the greater hardness of the rock:

> *The rails are in some places nearly sixty feet below the upper surface. Its length is one mile and a half, and the quantity of material excavated was 1,000,000 cubic yards. The nature of the soil rendered the whole of the operation extremely difficult; and as the contractor was unable to accomplish his work, the Company were obliged to execute the greater part of it.*

According to Bourne, 3,000 barrels of gunpowder (each of weight 100lb) were needed to blast through the rock, and this method had been used elsewhere on the line where the geology was adverse. The cost at Blisworth was twice the initial estimate, a familiar story elsewhere on the route of the railway. At the station built at Roade, passengers could alight for coaches to carry them to Northampton and elsewhere. But there was a limit to the depth which could be excavated by hand (and explosive), largely dictated by the cost of the operation. At some point it would be more economic to drive a tunnel, and just this happened at Kilsby. Different engineering skills were needed, those of mining. In the event, the work was harder than had been thought, largely because of unexpected strata, layers of porous sand through which water poured to flood the tunnel. Owing to many similar engineering problems, the tunnel was the most difficult project of all those needed for the new line. The problems in driving the tunnel delayed the opening of the complete line by many months, and increased the cost of the project, just like so many of the other large engineering projects.

The tunnel was built from shafts cut vertically at regular intervals (eighteen in all) plus another two shafts left in place for ventilation, was 2,442 yards long, and required no less than thirteen steam engines and extra horse gins to remove the water from the workings. It was by far the longest tunnel then being built anywhere on the rail network. Stephenson built the tunnel much larger (28ft high) than was strictly needed for simply allowing passage of trains. It was done to relieve fears of suffocation of train passengers by steam and smoke from locomotives, which were prevalent at the time. Indeed, rail tunnels were places of great hazard, as future accidents would amply demonstrate. The Clayton tunnel disaster (1861) revealed the problem of trains travelling too close on the same line, a problem associated with time-interval working.

Shorter tunnels had already been widely used closer to London, including the Watford, Primrose Hill and Linslade tunnels. The former had encountered several problems, including sudden floods of water released from newly exposed strata in the sides of the excavation. One had been so bad as to kill ten workmen in the tunnel at the time.

So the problems of the Kilsby tunnel were not isolated or unique, and had been encountered years earlier in driving the narrower tunnels needed on the Grand Union through geologically similar strata. The nearby Braunston tunnel is 2,042 yards long, nearly 16ft wide and 12ft high. Construction in 1796 encountered quicksands, and additional shafts were sunk. They were needed to correct poor alignment of the tunnels being driven from either end. The engineer for the shorter Crick tunnel was Benjamin Bevan (the same engineer who designed the Cosgrove aqueduct); it is 1,528 yards long, and suffered similar problems with quicksands.

But it was Blisworth tunnel on the Grand Union which suffered the longest delays, taking twelve years to build, (between 1793 and 1805). It is the longest tunnel on the waterways of Britain, being 3,076 yards long (over 1¾ miles), in total. Nineteen shafts were sunk on the alignment, and like the other tunnels nearby, suffered water ingress. Such was the pressure to use the canal, due to the delays in finishing the tunnel, a toll road and then a tramway were built to carry goods across the hill. The tramway, three and a half miles long, was designed by Benjamin Outram, and engineered by Jessop and Barnes. So it cannot be said that Stephenson had not had fair warning of the potential geological problems before Kilsby tunnel was built in very similar ground.

The fear of fume suffocation in such narrow and poorly ventilated tunnels was fully justified, as shown by an accident in 1861, when two bargees were killed by fumes from a steam barge using the Blisworth tunnel. As a result, more ventilation shafts were added, bringing the total to seven. The exhaust gases from all combustion engines are rich in carbon monoxide, a highly toxic gas produced in high quantities by incomplete burning of the fuel. The gas reacts with the blood more readily than oxygen, so the vital oxygen is displaced, and the victim dies of asphyxiation. It was the most common cause of death in the many pit disasters of the era, for example, when coal gas or dust explosions occurred underground. Those who were not killed by the violence of such explosions usually succumbed to the deadly gases left behind, the dreaded 'afterdamp', a mixture of gases of which the most toxic component is carbon monoxide.

Blisworth Railway: Grand Junction Canal

While the tunnel was being built, there was a problem in carrying goods on the canal, much of which had already been opened for business. A toll road was thus opened between Stoke Bruerne dock and Blisworth wharf, so that they could be carried across the intermediate hill. Pressure for raising revenue was always present in such an expensive project as building a canal. But the road proved a poor substitute, and so a railway was proposed by Jessop in 1799. Originally, when the Wolverton section had not been completed, it was suggested that the railway should run all the way to Old Stratford. But since work had already been started on this section, it proved more sensible to make it a much shorter affair, simply replacing the existing toll road from Stoke Bruerne. This was a wise decision, given that building a line was considerably more expensive than a road of the same length. The greatest expense lay in the cost of the cast-iron rails, the material still being an expensive commodity. But growth in its use had been stimulated by Thomas Telford and others, so prices were starting to decrease. Benjamin Outram designed and built the new railway, using L-shaped cast-iron rails (facing outwards), which allowed flat wheels to be used on wagons containing the goods. They were hauled by horses, as used elsewhere on tramways. Outram undoubtedly used his experience of colliery railways to build the line, and several Grand Junction engineers visited coal mines in Derby to see the system working first-hand. The tramway gave good service while the Blisworth tunnel was being constructed. When no longer needed, it was dismantled and used to construct another line to Northampton, while a branch canal was being dug from the Grand Junction. Many artefacts from the railway are on show at the Canal Museum in Stoke Bruerne, but little is left of the old tramway, apart from a bridge over the route halfway along its line between Stoke Bruerne and Blisworth.

So the drive to establish working lines of communication could use all the available technology to improve revenue and so satisfy the burgeoning demand for goods. Establishing one kind of communication link stimulates development of others, and continues to the present. Far from being competitors, the canals and railways often worked together in transporting goods. Barges (70ft long by 14ft wide) were well adapted to carrying long, heavy objects such as cast-iron girders, for example, when compared with small railway wagons. The large holds of barges were also well adapted for transporting bulk supplies such as bricks and stone and timber beams, all of which were needed for the construction of the railway infrastructure.

National Network

Completion of the L&BR and the Grand Junction Railway now linked London and Manchester, and further lines would expand across the country. The main lines stimulated branches, an activity well under way on the L&MR while it was being built. The new Manchester Railway created a corps of workers who would be kept employed on similar projects for many years to come. The engineering expertise would be honed and developed on the model created on the new line, using low gradients and straights at best, or smooth curves, for rapid and easy transportation. Train speeds would increase as locomotives improved, increasing competition with canals and turnpikes. Many standards were created by the first railway at Manchester, not all of which were adopted by other major projects, the most notable exception to the standard gauge (for example), being the much wider gauge of the Great Western Railway. The company owned and operated lines mainly in the West Country but their reach extended as far as Oxford and the South Midlands, with its London terminus at Paddington.

However, many areas of the nation were barely covered, if at all. Wales was especially bereft of new lines, the main problem being the mountainous geography, where low gradient railways would be more expensive to build. The bridges needed would necessitate longer spans than ever before, especially in the north at the Menai Straits, and in the south over the river Severn. Those challenges would be met by entirely new designs, or scaled-up versions of existing bridges.

The materials available for these structures would create problems for the design of the bridges, but pioneering research would show the way forward in bridge construction. The work would also highlight the special problems of railway bridges. There were many warnings of the problems of using cast iron.

4

The Great Project

The completion of the Grand Trunk line from Manchester to Birmingham, and the London to Birmingham lines, gave the country the backbone upon which other lines could be attached. Lines converged on Chester both from Birmingham and Manchester, but a link to Holyhead and then Ireland had yet to be achieved. The project had political overtones, because Ireland was an integral part of Britain, yet, in the 1840s the country was suffering from a series of deadly blights affecting their staple crop, the potato. There had been agitation in Ireland against absentee landlords, and there was deep malcontent with rule from the mainland. Holyhead was relatively close to Dublin by sea, so the route both by road and rail to Anglesey was strategic for policy makers in London. For example, better communications would greatly help relief aid such as food reach the people more quickly and help alleviate the suffering of the people.

The London to Holyhead railway line was one of those great Victorian projects which emerged from the frantic construction of a national rail network in the UK in the 1840s, a period known as 'railway mania', when the growth of the new railway network stimulated investment on a grand scale in many new and radical proposals for new lines. All had to be approved by Parliament, which was overwhelmed by the escalation of proposals. Many of those proposals were spurious, and were never realised. There was extensive speculation in railway shares, with some operators of existing lines not just manipulating the market, but manipulating their own balance sheets.

As one of the principal pioneers of the rail network, Robert Stephenson was appointed engineer of the final link in the line from London to Holyhead. It was possible by now to travel by rail from London to Chester, but no further into Wales. There were many engineering challenges on this line, the greatest being the Menai straits, but the estuary of the river Conwy on the coast of North Wales and the nearby cliffs at Penmaenmawr also presented major difficulties to overcome.

Railway Progress

The railway pioneers had visibly demonstrated the great success of their new lines, especially the L&MR, the London & Birmingham and the Grand Junction lines. Although very expensive in terms of the engineering works needed, the purchase of land along the route, and the plans needed to convince Parliament, the revenue had generally exceeded expectations. Moreover, the basic engineering skills were well developed, these skills mainly comprised making cuttings, building embankments, driving tunnels and constructing small bridges to cross roads, streams and small rivers. Contractors such as Thomas Brassey of Chester had developed managerial skills in marshalling teams of navvies in the extensive labouring needed.

The first lines had now found solutions to many of the problems which occurred to trains working their lines. Crude mechanical signals had been invented and were being used on the new lines, and the technology of manufacturing meant that wrought-iron rails were well established. Problems of communication along the line were still present, but help had appeared in the form of telegraphy, transmitting messages along wire conductors laid beside the track, and linked to dip needles in the signal boxes being built at regular intervals along the tracks. Wheatstone's new apparatus was destined to be highly popular as the most reliable means of communication between stations along a line, but why was it important? It could perform a vital role in warning stations of the impending arrival of trains, advising them of any hold-ups or breakdowns, so that the travelling public could be assured of the situation if their train failed to arrive on time. By the same token, stations could warn stations ahead of the safe leaving of a train. In the event of a train breakdown, following trains could be stopped from proceeding, and so collisions with the stopped train could be prevented. Communication was essential in the case of the fixed engines at the head of the inclined planes between Wapping and the entrance to the tunnel on the L&MR, and between Euston station and Camden on the L&BR. The engine man had to know when to release the clutch and so haul the train from the station. The only method then available was a pneumatic tube, where vibrations were transmitted from one end to the other along the air passage. Pressure at the sending end would activate a whistle at the other end. Fine for short distances, but impossible on long reaches. Michael Faraday had already demonstrated the significance of electricity and its interesting properties, and inventors soon took up at least one possible application in sending electrical pulses along a wire. Wheatstone and Cooke developed the first electric telegraph, an invention which would ultimately transform communications, not just on the railway, but in everyday life. The telegraph was first used on the L&BR, and then the GWR in the late 1830s.

Breakdowns were not infrequent events given the ongoing problems with the mechanical failure of moving parts on engines (wheels, axles, pistons etc) as well as broken couplings between carriages. Wheel breaks on carriages were also fairly common, despite their lower loading than engines. All such problems increased with the age of the equipment, as wear and fatigue took their toll on moving parts, and corrosion ate away at metal components. Although external metalwork could be protected by liberal and frequent application of oil and grease, inner parts could not be protected so easily. It would be a growing problem as locomotives aged, especially at critical parts of fireboxes and boilers. The latter were constantly exposed to water at various temperatures, and often water of variable composition. Locomotives were becoming larger, giving greater power and, inevitably, greater speeds.

Such problems could not be ignored, but they could be controlled by regular maintenance of hard-used equipment. Engineering problems on the larger scale of making lines had been solved, and there seemed to be no reason why bigger problems should not be tackled. The engineers were confident, although some of the problems facing them in some of the new proposals were daunting. Nevertheless, their self-confidence engendered a sense of confidence among the investors who were needed to supply the working capital to a new railway company.

Ireland

The link between London and Manchester had been established by the Grand Junction and London & Birmingham Railways in 1838, and work was afoot on the creation of numerous branch lines from the major trunk routes. Just this had happened with the L&MR, with branch lines to Leigh and Wigan, amongst others. The same effect occurred on the two long lines between the large towns, one such being a link from Crewe to Chester. Crewe was rapidly becoming the centre of the Grand Junction Railway, with workshops, marshalling yards and warehouses, just as Wolverton and Swindon were emerging as the centre of the L&BR and the GWR. Crewe, in particular, was to become a hub of links to other parts of the country.

The issue of a national rail network was becoming a hot political topic, especially the link from London, the centre of political activity, and Ireland. It was an integral part of the country then, and sent many members to Parliament. And those Irish MPs were very active and vocal in arguing for their needs, both practical and political. The Irish Problem was a regular topic in Parliament owing to the pressure for religious freedom for the bulk of the Catholic population, the need for reform of the feudal land polices then in operation, and improvement of the basic standard of living of the people. Ireland had little native industry, and had not seen the immense changes experienced on the mainland. The north had a small textile industry (linen produced from home-grown flax), but there were no coal deposits to support industry, and the bulk of the population was employed in agriculture, on very small plots of land of low fertility. As a result, emigration to England was high, especially as large numbers of labourers were needed on engineering projects such as the canals, railways and much else besides. The population was very much larger than it is today, about 8,000,000 compared with the current figure of about 4,000,000, showing how many Irish people emigrated during the Victorian period and later. The aristocracy owned large areas of Ireland, and their income from rents was sacrosanct. Some progress had been made to greater religious tolerance by the Catholic Emancipation Act of 1828, but prejudice was still common. The Act enabled Catholics to be elected to the House of Commons, from where previously they had previously been barred.

A link to the port of Holyhead by rail would improve communications with the island, and the possibilities included faster mail delivery and quicker export of goods (especially food). Investigations were started in 1839 with the appointment of a commission to study the problem of new networks on the mainland, as well as starting new networks in Ireland. They consulted widely and discussed the various proposed routes, eventually coming down in favour of a line running along the coast of North Wales, so avoiding all the mountains which dominated the hinterland. Inland routes via mid-Wales, such as the one proposed by I.K. Brunel, were rejected. George Stephenson's proposed route was lower in cost than alternative suggestions. Holyhead would make the best terminus since a good harbour existed here for ships to Dublin. Their final report in 1840 recommended

Stephenson's route from Chester via Bangor, but there were key gaps at the Conwy estuary and the Menai Straits. How would they be crossed?

Early Suspension Bridges

Comment in the technical press questioned whether or not a suspension bridge (like Thomas Telford's road bridge over the Straits) could withstand the greater weight of trains, and there had already been problems with the stability of the deck in high winds. Just a week after opening, on the night of 7 February 1826, high lateral winds destabilised the deck so that users could not travel across. Six suspension rods of wrought iron were found fractured the next day, and much of the deck was seriously damaged. Then, on 19 February, another gale broke twenty more suspension rods, with a further fifty bent, presumably by violent deck movements. A stagecoach had crossed safely, but on 1 March the movement of the deck had been so bad that the horses had fallen and become entangled with one another, needing to be cut free. The upshot was clear: the structure had to be modified by using stronger suspension rods and connections to the deck, which itself was also strengthened. The designers of other suspension bridges should have been more aware of the problem of wind-induced oscillations, but, unfortunately, they repeated the same mistakes made by Telford. Much later, in 1839, the structure suffered serious damage from a gale, and it was not the only bridge of similar design to have been damaged in that decade. The bridge at Montrose suffered severely in 1836 from wind damage, and the famous Brighton chain pier was effectively destroyed by a violent storm in 1836. As with earlier damage to this structure (which was effectively three suspension bridges linked to one another extending into the sea), the pier was repaired. The pier had been designed by Captain Samuel Brown and extended 1,300ft into the sea when finished in 1823. It served as a docking point for cross-channel ferries (or 'packets'). Brown had patented his way of constructing the main suspension chains in 1817, and had also built the Union bridge near Berwick-on-Tweed in 1820. It was the first suspension bridge ever to be designed for vehicular traffic, and still carries it, although use is limited to one car per crossing. It was not the first chain suspension bridge, there are earlier examples from the USA, including James Finlay's chain bridge of 1801 at Jacobs Creek, Pennsylvania, and White & Hazard's wire-rope bridge at Fairmont, Philadelphia, 1816 (both now demolished). They mainly used conventional wrought-iron multiple link chains from which the deck was suspended, rather than the eyelink system patented by Brown.

However, to suggest that a suspension bridge could carry heavy trains and remain stable seemed highly unlikely. So an entirely different kind of structure would be needed to cross the Menai Straits.

Final Approval for the C&HR

Another government report produced in 1842, this time concerned with Post Office Communication with Ireland, approved the Stephenson scheme. Sir Robert Peel was now premier, taking over from the reformist Whigs in 1841, but he was now imbued with the idea of yet further reform, having opposed the 1832 Act. He had clearly been persuaded by Whig policies, such as Catholic emancipation in Ireland (he was also MP for an Irish seat), the abolition of slavery, and the establishment of non-sectarian Universities. Lord Brougham, a prominent Whig leader and Lord Chancellor in the previous government had, for example, helped found University College, London. Agitation continued in the country, albeit muted compared with the earlier disturbances, and the causes this time were espoused by the Chartist movement and the Anti-Corn Law League. The defects of the 1832 Reform Act were plain for everyone to see: by putting a financial sanction on the right to vote the vast mass of working people were excluded. And Parliament was still largely dominated by the aristocracy, although they were elected by a uniform ballot across the country. Peel was strongly supportive of the new railway proposal, particularly as better links could improve the lot of the Irish.

A further report was called for, in this case, from James Walker, an eminent civil engineer. He had worked with Thomas Telford on the Caledonian Canal, and much of the new system of docks in London, including the East India, West India and Surrey Docks. He would later design several important lighthouses (especially Wolf Rock, and Bishops Rock), and many canals, but his experience of railways was more limited. He preferred an arch bridge over the Straits, and was rather critical of Stephenson's proposed line, especially along the rocky coast of North Wales. Despite these misgivings, Parliament approved the Act establishing the C&HR in 1844, the bridge over the Menai Straits required separate approval.

Railway Inspectorate

But the government was now becoming more interventionist with all railway schemes, this was because the government would be partly financing the new Holyhead railway through a Royal Mail contract to carry letters and parcels; the penny post had been introduced in 1839, and carrying the mail was an important revenue-earner for all new railways. The power to negotiate with the railways had been activated by an Act passed in 1839. The public had responded to a faster communication route for their writings with a much increased output, although the telegraph system would later increase the speed of communication. However, the telegraph system was still being developed at this time, with no national system yet in existence.

And secondly, the public concern over railway accidents had led to the first Regulation of Railways Act in 1840. This first Act of Parliament directly related to controlling the system, required the railway companies to collect data on their total traffic, and accidents on their lines. It was to be a major exercise in data collection, and statistical analysis of the results was published for public consumption. It was an important innovation, because it enabled the government to assess the gravity of a particular technical problem causing accidents involving personal injury, and possibly regulate accordingly. It also established the Railway Inspectorate to provide independent reports on accidents, and make recommendations to improve particular aspects of the evolving railway system. However, their recommendations could not be enforced without new legislation. The reforming Whig government of Grey and others had already created a precedent for an independent and paid inspectorate by the Factory Act of 1833 (promoted by Lord Althorp), which controlled working conditions in factories. The Factory Act controlled and limited the length of the working day, for example. Further acts prohibited the employment of children in mines and other hazardous places, such as chimneys.

The first Inspector General appointed by the government in 1840 was Lt-Colonel Frederic Smith, but he only held the post for a year before taking up the job of Director of the School of Military Engineering at Chatham. He was succeeded by Major-General Charles Pasley (born in 1780), the previous Director at Chatham. He was an expert in siege warfare, having participated in the siege of Copenhagen of 1807. General Pasley was a hero of the Peninsular War, when, as ADC to Sir John Moore in the retreat to Coruna in 1809, gave his horse to a wounded soldier, and finished the retreat on foot with only one boot. The commander was killed in the battle, and his burial gave rise to a famous poem *The Burial of Sir John Moore* by Charles Wolfe, a poem well known to generations of schoolchildren. Pasley started the School of Military Engineering in 1812 with the help of Wellington, and was appointed a Fellow of the Royal Society in 1816. He was a specialist in subsea diving and telegraphy. His main area of expertise was in the semaphore telegraph developed for purely military reasons in the Napoleonic Wars, but he was also of great assistance in their use on the railways. In 1838–40, he was involved in the destruction of the *Royal George* using a new diving suit to lay explosive charges. The wreck blocked a channel leading to Portsmouth harbour. He was promoted to Major-General in 1841 when he became Inspector General of Railways.

All inspectors would be recruited from the Royal Engineers, presumably because they had extensive experience in both civil and mechanical engineering. Artillery and muskets needed just as much care and attention to function correctly as a locomotive, and active military experience demanded discipline and training. Indeed, some officer inspectors would return to active service after a spell on the Railways and gain high office. On the other hand, they could not have had much experience of railways, and learning on the job would be a vital skill. Liaison with railway staff involved in an accident would involve tact and diplomacy.

But, perhaps most important of all, investigating accidents needed keen observation, just as much as any detective, to spot incongruent details, the broken part perhaps, which caused the accident, rather than being caused by the accident. The remains should be kept intact until the inspector arrived, a task usually assigned to the policemen working on the line. The temptation to clear the line would be great in order to get traffic moving again, but it was far more important to establish the causes of an accident so as to prevent future accidents of the same kind. Inspectors would need to question eye witnesses to determine the exact sequence of events during and prior to an accident. This was not always a straightforward job, perhaps because a witness may have been a participant in the accident. The most important witnesses in many accidents would be the driver and brakeman (or brakemen), and in collisions they might also be victims, and in the worst cases, dead, so vital testimony would be missing. Many of the first accidents to be investigated were in fact reasonably straightforward, so the first inspectors were able to build up their expertise to be used when more problematical accidents occurred.

First Investigations

The very first accident to be examined by the new Inspectorate occurred on 7 August 1840, when a heavy casting fell from a wagon next to the engine of a passenger train. It derailed several coaches and four passengers were killed. It happened on the Hull & Selby Railway near Howden. The facts of the accident were only too clear, and the recommendations fairly obvious. Care was needed in loading wagons so as to ensure a stable load, and stable not just when static, but also when the wagon was moving.

The next accident involved another derailment, this time on the North Midland Railway between South Wingate and Ambergate, killing two passengers, just a month after the Howden accident. The following day, a train collided with another travelling in front, killing one passenger; it happened at Bow on the Eastern Counties Railway. It illustrated the problem of the time interval method of controlling train movements, and the inspector, Lt-Col Thomson, recommended that drivers should be trained in the arts of controlling a large locomotive and its train, that there should be a minimum time interval of thirty minutes between trains, and that mileposts should be erected along lines so that passengers should be able to measure their train speed with a watch. The first proposal seemed rather optimistic, given the pressure on the new railways to increase traffic and so increase revenue.

In the very next accident, another collision occurred when a goods train ran into the rear of a passenger train, killing two passengers. The accident was on the York & North Midland Railway at South Milford Junction on 11 November 1840. Sir Frederic Smith recommended that no train should be allowed to leave less than ten minutes after the preceding train, a much smaller margin of safety than thirty minutes. He also recommended that a red flag or lamp be displayed to warn oncoming trains, preferably mounted on a post. The problem was compounded by the variability of time recorded on station clocks, because when Captain Melhuish inspected the Birmingham & Gloucester Railway, he found that Down trains used Birmingham time and Up trains Cheltenham time. The times varied between ten and fifteen minutes apart! He made a strong recommendation that time should be standardised so that no ambiguity could occur in future.

The problem of standardisation of routines and equipment across the country would come to a head with the battle of the gauges, but was not to be completely solved until much later in the century.

Sonning Accident

One of the first accidents to cause multiple casualties occurred at Sonning in darkness at 4.30 on the morning of Christmas Eve 1841. The accident was caused by a landslip blocking the line, with which the train collided. The landslip, induced by heavy rain during the night, occurred in a particularly deep and steep-sided cutting on the GWR line between Reading and Twyford. It bore some comparison with the Tring cutting, being a mile long and 60ft deep. The passengers were standing in open-sided, unroofed wagons, and many were thrown out or crushed between the wagons. As a result, eight people died and there were seventeen injuries. Many of the dead and injured were artisans returning home after working on the new Parliament building in London, the open trucks and mix of goods and passenger wagons increasing the severity of the accident.

The inspector was Lt-Colonel Frederic Smith, and his report could not find any fault with the construction of the cutting itself. Trains on the GWR at this time were probably the fastest of any on the network, their locomotives by far the biggest owing to the broad gauge used on the GWR, and were capable of 60mph. The locomotive was *Hecla*, a near new 2-4-0 engine, she was hauling the train from Paddington to Bristol. The long train comprised two third-class carriages, a covered parcels van, and no less than seventeen goods wagons. It was likely that the train was travelling at high speed when it collided with the mass of earth blocking the line, and there can have been little warning given the poor illumination shed by the loco's lights. However, the inspector did criticise several features of the train itself. The passenger carriages were immediately behind the engine, followed by the goods wagons. It meant that the heavier wagons at the rear crushed the passenger carriages on impact, and the luckless passengers stood little chance of escaping without injury. His report detailed the condition of the passenger coaches. They were not equipped with spring buffers, so there was little resistance to the momentum of the goods wagons. The passengers were almost completely exposed to the winter weather, only being protected by a 2ft-high board around the sides of the coaches. The seats were rudimentary to say the least, being planks raised just 18in above the floor. And the GWR was by no means unique in running such poorly equipped trains: the practice of mixing goods and passenger trains was commonplace on the growing network.

If this was an example of a problem occurring across the network, it was a chance for the government to show its mettle. By this time, 1,556 miles of railway were open to the public, and over 20,000,000 passengers were carried that year.

George Stephenson's Letter

The following March, Parliament was hearing evidence before a select Commons Committee, and received a letter from George Stephenson regarding safety on the railways which he had done so much to create. The letter supported the case for greater government control:

> *I am quite sure that some interference on the part of the Government is much wanted … I am convinced that some system should be laid down, to prevent wild, and visionary schemes, being tried, at the great danger of injury or loss of life to the public. I consider it right that every talented man should be at liberty to make improvements, but that the supposed improvements should be duly considered by proper judges.*

After emphasising the need for engineers from different companies to work in collaboration, he then made his own specific proposals:

> *I should propose for the consideration of the different Engineers that the speed of Locomotives should not exceed forty mph on the most favourable lines, excepting on special occasions: curved Lines to diminish*

in velocity, according to their radius. I am quite aware that this cannot be carried out to any great nicety, but it would still be a check on the Drivers. Collateral Lines require government consideration is a very strong point of view. Uniformity of signals is another desirable point. As several persons are now turning their attention to the construction of self-acting breaks [sic], it will soon appear that great benefit and safety to travelling will be found by their adoption.

Six wheeled Engines and carriages are much safer and more comfortable to the travelers than four; any person riding one hundred yards upon an engine or coach constructed upon this plan would discover the difference. The rim of all Railway wheels ought to be made the same width, and the axle trees for all coaches of a strength approved of by the Engineers, both wheels, springs and axles should bear the government stamp, to being made of the best materials, as every practicable means ought to be made use of in order to have these made of the best iron.

Some of his comments perhaps reflected the recent tragedy at Sonning, especially the comment about train speed, and others concerning the quality of wrought-ironwork, the continuing problems with broken wheels, axles and springs. In hindsight, the geometry of their form will have been almost as important as the material of which they were made, but engineers were only just coming to appreciate the importance of metal fatigue.

Inspecting New Lines

As a result of their experience, the Inspectorate made forceful representations to the Board of Trade to tighten the existing regulations. The most important new power requested by the inspectorate was to be able to examine new lines before trains were allowed to run upon them. Such an examination would reveal the state of the track (a problem highlighted by the Sankey viaduct derailment of 1830 on the L&MR), and the condition of structures such as bridges, embankments and cuttings. Many entirely new railways were coming into being in the 1840s, and the inspection of the much greater length of tracks being built would be a time-consuming but essential role for the inspectorate. It would also help to reassure the travelling public if a new line had the government's stamp of approval. The power was duly granted in the new Act of 1842, and included the important safeguard that opening a new line could be refused, if found to be dangerous, defective, or incomplete in some way. The power would be exercised in the future, showing that the inspectorate was not a toothless quango.

Further Legislation

William Gladstone was a rising star in Parliament, having at first been a Tory in the previous Whig government he had, like Peel, been converted to the progressive camp. He was appointed by the premier to the post of president of the Board of Trade in 1843, a post he was to hold for two years. The Sonning tragedy stimulated Gladstone, in what came to be known as 'Gladstone's Act', to introduce new legislation in 1844 to improve the railway network, further regulating the way the network operated.

The new act introduced several innovations. The increasing power of the railway companies on the national scene prompted the government to award itself the power to nationalise the railways, should the need arise. Gladstone also instituted a new procedure for examining new proposals, an Advisory Board, so that such schemes could be seen in the larger context, rather than in purely local terms. Thirdly, the Act ensured that cheap travel was provided for the poor, by insisting that the companies run trains which offered tickets at no more than one penny a mile, the so-called 'Parliamentary' trains. And finally, it authorised the electric telegraph to be used alongside all railway lines, for their own use as well as by the government and the public. The last provision was to be the most important for rail safety, because telegraphy allowed almost instant communication between stations and signal boxes. Trains could now be tracked, and in the event of breakdown, others could be warned of a blockage on the line.

Gladstone showed great perspicasity in his bill, the cheap train proposal being well received by working people, who had been neglected by the companies up till then. They had been more interested in catering for the upper classes, who naturally paid more than artisans. The Sonning accident highlighted the way in which they treated the bulk of the population: conveying workers like goods. Perhaps the fact that many of the victims had been working on the new House of Commons swayed opinion in Parliament. The nationalisation clause was not activated until the next century.

Railway Mania

Although the economy had been severely depressed in the early 1840s, the rapid growth of railway lines on the ground prompted an era of speculation in railway shares, which came to be known as 'Railway Mania'. Schemes for new railways multiplied fast, especially where the geography was easy, and the engineering costs would apparently be low. Because the first railways, especially the L&MR, L&BR, Grand Junction and GWR had proved so successful, with a myriad of other railways now criss-crossing the country, there seemed limitless opportunities for investors in new links and branch lines, as well as bigger projects such as the C&HR, and major lines for Wales and Scotland. The success of the new railways was visible to an increasing number of the population, especially in the fixed assets such as viaducts, stations and other engineering works.

The depression of the early 1840s gave way to increasing prosperity, and in 1844, the Stock Exchange gave opportunities for new listings. The market was dominated by a handful of the large established companies including those already mentioned, as well as the Midland, London & South Western, South Eastern, Eastern Counties, Newcastle & Carlisle, Manchester & Leeds and the Birmingham & Gloucester.

The key year for the railway network was 1845. Parliament sanctioned 2,816 miles of new railway that year, equal to the total approved since 1821, when the Stockton & Darlington Railway was sanctioned. It was clear that the new Advisory Board would be very busy. It was chaired by Lord Dalhousie (later he was to create the Indian Railway system), and included General Pasley and three other members. Its terms of reference were headed by the need for public safety, and the rest of the remit focused on ensuring that all the schemes were substantive

LORD BROUGHAM'S RAILWAY NIGHTMARE.

(4.1) Punch cartoon, 1844.

rather than speculative operations. One of their objectives was to lower capital expenditure by recommending alternative routes using existing lines, a useful razor given that no less than 240 new railway bills had been presented to Parliament by May 1845. The committee was to be grossly overworked, as *Punch* showed in a famous cartoon of the time *(4.1)*. The committee certainly cut the mass of proposals down, but it engendered powerful opposition and was eventually abolished. Their work brought attention to the problem of different gauges, mainly the Stephenson gauge of 4ft 8½in and the Brunel broad gauge of 7ft. Tests were conducted by Sir Frederic Smith, G.B. Airy, the Astronomer Royal and Peter Barlow of the Royal Academy, Woolwich, but were inconclusive.

It was a time of endless inventions to improve the railways, and one proposal seemed, on the face of it, to save energy and provide smoother travel: the atmospheric railway. Principally supported by I.K. Brunel, it replaced the steam engine with a pneumatic tube running along the track. The air in the tube was evacuated by a steam engine, and the train was connected to a piston in the tube. The train would be driven by the air pressure acting on the piston. The idea passed many tests, and a railway on the south coast of Devon was built at great expense by Brunel. It failed dismally owing to poor seals for the vacuum, and the line was converted to conventional engines, leaving the investors and Brunel with egg on their faces.

But there were other worries about the railway network, especially the nature of the materials being used by railway engineers in the many structures needed to create it. The concern arose from a quite different source: failure of cast-iron beams in fire-proof mills and other buildings. Just such a new mill had collapsed suddenly during restoration work, and the disaster was analysed in detail to find the causes.

Collapse of Mill at Oldham

In late 1844, a fire-proof building collapsed suddenly, killing twenty mill workers, and injuring many more *(4.2)*. The disaster was reported widely, and at a national level in the new *Illustrated London News*. Improved printing methods giving faster turnaround produced many new journals, including the celebrated *News*. Like many other similar papers, it sought to provide its readers with the latest news from home and abroad, and included the most sensational disasters, illustrated wherever possible with pictures of the ruins. Quite apart from the serious death toll, it was an important story because cast-iron beam buildings were in widespread use in all parts of the country, and not just for mills and factories. Many large public buildings in London used cast-iron beams as primary supports for floors, such as Parliament and the British Museum.

The inquest was held locally at the Black Swan Inn, Mumps in Oldham. It produced some graphic accounts of the way the collapse occurred, such as that from William Mills. He had been mending a dropped jack arch on the top floor of the six-storey building on 31 October 1844:

> *I am a bricklayer, and was working at Lower House Mill, Messrs Radcliff and Sons. One of the arches in the flooring of the top story had given way about five inches in the crown, and I pulled about a third of it out, and put it in again … I took it out on Tuesday night, and on Wednesday it was got ready for me, and I put one length … in on Wednesday night … It was flagged over the top, and the flags of the next bay had given way, and showed it to the master … One of the ends of an iron beam had broken … and I showed it to Mr Radcliff, and he said it was a pity they broke that way. The beam had lost only one ear, and had not lost all its bearing on the pillar. I had just pulled the middle part out, when I saw the gable end fall*

Worse was to follow as the initial failure set off a chain reaction:

> *One of the men working near the end ran, and before he could reach it, it went down, and him with it. It went bay after bay, the roof following the floor, beginning with the gable.., and coming towards me, and I saw it going bay after bay, for perhaps a minute, and when it came to me, down I went with it. My head was badly cut, but I was never insensible.*

He was lucky to have escaped the sequential collapse, and his statement was supported by his fellow bricklayer, Thomas Mellor. But what had caused the accident? The jury asked for an expert opinion and called for William Fairbairn, the engineer who had made the Water Street bridge on the L&MR. He had gained a national reputation for his development of new machines and components, such as his Lancashire boiler for steam engines. His experience was called upon to investigate boiler explosions, which usually caused utter devastation to the surroundings, often bringing mills and factories down. He

(4.2) The collapsed mill at Oldham.

RUINS OF THE LOWER-HOUSE MILL, NEAR OLDHAM.

was the natural choice to investigate this disaster, and was accompanied by a colleague, David Belhouse, an architect. The testimony and visible remains pointed to brittle fracture of one or more of the beams, which then set off a cascade of other failures. The mill had been extended by adding an extra wing in May 1844, so was only six months old at the time of the accident. Although the boilers were inundated with falling debris, fortunately they did not explode.

The testimony of the bricklayers pointed to the jack arch, which they had been restoring, as the source of the collapse. The broken girder had fractured laterally as a result of sideways pressure from the other arches, despite support being given by temporary wood beams inserted to take the pressure. The iron beam broke near the supporting column *(4.3)*. The long iron beam next to the one which cracked and adjacent to the gable end was more heavily loaded owing to the greater width of the bay, so the initial break destabilised this beam, which cracked in turn and the gable end fell away.

Fairbairn considered that all the cast-iron beams were under-designed for the loads they would have to bear, with a breaking strength at the centre of about 10 tons, apparently equivalent to a uniformly distributed load of 20 tons over the entire length. However, the load from mill equipment above was distributed unevenly, giving a lower breaking load of 15 tons. The actual load was 13.75 tons, so the safety factor was only about 1.09, far too close to prevent failure if there were hidden flaws in the castings. Extra loads were imposed by the temporary work replacing the jack arches. Since all the beams were of the same nature, when one small failure occurred, the overload made failure of the entire structure inevitable.

The disaster so raised public concern that an official report was commissioned from Sir Henry de la Beche, a distinguished geologist, and Thomas Cubbitt, an eminent engineer and builder. They probed further than Fairbairn, and found that many of the broken girders from the mill showed brittle cracks, some of which probably pre-dated the disaster. They were caused by cooling the castings too quickly, then by removing them when

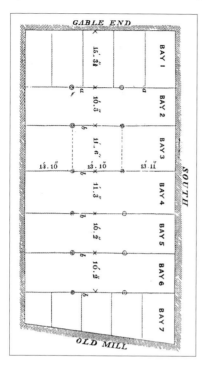

(4.3) Plan of top floor of Oldham mill showing floor girders and support columns; the collapse started at the gable end.

red-hot from the casting pit. We know today that fast cooling can induce hidden stresses within the structure, a problem known as 'residual stress'. It is caused by uneven cooling as the material contracts. De la Beche and Cubbitt recommended improvements in practical casting methods (allowing them to cool slowly to ambient), and also that wrought-iron girders be substituted for cast iron using riveted rolled iron sheet, a material promoted by William Fairbairn in many different kinds of structures.

The enquiry also looked at the source of iron itself. There were numerous foundries supplying cast iron, and there seemed to be large variations in quality between the various iron ores used in the blast furnaces. The eminent chemist Lyon Playfair was to provide evidence to the enquiry, as did other chemists. Chemical analysis of iron was a primitive science then by comparison with today, and we know now that minor elements in the iron can have a big effect on quality. The elements which are important include silicon, sulphur and phosphorus.

It is interesting to observe that the problem of low strength cast-iron beams was not new in 1844. The Beche/Cubbitt report included a discussion of the failure of such a beam in a cotton mill at Salford on 13 October 1824. The mill was also six storeys high and of similar width. A cast-iron beam suddenly fractured on the top floor, and caused a part of the building to collapse, killing seventeen mill workers. A news article in the *Manchester Guardian* (in an early example of investigative journalism) concluded that the centre of one of the beams on the top floor broke suddenly near its centre. The intrepid reporter found what he thought was probably the cracked beam, and was able to find the matching part, the fractures fitting together perfectly. However, the crack also exposed a flaw, perhaps a blow hole, which covered no less than a third of the section, so weakening it drastically. That part of the mill had only just been occupied by a company which carded cotton, and the extra weight of the new machinery probably overloaded the beam sufficiently to cause a catastrophic extension of the flaw.

The Beche/Cubbitt report was widely circulated as a government paper, and recognised the importance of investigating failures, consulting widely as to causes, drawing appropriate conclusions, and making recommendations to government. It was a forerunner of the many public reports made by the new railway inspectorate on railway accidents, as well as other major public problems.

Trussed Cast-iron Beams

Be that as it may, engineers continued to make widespread use of cast-iron girders, especially on the railways, but also in mills, factories and government buildings. The former would be more vulnerable since their floors would always be more heavily loaded than museums and art galleries.

Awareness of the brittle problems of such girders led to an interesting design modification. It was argued that since wrought iron was tough and ductile, a cast-iron beam could be strengthened by fitting it with a truss, or several trusses. In the event of a brittle crack in the beam, the wrought-iron trusses would hold the parts together, and so prevent a sudden collapse. The trusses ran either side of the beam, from the upper outside corners to the lower centre of the beam, where tensile stresses would be greatest when the beam was bent. The line of reasoning went even further, because two or more cast-iron girders could be fastened together to make a longer beam, also trussed, and therefore as safe as a single trussed beam. The principle was widely used when wooden beams (for example) were used in building roofs, and extra strength was provided by threading a wrought-iron tie rod through the members. However, wood is itself a tough material and much less stiff than wrought iron, so the effect is real and genuine with these two materials. Cast and wrought iron are much more similar, however, and the effectiveness of the supposed strengthening effect is highly dubious.

Trussed cast-iron girders had been used for some time on the new railways, apparently as early as 1831, being said by a recent author, Rennison, to have been first developed by Vignoles, another pioneer railway engineer. The Stockton & Darlington Railway had wanted to extend its line from Stockton to Middlesborough across the river Tees, and duly applied to Parliament in 1828. There were several proposals for the design of the bridge, but since the span needed was very large (281ft), a suspension bridge was chosen to the design of Captain Samuel Brown. As discussed earlier, he had designed the first eyebar suspension bridge in Britain, as well as the famous chain bridge pier at Brighton. The bridge was built, but needed immediate strengthening since the deck appears not to have been strong enough to carry heavy trains. It lasted until 1841, following deepening of the river channel, when a new bridge was proposed. This time, two masonry piers would be erected in the river bed to support a trussed cast-iron girder bridge. Robert Stephenson was the engineer for the structure, which consisted of two 86ft-long girders, each of which consisted of three giant castings bolted together and trussed, to cross each of the main spans. It was quickly finished, as one might expect for such as simple superstructure, opening on 18 March 1844. Stephenson called it:

> ... *one of the finest specimens of architecture of this description in the north of England, or, perhaps, in the known world.*

Such effusive comment would come to haunt the great engineer, because, according to Rennison, a brittle fracture was found in the girder just after completion of the bridge, and it demanded immediate remedial works. We are not told what those works entailed, but for such a serious defect they would have replaced the entire casting in which the crack had been found. Each span was 87ft, so each casting will have been about 27ft long; they were also 3ft deep, so replacing one rotten casting will have required bridge closure and dismantling of the affected span. From contemporary drawings of the spans, it is clear that they were given recessed box mouldings on the visible sides, like the Water Street bridge, perhaps to show the world that engineers could design aesthetically pleasing structures.

There were many other trussed girder bridges which had been built in the frenzied activity to complete new lines, judging by the survey which was done by the BoT after the Dee accident. One such bridge was at the Minories in the City of London. It was at the city terminus of the London & Blackwall Railway, a line only four miles long connecting parts of east London with the Docks, and beyond. The line was unique in being run only by fixed steam engines, which hauled the carriages by means of an endless rope made of hemp. It was completed in 1840, and the engineer was Robert Stephenson. The line was the first to be fitted throughout its length with the new telegraph, which enabled the enginemen to know when to start hauling trains. While a pneumatic tube might be fine for the half mile of the Euston incline, it became inefficient and thus redundant for the longer Blackwall line.

According to William Fairbairn in his book on fire-proof buildings, the principle had been first developed by George Bidder in one of the railway bridges over the river Lea at Tottenham on the Northern & Eastern Railway:

> *The span was 60 feet, and each girder was composed of two parts, instead of three parts, as was now found more advantageous. Each had been proved with 40 tons on the centre, and had borne the test without any permanent change of form. The trains ran over the bridge for some time, when, without any notice, one of the girders broke, where, it was afterwards shown, that an imperfection existed in the metal; the tension rods, however, supported the girder, and held the parts so tightly together, that the trains passed over as usual until the accident was repaired.*

The incident encouraged engineers to continue to use the trussed girders, although the precise design used on the Tottenham bridge is unknown today. On the other hand, architects had good reason to suspect the principle, according to Fairbairn, who relates that government offices in St Petersburg were built with trussed cast-iron girders, but one floor of the building suddenly collapsed when three such girders fractured. They were replaced with riveted wrought-iron equivalents. And the use of trussed girders did

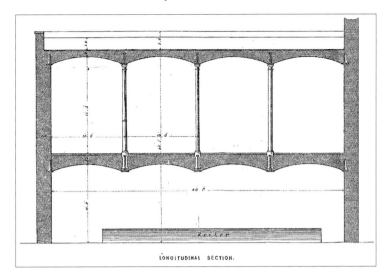

(4.4) Elevation of
the Manchester mill
before collapse.

not end there, because they were used both in the Winter Palace and St George's Hall.
A floor in the latter building collapsed, and they too were replaced. Snow loading was a
specific problem with the Russian buildings, a railway station roof having collapsed under
the accumulated weight of 10ft of snow on the roof.

Collapse of Manchester Mill

That there was a problem with such compound trussed beams was realised when a compound
trussed girder supporting a floor in yet another mill, this time in Manchester, failed suddenly. It
was Messrs J. and J.L. Gray's cotton mill. It was actually quite small compared with the Oldham
and Salford mills, being only 40ft long and nearly 32ft wide, and consisted of just two storeys
(4.4). It was also different in having a water reservoir sealed by asphalt on the roof, which
covered the whole of the top of the building *(4.5)*. The boilers and steam engine were situated
in the lower storey, with textile machinery on the second. The floor supporting the machines
was supported by three compound cast-iron beam and wrought-iron trusses of nearly 32ft
span. They were shallower than Stephenson's giant beams at Stockton, being only 2ft 3in deep
at the centre, and 1ft 10.5in at either end. Jack arches had been built across the lower flanges
as was normal with cast-iron beams.

The beam had broken just off the centre, in a vertical straight line, which Fairbairn (who
read a paper on the case to the Institution of Civil Engineers in late 1846), considered
as starting at the top, rather than at the base where the tensile stresses were greatest. The
quality of the cast iron was apparently good, in that he mentions no intrinsic defects,
but he estimated that the beam had been unfit for the load it had to bear. The weight of
brick arches was 20.5 tons and machinery 10 tons, it was assumed the weight was acting
uniformly over the length of the beam which ultimately broke, being about 15.25 tons.
The weight of water in the reservoir when full was substantial (14 tons) and the roof
weight was 23.5 tons, or 18.75 tons distributed. That gave a total of 34 tons, which with a

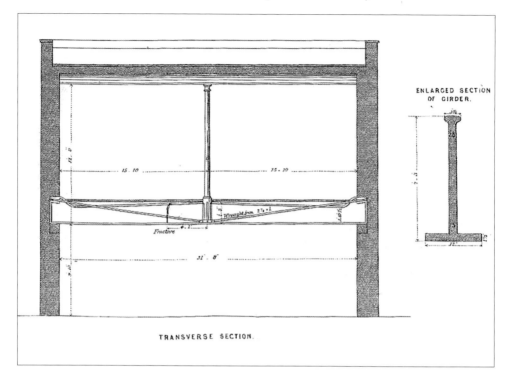

ENLARGED SECTION
OF GIRDER.

TRANSVERSE SECTION.

(4.5) Compound trussed girder in Manchester mill.

known breaking load of 36 tons gave a safety factor of only 1.06. Once again, the design was too close to call, and could, in the end, not resist any extra, unforeseen loads. The beam would be subject to cyclical loading from the roof pond, and vibrations from the machinery, which he thought would be injurious. He also opined that the trusses did not act in concert with the main girder and contributed little to sharing the loads on the floor, a damning condemnation of the entire principle of the trussed beam.

In his paper given at the Civils, there was a lively debate with much disagreement from eminent engineers in the audience, especially Robert Stephenson. Since he had already built railway bridges using such beams, he naturally defended the design with vigour. However, he had been warned of the potential for trouble ahead. Fairbairn had spent considerable effort in developing riveted wrought-iron sheet for structural purposes, and was actually working with Stephenson on the new designs for the Menai Straits and Conwy bridges. He would propose (and patent) a quite different design for spanning such large expanses of water: a wrought-iron tube. He had also recommended that Stephenson should use a wrought-iron girder on the Dee crossing.

Bridge Failure in Kent

During the winter months, on Tuesday 20 January 1846, a new wooden bridge over the river Medway failed on the South-Eastern Railway between Tonbridge and Penshurst

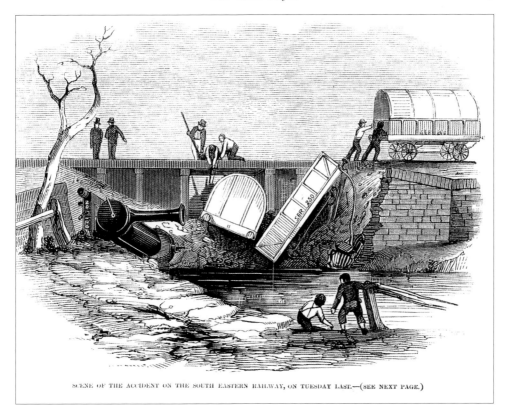

SCENE OF THE ACCIDENT ON THE SOUTH EASTERN RAILWAY, ON TUESDAY LAST.—(SEE NEXT PAGE.)

(4.6) Bridge collapse caused by floods, derailing train in 1846.

stations, probably the first ever bridge failure on the new system *(4.6)*. The railway had only been finished recently, and the driver had little chance of averting the accident since it occurred at night. The river had been swollen by rain, overflowing its banks and flooding a large part of the neighbourhood. The first intimation of disaster was a crash heard by the guard, who just saw a huge burst of steam and heated coke from the engine, which had clearly plunged headlong into the torrent below the bridge. The surviving staff surmised that the bridge had collapsed at the time the engine first passed over, and only the top of its chimney could be seen in the surging waters. The tender and some luggage wagons were also in the water. Both the stoker and driver were found on the bank, the former having dragged the terribly injured driver to shore. He had been almost cut in half by the accident, probably by jumping off the engine as it fell, but being caught between the colliding engine and its tender. The driver was still breathing when rescued by the stoker, but he died while being carried to safety. It appeared that the foundations of the bridge had been undermined, and the weight of the engine was enough to destabilise the structure.

Bridge piers in rivers would always be vulnerable to the scour problem, and this was not to be a unique example in the history of the railways.

(4.7) The railway viaduct over the Dee floodplain at Chester.

Public Concern

The same edition of the *Illustrated London News* fulminated in the editorial next to the report of the accident, about the rising accident rate on the railways:

> *Accidents are even more frequent now, after some years experience of the working of the system, than they were in its infancy. We are falling off in skill at the time we ought … to be nearing perfection. Whether this proceeds from desire of companies to make larger profits, by reducing the expenditure to a degree that ensures a saving to themselves more certainly than it procures safety to the public, - or from the carelessness of well paid officials, who ought to be better disciplined – or lastly, from some of the lines having in the course of years got somewhat out of order, the inevitable wear and tear having escaped due attention, - it matters not: in either case the travelling public is placed 'in jeopardy' every hour, and a feeling of dissatisfaction and mistrust is growing up, the deeper because the public has no remedy.*

The writer went on to castigate the inspectorate:

> *If an accident takes place, down posts General Pasley, looks at the torn-up rails and broken engine, rides back, trying an experiment or two by the way, gives his evidence before the Coroner's jury, and explains elaborately what every body knew – how the calamity took place, but has little to say what all are most anxious to hear – how such accidents can be prevented for the future.*

(4.8) Present railway bridge over river Dee from Saltney cutting.

Changing practices or introducing new safety measures would always be voluntary in the spirit of this entrepreneurial Victorian world, with the inspectorate in the firing line of the emerging opinion makers of the press. But matters were to worsen for General Pasley.

Bridge on the Dee

When the C&HR began construction of their railway in 1846 the river Dee just outside Chester presented hardly any apparent challenge at all when compared with the Menai Straits or Conwy estuary. It is only about 250ft wide, compared with 400ft at Conwy and 700ft at the Menai Straits, and is subject to the scouring action of ebb and flow from the tide. In the first design, the river was to be crossed by means of five masonry or cast-iron arches with individual spans of 60ft. The foundations, however, were thought to be insecure for a heavy masonry structure, and there were objections from river users to the proposal. Chester had been an important inland port in the Middle Ages, with moorings below the castle, half a mile upstream from the proposed crossing. In the end, Stephenson opted for just two masonry piers in the river bed to be bridged by iron girders.

The approach to the bridge across the flood plain was constructed in the conventional way with brick piers and arches *(4.7)*, the present bridge adopting the same course as

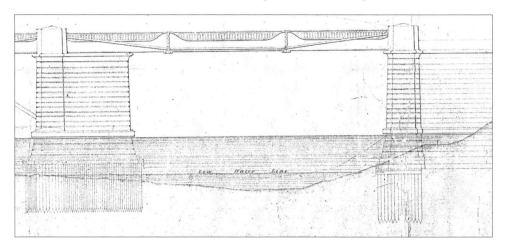

(4.9) Elevation of the trussed bridge over the river Dee at Chester.

the first structure. In addition, a cutting was needed where the line met the other, much higher bank of the river *(4.8).* The line met the river at an angle of about 50 degrees, just by Chester race course, and then curved away to Saltney station about half a mile away on the other side of the river.

The bridge was built during 1846, and was formed by laying cast-iron girders across each opening of about 98ft between masonry piers. Each track (the up line and down line) was supported by separate girders, so twelve were needed in all. Each girder was made by bolting together three smaller castings of roughly equal length, which were reinforced by wrought-iron trusses running the entire length of each composite structure *(4.9).* It was very similar in design to the Stockton bridge. The line itself was laid on thick oak beams which were supported at each end on the lower flanges of the I-shaped cast-iron girders.

The bridge was opened to local freight traffic on 4 November 1846, after inspection and approval by General Pasley. In the early days, large deflections of several inches were observed by painters working on the structure when trains passed over. Such observations seem not to have been communicated to Stephenson or his staff, but emerged later at the inquest. If he was told, then he must have regarded the movement as normal. A short time before the bridge was opened to the public, a small fracture was seen in one of the cast-iron girders near a joint, and it had to be replaced by a new casting. Stephenson thought that the fracture had been caused by a casting defect, and the girder had to be supported by piles while the new casting was made.

Replacement was not an easy job. It must have been a back-breaking task, given the size and weight of the castings, which, after transport by the railway to the spot, needed assembling together to form the compound beam, followed by attachment of the wrought-iron tie bars. Then the tie bars would need tensioning before the girder was hauled over the span. Great care will have been needed to ensure that the girder could not break under its own weight while being manoeuvred into position, presumably using block and tackle on a trestle above the level of the bridge, and on the opposite side of the span.

5

Disaster!

On the morning of 24 May 1847, six trains had passed over the bridge without a problem. The new bridge was inspected by Stephenson that same day. He was worried about the exposure of bare wood to sparks and ashes from passing trains, especially as it recently destroyed a bridge on the Great Western Railway. He personally ordered a local contractor to lay about 5in of ballast over the timbers, apparently equivalent to an extra load of about 18 tons imposed uniformly on each girder of the bridge. The extra dead load on one girder would thus have been about 9 tons. The ballast was laid in the afternoon, with the next train after the operation the 6.15 p.m. train from Chester. The train weighed roughly 60 tons and was travelling at about 30mph towards the bridge, according to an estimate made later by Captain Simmons, one of the accident investigators.

It never reached its destination. As it was passing over the final span, the outer girder cracked and the carriages fell through the gap into the river below. The driver described how he felt the train sinking beneath him, so he put on full steam and just reached the far bank with the tender. However, all the carriages fell about 36ft to the surface of the water with the bridge, killing four passengers and injuring many more. The stoker was killed when thrown off the tender, which was derailed and struck the stone parapet of the bridge. It was left standing about 50ft from the water's edge, and 3ft off the rails. An engraving published in the *Illustrated London News* two weeks later shows the accident scene in some detail *(5.1)*, but no photographs (Calotypes or Daguerreotypes) appear to have been taken, or if they were, to have survived. There are some spurious additions in the engraving, such as the fanciful backdrop showing berthed schooners and other ships, an impossible vista from the position taken by the artist in the picture. The article accompanying the engraving says that all the debris had been removed by the time they arrived on the scene, so the picture was to be read cautiously. For example, six carriages are shown in the water, while it is known that there were only five.

However, the foreground bears some comparison with the known facts as surveyed by the accident investigators, and other engravings of the time *(5.2)*. The top part of the broken girder is shown poking up above the water level between the foremost carriages, in roughly the same spot as shown by the official report. The driver (Clayton) was the only uninjured survivor, and he, with great presence of mind, drove the locomotive another half-mile to Saltney station, where he raised the alarm. He then crossed over onto the opposite track, and recrossed the bridge to Chester station, so that he could warn other trains of the danger. Given that part of this bridge had just collapsed, it was an action needing some courage.

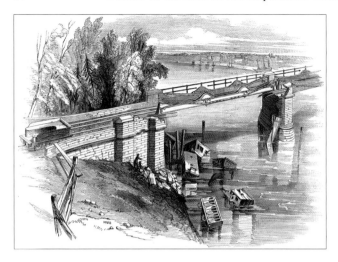

(5.1) The collapsed bridge showing tender off rails at the left and carriages in the river.

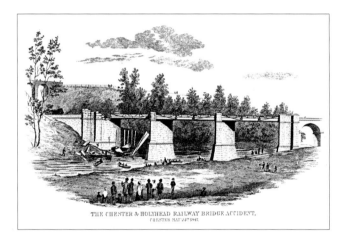

(5.2) View of the collapsed bridge from the floodplain.

Fortunately, there were many locals who had seen the accident and the survivors were soon rescued from the river.

The Official Investigation

The Railway Commissioners asked Captain Simmons RE, the Inspector-General of Railways, to investigate the disaster. He was helped by James Walker, the civil engineer who had been closely involved with the C&HR, and they produced a report in the remarkably fast time of about three weeks. Simmons made two visits to the site, where he was presented with a description of the original design, made a detailed inspection of the broken parts and carried out extensive tests on the girders still intact on the bridge. Their joint report provides very detailed drawings of the design as well as the remains left after the disaster.

The three castings were bolted together to form the composite span of 98ft, and were tied together at the joints by massive semi-circular castings at the top of each joint *(5.3)*.

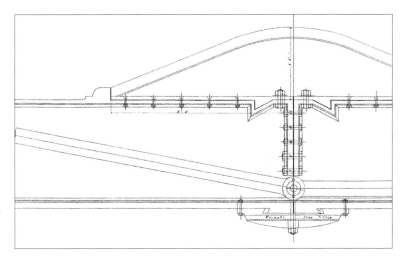

(5.3) A section of joint in the Dee bridge.

Each girder was reinforced by longitudinal wrought-iron tension bars attached to the girder at end flanges at some distance above the main axis of the ends, as well as at several points along the axis. The tension bars were provided in the form of a chain, as the elevation of one of the joints shows *(5.4)*. They were also tied together laterally by wrought-iron tie bars attached to dove tail sockets cast into the structures (left-hand plan in *(5.5)*). The large oak joists (10in x 10in) were laid loose onto the lower flanges of the girder, and supported 4in planks onto which the rails were laid *(5.6)*. Inside the main rail was a duplicate set, which acted as a guard rail to prevent sideways toppling.

Simmons found the girder broken in two places, one near the centre of the middle casting, the other at the abutment girder near one of the joints. The form of each break appears, on the evidence of the contemporary drawings, to be very similar. However, his description notes several differences. The fractures on the abutment girder led down to the lower flange, which was broken in one place only. The fracture in the central girder was more complex, he states, consisting of several pieces, some of which were still in the river at the time of writing of his report. No detailed drawings of the fractures appear to survive. He attributed the damage to the stone abutment to the derailment of the tender *(5.7)*.

Damage to the upper masonry courses of the river pier and Saltney abutment was severe, as the contemporary engravings clearly show. A corner stone from the river pier had fallen into the water, and one end of the broken casting leaned at a precarious angle against the remaining part of the pier.

Captain Simmons presented his and Walker's conclusions towards the end of the inquest, and they were to be crucial to the jury.

The Inquest

The formal legal investigation opened at Chester Town Hall on 4 June, just ten days after the accident. The inquest was held before a jury of local ratepayers. They were drawn from the voting list, which was (even after the 1832 Reform Act) much more limited

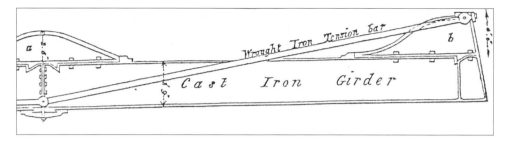

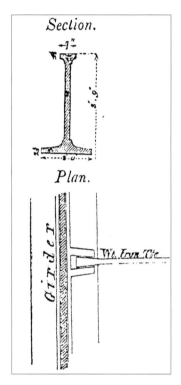

Above: (5.4) Elevation of end casting showing the truss attachments.

Far left and left: (5.5a and b) Girder casting with sections and plans.

than today's universal suffrage. In fact, the Chester jury consisted of local worthies who had no inhibitions about intervening in court proceedings. The inquest was reported very widely in both the national and local press, including *The Times* and the *Chester Chronicle*, with detailed transcripts of the oral evidence given to the court. The city coroner, Mr Hostage, was assisted by James Walker, who had previously reported to the government on the C&HR plans. He was able to suggest technical questions for the expert witnesses. The *Chronicle* reported that the court was packed not just with locals, but with reporters and government officials from the Board of Trade and the Admiralty.

The behaviour of the structure in its short history since opening would be the subject of immediate interest, especially if it gave any clues as to how the bridge failed. The first witnesses were painters who had been employed in April and May 1847, immediately before the accident. They had seen substantial deflections on the girders when trains passed over. One witness, William Clegg, said:

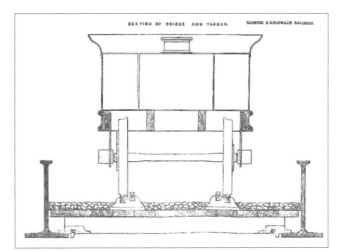

Right: (5.6) Track platform supported on inner flange of girder.

Below: (5.7) Damage to masonry of Saltney abutment.

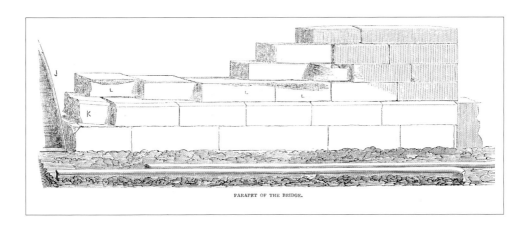

In the months of April and May last year, I was employed in painting the girders … When a ballast train passed over I noticed the deflection of the middle girder to be from an inch and a half to two inches. I also observed the deflection when the passenger trains went over; they went faster than the ballast trains considerably; the extent of the deflections was 3½ to 4 inches; I got my rule and put it under the bridge and noticed how much it went down…

The next painter to give evidence, William Clarke, went further because he had observed a critical girder himself:

… when passenger trains have gone over the deflection was according to the speed; in one instance it was as much as 5 inches; it was the outside girder in the middle arch, which afterwards broke and had to be replaced; I measured it with my rule…

The deflection was downward but also the base was seen to 'elbow outward' while the top moved inwards. Clarke is presumably referring to the girder replaced by Stephenson before the accident.

The foreman of the Jury, Sir Edward Walker, asked Clarke if he had mentioned the deflection to anyone. He received the reply:

> *I told someone who had charge of the bridge, but I do not know if he was the engineer.*

Such large deflections of the main girders should have raised some concern about the integrity of the structure, but no action seems to have been taken.

Eye Witnesses

There were witnesses of the accident who actually saw the bridge fall, and described very vividly the sequence of events, such as Thomas Frith, a fifteen-year-old boy working in the town clerk's office, who had been fishing in the river at the time of the accident:

> *… I was on the Saltney side; I was from fifty to one hundred yards above the bridge: I saw the train come up about half way on to the middle arch; I saw it on the last arch; there was a tremendous crash; a large piece of girder fell from the middle buttress; also a lot of rubbish and the carriages; the last carriage dropped first, and the rest followed. I ran to the spot; I found a large coping stone and rubbish, a quantity of timber, and people lying amongst them…*

He was also there on the morning of the disaster, and went on:

> *I stood under the arch next to the Roodee; when a train went over, one of the girders bent down between four and five inches; it was the inside girder of the first arch on the going out line; the girder bent down, about the middle … he noticed it because his brother had called his attention to it; I was bathing there one morning when a train passed over, and saw the girder belly down.*

It was strong corroboration of what had been observed by the painters, that the main structural elements of the bridge, the massive cast-iron girders, deformed under the load of passing trains.

Another local witness was Thomas Barlow:

> *I was mending nets at the time of the accident on the marsh below the Dee bridge, about four hundred yards from the railway bridge; I was on the west side; I saw the train coming; I saw it on the last arch, when it all went down, except the engine and the tender. I and my father got to the place as quick as we could in the boat; ours was the first boat there; we found a lady dressed in black; with assistance we got her into the boat; she was alive; a young lady was also got into the boat; I did not see any parties who were dead; we got a boy out whom we thought would not recover; the coping stone of the bridge was on the ground; it was on a railway carriage which was knocked all to bits…*

Other witnesses gave evidence of their involvement, including Henry Thomas:

> *I was at my own door Greenway Street, Handbridge when I heard the crash of the accident; I found Charles Nevitt lying dead at the bottom of the abutment close to the water edge; one of his legs was shattered all to bits; he was close to a second-class carriage, but nothing was on him; the carriage was on the land, and not much broke; I saw Roberts the guard in the boat; he appeared to have life in him then; I took Roberts to the workhouse.*

A police constable gave his statement of how he had reacted:

> *I was on duty on the evening of the 24th near the railway bridge; I was at the place directly after the bridge fell; I saw John Matthews; his head was under one of the carriages; he was dead; I took his body to the workhouse ... I assisted to get Roberts out; he was not dead; I directed some parties to take him to the infirmary...*

Another local who had given help to the injured at the scene of the accident was James Jones, a cabinet maker of Chester:

> *... I was working in Paradise Row at the time of the accident; heard the crash and a scream, and I hastened to the river; I and three others crossed in the railway boat; the first I saw was the heel of a child which was alive; we turned over the top of the carriage; part of it was in the water; under it were three bodies; one was Isaac Jones; he was then alive; he was hurt about the head and back ... I assisted to get seven out altogether.*

Dramatic evidence of the way the accident had occurred was revealed by Thomas Jones, a local milkman and publican:

> *I was on the Grosvenor bridge at the time of the accident; I saw the train at the ship yard; I put my milk cans down and watched it across the bridge; when the train got on the furthest arch on the Saltney side, I observed a crack open in the middle of the girder; the train and tender were about the centre; the crack opened from the bottom; the engine had passed the crack, and the tender was right upon it; the engine and tender went on, and I saw the tender give a rise up; the carriages gave a jump and fell backward; the last carriage went down first according to my judgment; the next I saw was the large stones fall off the wall on the Saltney side; I heard a crash when they fell; I am certain the girder opened up from the bottom...*

The surgeon, Samuel Jones, who attended the victims at the Chester Infirmary confirmed their state:

> *... I saw the body of George Roberts on the Roodee; I saw him afterwards at the infirmary; he had severe lacerations of the skull but no fracture; he had died from the injury to the head and concussion of the body; Isaac Jones died from wounds on the head and general injuries, a few minutes before two o'clock on Wednesday.*

The jury foreman, Sir Edward Walker, made a significant point after this harrowing witness testimony, saying that in view of the plans for iron bridges on the Voryd, Conwy and Menai Straits, he had written to the Railway Commissioner, Mr Strutt, urging a full and satisfactory enquiry into the Dee bridge tragedy. Mr Strutt replied that Captain Simmons and Mr Walker had been instructed to investigate the disaster.

The testimony of Thomas Jones was heard late in the proceedings, and although he was much further away from the bridge than the other eye-witnesses (about 690 yards, as the court afterwards determined by direct measurement), it was very strong evidence for the course of events. It is unlikely that a crack would be visible from such a distance, the present bridge being only just visible in the distance from the parapet of the Grosvenor bridge. The latter is a single arch masonry span across the river, upstream from the railway bridge in question (and itself one of the longest single arch masonry bridges in the country).

Engine Driver

James Clayton was the driver of the train, and his evidence was also important in the quest to arrive at the true circumstances of the fall of the bridge. He said:

> ... *the train proceeded across the Roodee arches about 15 or 20 mph; when I approached the first arch I felt nothing, no vibration; when I got onto the arch which gave away, I felt a sudden sink; the engine made a rear-up; I gave her all the steam which I had, which plucked the tender away; the tender sunk with the bridge, but we plucked it out; the tender was thrown off the line; I did not see what had become of the carriages; I saw Thomas Anderson [the stoker] fall off the tender on the right hand side; he fell with his head on the rails, on the place shown to the jury as covered with blood; I soon after stopped the engine, and could not tell what had become of the train, but I judged that the arch had fallen in...*

He related to the court how he had then proceeded:

> ... *I then went on to Saltney junction; I saw some bricklayers, and made motions that the arch had fallen in; I went to Saltney station, and then got the engine on the down-line; I told the persons at the station that I though the bridge had given way, and also that the fireman was killed; I came back with the engine and stopped at the Dee, where I saw persons assisting the sufferers in the water; I saw the fireman lying dead where I saw him fall; the train was all fallen below; one arch had given way, that nearest the Saltney end; I then went on to Chester; I gave notice of the accident at the station; I have been employed on the line since November last; I have never felt any vibration in passing this bridge to alarm me; I have never felt any sinking of the bridge when I passed over it; ... I have never felt any vibration at all, at any time.*

He mentioned that he had driven both long and heavy trains over the Dee bridge and not noticed anything at all unusual. In answer to the jury foreman, he said that his hand was on the engine regulator, but he had no premonition that the bridge would give way. The answer clearly showed how he was able to give the engine extra steam, probably as a reflex action when he felt the engine sinking beneath him.

It is interesting to note that he denied feeling any sensitivity of the structure to load from his locomotive, despite the observations of many witnesses of girder distortion. It is likely that the vibrations of the locomotive itself masked any external movements of the bridge, until they were so large that they signified total failure.

Train Passengers

So what did the surviving passengers have to say? Samuel Tomkinson, a merchant from Liverpool, was travelling in the second compartment of the carriage immediately behind the tender:

> *… I was engaged in a conversation with Mr Grote before entering the bridge; the rumble caused it to cease; I had my back to the engine and was looking at the Roodee race course; just as we were on the last span of the bridge I felt the line sinking under the carriage; I think we were about the centre of the span; we dropped for a moment; but there appeared a violent lift of the carriage, and we fell a great height, and all was dark in an instant; we struck upon the bank, and the carriage rolled over once or twice on the bank; I appeared to be on my head once or twice in the carriage; the carriage was crushed; when the rolling ceased I found myself on the cushions all of a heap; I sprang up and found I had no bones broken; the wheel of the carriage was close to my head; I found Mr Grote was comparatively uninjured; I looked at the wreck; several of the carriages were on the bank, and one in deep water; a woman was struggling in the water; I went into the river and drew her on the side; she appeared confused…*

The jury foreman questioned him on the derailment theory, but Tomkinson said he had heard nothing to suggest that the tender had hit the girder or any vehicle had left the line: he just felt the sinking movement. His testimony was corroborated by another passenger, Alexander Macgregor, who was in the luggage van, the last carriage but one:

> *Matthews, Nevitt, and Roberts, the guard were with me; the train was going about twenty miles an hour; when on the first arch I directed the guard's attention to the Saltney signal; I was on the right hand of the carriage, being next to the down line, with my hand on the side of the van; I was looking along the train; the guard said he never saw the signal that way before; Matthews asked what was showing the guard; I heard a crash and then observed a deflection in the carriages; I did not observe any carriages off the line; I should have observed them if they had been off; I had the advantage of the curve, which brought the train more fully into view; jumped off the carriage, and after that I knew nothing; the next thing I recollect was someone picking me up; they said 'this poor fellow's dead'; I said 'I wasn't'; don't know where I was when I was picked up; the other three were killed on the spot.*

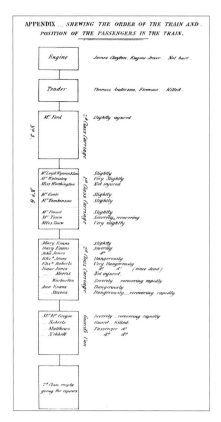

(5.8) Injuries to passengers and crew on the 6.15 a.m. train from Chester.

Macgregor's escape was very lucky considering that his three companions were killed. *(5.8)*. When asked by the foreman of the jury about derailment, he said it could not have left the line because he was observing it at the moment of the crash. So both of the passengers were in complete agreement about the lack of derailment at the time of the initial crash. That left only one possibility: that the girder had fractured under the train.

The tide was probably out when the accident occurred judging by the comments about carriages hitting the banks; it may have saved many passengers because the soft mud will have cushioned the fall, and saved some from drowning. Nevertheless, five were killed immediately, three of them from the penultimate carriage from which Macgregor had such a lucky escape.

Foundryman

The way the castings were made and tested were also of great interest, because defective casting practice was a well-known source of weakness in cast iron, especially after the Beche/Cubbitt report from two years previously on cast-iron girder failures in buildings.

A key witness was Robert Board, superintendent of the Horsley ironworks, who had made the castings for the bridge. He testified that all the castings had been tested before being supplied. Each girder had been placed side-by-side and 50 tons' load suspended from the centre, deflections of the beam being recorded every 5 tons. Unfortunately, he could not supply those results to the court. He thought that the load from passing trains could not exceed 50 tons. The test however, did reveal that one casting was flawed with 'honey cake', presumably a blowhole with foamed interior. He had examined the same casting after the accident and found that it had not caused any failure, the actual fractures occurred in sound metal. He had superintended installation of the castings into the bridge, and said that experience with trussed girders was good:

> There are many railway bridges of the same kind. On the Trent Valley line, there are eight of the kind. It is not opened to the public as yet, but on the Blackwall line there are several that have had heavy trains passing over them for years. The one over the Dee is the largest. I have not heard of any of them giving way. Had been several times to view the bridge when trains were passing over it, and found the deflections very trivial, not much more than an inch.

The trussed bridges on the Blackwall line (opened in 1840) were smaller than the Dee bridge, however, and not as highly loaded. They only carried carriages without locomotives, the trains being hauled by an endless loop of rope powered by fixed engines. The locomotive was by far the heaviest component of any train. When locomotives were introduced in 1849, such bridges were replaced by stronger structures, the station at the Minories being closed with the opening of Fenchurch Street station. The trussed bridge at the Minories was unique in being enclosed totally so that the trains could not be seen by city gents.

But Robert Board did confirm what the painters had said about the girders deforming under load. Whether or not deflections of 'not much more than an inch' were trivial was really up to others to decide. The tests done in the foundry could also be very misleading, because they did not correspond to the way the girders were actually loaded, at the flange rather than from the top. Loading from the top of the centre of a girder also produces a more complex loading pattern than compression at the top and tension at the base, and in this case, is likely to have given wildly over-optimistic values of the strength.

Ballast

The contractor who put ballast on the track on the day of the accident was called to give evidence. Mr Mark (an agent of the contractor) said that the ballast was added to prevent passing engines from setting the timber decking from catching fire. He estimated that between 8 and 10 tons were used to cover all the track to a depth of 3 or 4ins, and the job was finished about an hour before the train was due to pass over. Another agent was also called and said that forty wagons carried the ballast to the bridge, suggesting a much greater load than '8 or 10 tons'.

It was a gross underestimate, a figure of 18–25 tons had been calculated by the expert witnesses, spread to a depth of 5in over each span. According to Henry Robertson, the engineer of the Shrewsbury & Chester Railway, it was composed of broken red sandstone. Like the other experts, apart from Stephenson (who had ordered the ballast laid), it was regarded as a significant factor in the fall of the bridge. After all, six trains had passed safely over the bridge that day without a problem, but they had crossed before the ballast was put on the track. It was only after the ballast had been laid that the first train through had fallen through the girder.

General Pasley

Since the Inspector of Railways had seen and checked the construction, his evidence was clearly important. The inspection had taken place on 20 October 1846, and he had compared the construction with the detailed plans. He considered the wrought-iron tie bars to not be of much use in reinforcing the massive cast-iron girders, but, on the other hand, none of the many which had been installed elsewhere had failed so catastrophically as at the Dee bridge. However, the span at the Dee was the greatest of any he had encountered, longer than a bridge over the Ouse at York (70ft) and the Stockton bridge (87ft). Indeed, Bidder and Gooch, two well-respected railway engineers, had tested a cast-iron girder with and without trusses, and found no difference in strength. So to what did he attribute the accident? First, he mentioned that one of the girders had fractured after installation and without load, but he had not been informed about this at the time. He felt that cast-iron girders were unsafe, and overly dependent on the quality of the castings used. He also noted that the ends of the tension rods on the Dee bridge were attached to the girder ends rather than independent supports, unlike earlier trussed girder bridges. He therefore believed that the girder broke because of the extra load of the ballast added by Stephenson together with the load of the train.

To counter other theories, he felt that the masonry supported the girders quite adequately, and that the check or guard rails (an extra line of rails beside the main rails) would have prevented any serious derailment. The jury foreman, Sir Edward Walker, then asked the General a very direct question. Assuming the bridge was repaired, would he be prepared to travel over it? He replied:

> *No, I would not, as I am not infallible. Although I did sanction its opening, I should not now allow trains to pass over it without fixing independent supporters. For my own part – and I am not troubled by nervousness – I certainly should not like to travel over it until it is secured as I have stated.*

So Pasley agreed with the eye witnesses that the girder had collapsed under the weight of the passing train, aided by the extra weight of ballast added just before the train arrived.

According to L.T.C. Rolt, Pasley was barely audible when he gave his testimony to the court, and was clearly shocked by the whole affair. His contemporary diaries (in the British Library) reveal many notes taken during the inquest, as well as newspaper reports on the affair.

Conflicting Theories

The first theory on the failure not involving direct fracture of the cast-iron girders came from Thomas Yarrow, bridge-master in Chester and appointed by the inquest to report on the accident. He did not think that fracture of the iron beam was relevant to the accident. His examination of the broken end of the casting revealed no inherent defects. He estimated the total strength of the casting at 206 tons, without considering the additional strengthening effect of the wrought-iron tie bars, so he felt it unlikely that failure of the girder caused the disaster. This breaking load was apparently far greater than the load of the locomotive and tender of about 30 tons, the whole train weighing about 60 tons.

He then turned his attention to the masonry of the piers, a topic with which he would have been very familiar. The masonry of the Saltney abutment had been damaged, with two large bedding stones having fallen with the girder. The river pier showed that the one of the large corner stones had also fallen during the accident. It overhung the pier itself to a considerable extent, and was not attached by cramps or ties to the adjacent stones. Since the axis of the bridge was at a skew angle, this stone would have been subjected to lateral forces every time a train passed over the bridge, tending to loosen it from adjacent masonry. He thus thought that the fall of the corner stone destabilised the girder, which then fell and broke.

However, there were very serious objections to the theory. In the first case, the stone on the pier was under the girder, and therefore was held down by the great weight of the castings. Any supposed movement of the stone was not seen by anyone before the tragedy, especially those working on the bridge on the day of the accident, including the engineer himself, Robert Stephenson. Finally, it was difficult to estimate the lateral forces exerted on the stone by passing trains. Most of the force from the train will be downwards from its weight passing over, with minimal lateral force.

The theory was quite speculative, and at odds with the evidence of failure of the girder itself. Why, for example, should the girder be broken in two places, in the centre and at the furthest point from the river pier? There was no way of explaining such fractures if the top stone had fallen. If the stone had fallen out of place the girder would surely simply have dropped a few inches onto the next stone on the pier, rather than ending up in the river in several pieces.

Stephenson's Theory

The most serious objections to the simple failure at the centre of the mid-girder theory were presented by Robert Stephenson, and he was supported by an array of distinguished engineers including Locke, Vignoles and Gooch. Stephenson claimed that the bridge failed when the train derailed and struck the inner side of the bridge, and fracture of the castings of the last span followed. He had prepared a written statement of his observations and inferences, and he made some preliminary comments concerning his actions on the day of the accident:

> *You are already aware that … I narrowly inspected the bridge on my way to Bangor. I saw nothing to indicate weakness, neither could I perceive any imperfections in the manner in which the work had been fitted.*

He then turned to the visit he had made to the scene of the accident.

> *I minutely examined every circumstance which appeared ... to cause the accident ... and the following appeared most prominent:*
>
> *1.) The masonry of the wing parapet on the Saltney side was much shattered and displaced, bearing evident marks of having received a violent side blow.*
>
> *2.) On examining the tender ... it was clear that it had come violently in contact with the masonry and caused the disturbance just alluded to.*
>
> *3.) All the lateral ties which bound the girder together sideways (thirteen in number), each measuring 4 by 1 inches ... were torn from their sockets...*
>
> *4.) That portion of the broken girder ... lying against the pier at a considerable angle ... must have fallen back with great force...*
>
> *5.) On examining the wrought iron work of the girder the whole was found sound, except one of the leaves of the wrought-iron link, against which the tender of the carriages would necessarily strike on leaving the rails, and which was severed about 18 feet from the Saltney abutment, and near to the point where the first fracture of the girder itself took place.*
>
> *6.) On examining the broken girder itself the fracture was precisely such as might be expected from a lateral blow, a large piece of the vertical rib being broken out of the girder, and separated from the lower flange, which remains perfect; a description which could scarcely be produced by vertical action.*

So what explanation was there for the accident? He felt that there was no evidence of a vertical force acting on the girder which could have caused the visible damage. The tender coming off the line and striking the abutment was clear evidence of a lateral force, but what had caused it to derail? He thought that since a wheel on one of the carriages was broken (and all the others were intact), this was likely to be the true cause of the tragedy.

Stephenson estimated the breaking load of the two girders together to be about 280 tons distributed over the whole span (without allowing for the wrought-iron tie bars). Taking away the self-weight of the structure itself of about 90 tons, that left 190 tons leeway to support any other superimposed loads. It should have been more than enough to support a train of 60 tons travelling over the structure. He had himself tested the Stockton bridge with 40 tons at the centre, producing a deflection of 4.75in. When the load was removed, the girder had returned to its normal position of rest. That bridge had conveyed 5,000,000 tons of coal since construction, and was still standing. With that proof before him, he had no hesitation in using the same design over the river Dee.

The counter-arguments to the theory were considerable. The tender had derailed *(5.1)*, *(5.7)*, but the eyewitnesses clearly said that it had occurred *after* the initial break in the central girder, and not before. The remains of the train were scoured for any support for the theory, but very little could be produced. The single broken wheel, for example, was claimed as strong evidence that one of the carriages had derailed, but eye witnesses said that the wheel had been broken deliberately to rescue the injured. Those passengers who were fit to give evidence concurred: the carriages had not derailed in the accident, a conclusion supported by Mr Clayton, the driver.

He also added that the ballast had been added to the track to prevent the timber catching fire from sparks ejected by passing engines, especially in view of a large bridge which had recently been destroyed by just such a fire on the Great Western Railway line from London. Such hazards were a new danger from locomotives, not just to wooden structures used on the new railways, but also to crops during harvest time where lines passed through the countryside.

Relying on the contemporary account of the inquest by F.R. Conder, L.T.C. Rolt relates that Conder had never seen the great engineer looking so pale and haggard. Rolt also goes on to say that Stephenson had been put up to the derailment theory by the C&HR solicitor as a way of denying liability for the accident. The theory could help to deflect some of the criticism, albeit only temporarily.

Eminent Engineers

Stephenson received strong support for his theory, however, from an array of famous railway engineers, who came in person to give their support. Joseph Locke (engineer of the Grand Junction Railway), for example, had inspected the remains of the girder, and thought that it could only have been broken by a side blow, and not by downward pressure. The tender was the obvious culprit, and he had found traces of paint on the inner tie bar which showed that the axle box of the tender had scraped along the tie bar, as well as the inner side of the masonry abutment. The tender then hit the pillar cap of the balustrade and knocked it into the river. He thus concluded that the tender derailed on the last part of the span, impacted the tie bar, and the casting broke under the sideways load. So he thought that it was not a derailed carriage which brought the bridge down, but rather the tender of the locomotive. On the other hand, the fact that a derailment could cause bridge failure implied that such cast-iron bridges were too fragile for safety. Indeed, he went on to state that he would not have designed such a bridge in the first place:

> I don't like cast iron girders of any shape; a brick or stone bridge would have been much cheaper; if the bridge was reinforced I should consider it safe; but if left to my own choice, it is not a bridge I would adopt…

So he actually gave a mixed opinion about the use of cast iron in railway bridges, despite supporting the derailment theory espoused by Stephenson. Vignoles also thought that derailment caused the bridge to fall, but would not use the design himself. His statement was not, however, backed by any chain of reasoning or observation. Thomas Gooch, engineer of the Manchester & Leeds Railway, arrived to lend similar support to Stephenson's theory; as engineer to the Trent Valley Railway, he had built or planned numerous trussed bridges on that line under Robert Stephenson, so had a material interest in the outcome of the inquest.

Yet another eminent engineer, James Kennedy, appeared for the defence of Stephenson. He had been a judge at the Rainhill trials on the L&MR. He gave more detailed testimony than either Gooch or Vignoles; he had personally inspected the remains and concurred on the quality of the metalwork, and supported Stephenson. However, he questioned the derailment theory:

> *I cannot understand how the tender could have left the rail, so well protected it appears to be, when going at twenty mph; I think it must have gone off the line at the end of the projecting rail; it could not then have caused the fracture; it has only one mark on the wheel … I am puzzled at only finding one mark on the wheel … I am quite astonished how the bridge has failed … I think the girder may have broken with the weight of the roadway, the ballast and the train … I have never known an instance of an engine getting off the rail with such a good check rail.*

Kennedy was split between his support for Stephenson, and his own observations, which ran against the derailment theory.

The jury themselves visited the scene of the accident (at least twice during the proceedings), and were able to assess for themselves much of the evidence said to support the derailment theory. They examined the paint marks and scrapes found by Joseph Locke on the tie bar and masonry, and could not accept the evidence. Some of the jury were conversant with paints, and could not agree that the marks were paint marks at all. They were not soap marks either, and the marks were easily rubbed off into dust.

The derailment theory suffered other objections as well. How could a lateral impact from the tender (or carriage) affect the girder lying behind? The diagonal wrought-iron tie bar at the end of the girder would act as a cushion, and any impact blow transmitted to the girder itself would be minimal, if the theory were to be true. In addition, the guard rail would have prevented a serious derailment on the bridge itself, and the visible evidence suggested that the tender only left the line after the guard rail ended at the bridge abutment.

Another witness who gave technical evidence was Major Thomas Robe, RA, who was called specifically by Sir Edward Walker, foreman of the jury. He had frequently inspected it while being built, and had concern about the lower flange on which the track platform was erected:

> *I expressed to Mr Munt, who gave me an order to go on the bridge, my apprehension that the bridge in one part was insecure; the part alluded to is the strength of the flange on which the floor of the bridge rests, which I considered insufficient to carry a road way for general traffic … one part is broken away from the flange; I am of the opinion that the flange should be tested separately, as the whole weight of the traffic goes over it.*

In court, Broad responded that the flanges had not been tested separately. The point made by Major Robe was very obvious from the section of the bridge, and is very striking to modern observers, especially those with an interest in structural matters.

Mr Tyrell, who said he had made the design for the bridge, as well as supervising the erection of the structure over the Dee, also gave evidence:

> *I have seen three engines and tenders coupled passing over the bridge; there would be about one hundred tons on the bridge; that was heavier than any luggage train; the centres had been taken away, and the*

girders were clear of the props; the two girders of every road are tied together by very strong iron rods; there are thirteen of them; General Pasley inspected the line in October last; he also inspected the bridge throughout; he certified that it was safe; he did not suggest any alterations.

Tyrell may actually have been describing a so-called proof test of the bridge, when a new structure is tested to much greater loads than normal. Any defects should be revealed by such a test, and close attention should have been given to any serious distortion in the girders when the coupled trains passed over. His response may have raised doubts in the jury about the thoroughness of General Pasley's inspection and approval of the bridge in October 1846, and there is some evidence that the General was at this time very seriously over-worked. A large mileage of track and associated structures had been opened in the preceding years, with only a very small railway inspectorate to check their quality.

Other Train Accidents

The papers during the inquest were full of news of more fatal accidents on other railways during the proceedings of the Dee inquest. *The Times*, in its edition of 2 June 1847, ran the banner headline:

Fatal Accident on the South Coast Railway.

and reported on a derailment on the Portsmouth extension of the Brighton to Chichester line. The accident occurred at Nutbourne, where an engine derailed, killing the driver. The accident happened on a straight and level section of the line, leading to suggestions of an obstruction, or alternatively, a faulty engine. It was a Stephenson engine, and allegations were made about its tendency to rock from side to side due to imbalance between the two pistons which drove the wheels.

A few days later, it reported on another accident, this time with even more serious consequences. The headline in *The Times* on 7 June 1847 read:

Frightful Collision on the London & North-Western railway.

and the paper proceeded to give a lengthy report on the incident. The accident occurred at Wolverton station on the L&BR on the night of 5 June 1847, when an express train from London was wrongly diverted into a siding by a policeman *(5.9)*. Despite the best efforts of the driver and guard in applying their brakes, and stopping off the steam to the engine, the train collided with a coal train standing in the siding, and seven passengers were killed in just one of the coaches, which bore the brunt of the collision. The train was estimated to have been moving at about 24mph at the time of the accident, showing just how much momentum a train possessed, even when moving at a rather slow speed by modern standards. Ironically, the two parcels wagons just behind the engine were undamaged. The bodies were laid out in one of the station rooms so that the inquest jury could examine them personally. There were also four injured travellers in the other coaches.

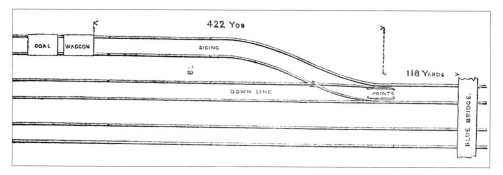

(5.9) The Wolverton accident.

The incident could only be attributed to human error on the part of the policeman, who had switched the points just before the train arrived. He was detained in custody at Newport Pagnell police station, pending the outcome of the inquest.

It was no wonder, then, that *The Times* published several letters about the state of the railways, and the hazards of travelling. One such letter was published prominently in *The Times* on 10 June 1847, under the title 'Railway Bridges', and it was laden with gloom about safety on the new railways, especially about bridge integrity:

> *... from the investigation at Chester we are doomed ... to glean nothing more consolatory to future integrity of life and limb than that, after a manifest difference of opinion in those examined, a board of directors came to the conclusion that 'no precaution or engineering skill could have guarded against the accident'; while, to crown the whole, we are furthermore told, 'there are many bridges of a similar description – as in the Trent Valley, Blackwall, Great Western and other railways' – over which, with these appalling deductions staring us in the face, and unalleviated by any further explanations, we are doomed ... to peril in future the lives of ourselves and families...*

The letter was signed anonymously by 'Prospector'. Several issues relating to train safety were discussed in yet another letter to *The Times*, this one on 14 June 1847, again anonymous, and signed 'An Engine Driver'. Most important was the problem of adequate brakes, and after a very long and detailed discussion, the writer advocated that every vehicle be fitted with its own brakes, so as to maximise the braking force in an emergency. The comment was, no doubt, of immediate interest following the Wolverton disaster. Other letters also raised the problem of railway safety in a very detailed and technical way, these were no doubt prompted by the spate of accidents that occurred in the spring and summer of 1847.

Yet another accident was reported on 19 June 1847, this time under the headline 'Frightful Accident and Loss of Life'. This incident involved the fall of a bridge on the London & Gravesend Railway at Great Russell Street in London. The arch was just being finished by removing the wooden formwork when a sudden cracking was heard, and the whole mass collapsed in a heap onto the pavement. Three severely injured pedestrians were found during the rescue operation, in addition to two corpses. The report does not give any indication of the cause of the accident, although faulty cement or brickwork seems the most likely explanation.

Meanwhile, full reports on the Wolverton inquest continued to be published. It was held in the infants school next to the station, and included Captain Simmons of the Inspectorate, who had to interrupt his investigation at the Dee bridge inquest to attend. As with the Dee Bridge inquest the proceedings were fully reported in the papers, with no details spared, including an extensive discussion of the lights used on the trains that night. Another question arose about the brakes then used on trains, Captain Simmons recommended that the number of brakes used should be proportional to the total size and weight of the train.

Robertson's Theory

The final expert witness called was Henry Robertson, engineer to the Shrewsbury & Chester Railway. He had also prepared drawings of the remains, and a scale model to help explain the sequence of events. He thought it likely that the fracture at the centre of the girder had occurred first, while that near the Saltney abutment occurred afterwards. Of the primary break, he opined that it had started at the top flange, and was caused by excessive compression brought about by the locomotive, the excessive vibration and the load of 25 tons of ballast added to the track just before the accident. He also thought that the tension rods, far from strengthening the girder, actually weakened it by putting the top flange into compression, a view uncorroborated by any evidence. He then proceeded to describe in detail the loads on the girder:

Weight of platform carrying track   = 19 tons 6 cwt

Weight of locomotive and tender   = 33 tons 10 cwt

Weight of ballast laid on track   = 25 tons

The self-weight of the girders is not explicitly mentioned by Robertson, but Simmons and Walker estimated that they weighed, together with the platform, about 90 tons in all. If Robertson's estimate of the platform alone at 19 tons 6 cwt is right, then the two girders making the trackway weighed about 70 tons, or about 35 tons each. This implies that each of the castings weighed about 10 tons. It is interesting to observe that their self-weight is by far the heaviest item in the total load on the structure.

Robertson also calculated the breaking strength of each girder, using a formula developed by Eaton Hodgkinson (a collaborator of William Fairbairn). According to the formula, the breaking load at the centre of a single girder was about 62 to 71 tons, depending on exactly which formula was used. Hodgkinson had performed many experiments with cast-iron girders of various shapes and sizes, but his formulae described the breaking strength, a measure now known to be very variable, and depended greatly on defects within the structure, and precise girder geometry. In other words, his estimate of breaking strength was actually less than the self-weight of the girder! Two girders forming the track should thus support a centre load of twice this range, or from 124 to 142 tons.

There were many issues raised by both expert and lay witnesses on the tragedy, some of which could actually be resolved quite quickly. The jury visited the accident scene and tested the credibility of the scrape and paint marks on the bridge, for example. The question of the broken wheel was also resolved by examining all the carriage wheels. The court called Thomas Truss, locomotive superintendent of the Shrewsbury & Chester Railway, to give evidence:

> *I was at the scene of the accident about an hour and a half or two hours after; I had my attention drawn to the general position of the carriages; I saw the wheel; some of the spokes were broken out; it was not denuded of all the spokes; two of the spokes were entire; two or three were injured and the rest were broken out altogether; the carriage to which the wheel was attached was turned upside down; it had fallen among the piles; the carriage was five ton weight, and I think the wheel was broke by hitting against a pile or stone; the tire of the wheel is entire; there is no indentation, and the timber is good of the portion of the spokes remaining in the boss; these kinds of wheel are considered the safest; I examined the whole of the other wheels; of some of the other wheels, some of the axles are bent; all the tires were in good condition except one, on which there was an indentation on the tire; the wheel may have hit a piece of iron; it had fallen amongst the wreck; I am satisfied that if the wheels had broken the chairs, there would have been more indentations in the wheels, as there was more than one chair broken; I think that if a wheel had made a dent in a chair, there would be a corresponding dent in a wheel … I am satisfied that the tender could not have rode up the tension rods as stated by Mr Locke as the axles boxes being slight would have broken away, or have been more broken than they are; the weight of tender and water would be thirteen tons; I examined what was called paint by Mr Locke; I call it a mixture of sandstone and marl; I am satisfied it is not paint.*

So here was careful inspection of the evidence to disprove Locke's assertions about derailment of either the carriage or tender to bring down the bridge. Carriage wheels would remain a composite wood and wrought-iron product for many years before being replaced by all metal constructions. The reference to chairs refers to the cast-iron seats in which rails sat, and which would have been impacted had any vehicle left the rails on the bridge, as opposed to at the end of the bridge. The local rock at Chester is red sandstone, and marl is a kind of clay. The piles in the river can be seen in *Illustrated London News* print as poles stuck in the river bed, and were presumably part of the formwork used during the erection of the structure.

Testimony from the passengers and eye witnesses all suggested that the girder broke in the middle, and the various other theories all lacked corroboration. The scene was now set for the railway inspectors to deliver their considered and detailed report on the tragedy. Their report was produced at the end of the inquest and they were present to answer any questions, which were very few. They had been present for little of the inquest, but were clearly aware of the testimony, judging by the facts they adduced. Simmons, for example, had to travel back to Wolverton to appear at the inquest there after the horrific collision between a London express and the coal train on a siding, which had killed even more passengers than had died at the Dee.

6

Official Investigation

Captain Simmons and Mr Walker presented their thorough inspection of the remains towards the end of the inquest. Their report is a model of detailed observation, and included many diagrams to explain the damage to the structure. It was by far the most thorough investigation undertaken by the new inspectorate to date. Like the other witnesses, they were not swayed by the eminent engineers who gave evidence: on the contrary, they approached the task with professional disinterest and independence, just what was needed when analysing a serious accident.

In addition to accurately surveyed plans and sections of the remains, they also produced extensive tables of the results of their experiments on the remaining girders still in position, especially the intact track by the side of the broken girder, which the driver Clayton had used to return to Chester after the accident. They conducted a series of experiments on the surviving girders and track with a locomotive to see how the girders responded to both static and live loads. It was important to examine the claims made by the witnesses about large deflections in the centre of the girders when trains passed. Simmons used an engine and tender of 30 tons, giving a distributed load of 15 tons on each girder. This was comparable with the accident locomotive, and did not include the carriages, but was still dangerous if there was a design problem with the cast-iron structure. On the other hand, Clayton had driven over the same intact track, so there seemed to be some assurance of his personal safety.

Dynamic Tests

Using a theodolite, Simmons observed a mean deflection of 2.36in at the centre of an intact girder with the engine at rest. The top flange moved inward by about ½in, the lower flange moved outward owing to the asymmetric loading on the girder. He repeated the measurements with the train moving at 15-25mph, the deflection decreased to about 1⅝ in. More significantly, he felt the bridge oscillating beneath him as the train moved across:

> … there is the shaking and oscillating motion caused by an engine going at considerable speed, the effect of which depends on degree, and is difficult of calculation, but is a constantly repeated force, which, upon a hard rigid body like a cast-iron beam, tends to weaken and injure it.

They distinguished the repeated intermittent action of trains passing to the oscillations of much higher frequency induced by moving trains:

> *In addition to this is the tremulous motion of the beam (like the wire of a musical instrument) when the engine is going over. This tremor was so sensible that Captain Simmons could not distinctly see the edge of the beam*

He felt that both effects acted to weaken the girders.

In their report, Walker and Simmons thought that the wrought-iron chain gave little or no reinforcement to the cast-iron girders since the ends of the chain were tied to the cast iron itself. So when the centre was loaded down by a train, the girder ends deflected inwards, nullifying the support given by the tie bars to the girder. To offer support to the cast iron, it would have been necessary to connect the ends of the tie bars to an entirely independent support. They actually measured the deflection of the ends where the beam was loaded centrally:

> *Then, also, the strain upon the girders tends to shorten the distance between the points of suspension of the tension-rods, by drawing down the end of the castings to which they are attached; these ends being raised so high above the level of the girder as to give a considerable leverage to the tension-rod in drawing forward the point to which it is attached. Captain Simmons observed, that with a load of 48 tons on the bridge, the point of suspension on one side moved 7/16ths of an inch, and if the other side did the same, the distance between them was lessened by 7/8 ths of an inch, and the tension bars loosened in proportion. The effect of this is to counteract the strain which takes place upon the horizontal or middle link of the chain when the load is upon the centre of the girder.*

So the tension bars did not reinforce the girder at all when trains moved over the bridge, quite contrary to assertions made by Stephenson in justifying use of trussed girders in long railway bridges.

Examination of the Broken Girder

Simmons and Walker also examined the fractures on the girder, despite the fact that they had learned relatively little from the remains. Superficially both main breaks seemed similar, with wedge-shaped parts being formed in both breaks *(6.1)*. Neither had much knowledge of metallurgy, and there was little or no tradition of examining fractures for the way in which the cracks had formed first, and then grown to a completion. Nowadays, it is a normal part of the forensic study of broken products. Comments typically made in the scientific or engineering press were usually limited to saying whether or not the fractures surfaces appeared 'crystalline' or 'fibrous'. No attempts were made, in the absence of detailed studies, to determine the direction of crack growth, for example. That knowledge can then be used to trace a crack back to an origin or origins, often a defect at the free surface of a product. Such defects include small cracks, for example, which actually had been observed and reported by Beche and Cubitt in their earlier report of beam failures in buildings. Thus Simmons

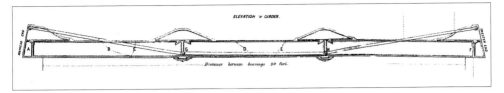

(6.1) Fractures in the cast-iron girder from the Dee bridge.

and Walker did not produce drawings of the fracture surfaces (as far as is known), which might have helped future investigators to unravel the sequence of events in the failure. They must have been aware of the importance of these and similar defects in cast iron, because they do make a specific comment about the absence of blowholes in the fractures:

> … *we may remark that the castings are what is technically termed sound, that is solid, and without hollows.*

They could not find blowholes in the fracture surfaces, but it seems clear that they went no further, by, for example, cutting the broken castings to investigate their internal structure. Today, it would be normal and essential to take sections of broken products to assess their quality.

However, they did notice the following feature of some of the castings:

> *We think that … [the inward deflection of the girder] … required a larger top flange than one fifth of the bottom flange, even if the girder-castings had been straight, which some of them are not, to the extent of three inches in the top rib … Whether this has arisen from the unequal cooling of … the casting, or from the mould being twisted, is of little consequence … Although the quality of the cast iron … is good, we consider the above as defects in the castings, which, in this bridge, have been injurious.*

What they are saying here is first, that some of the castings were twisted in shape, and second, that the top flange should have been wider to resist compression forces. The fact that some castings were distorted without any applied load (we are not told which castings) suggests that perhaps their manufacture may have involved quenching rather than slow cooling. This implies that there may have been high levels of residual stress, which would inevitably lower their strength. There is no evidence that Simmons and Walker retrieved all of the broken parts from the river, which, had they done so, would have enabled them to fit the parts together and determine if the broken beam was so twisted. Such reconstruction is a normal part of a modern forensic examination of broken parts to find out whether the original item showed any deviation from the specification drawing, for example. The search for missing parts is indeed a vital part of investigation of, for, example aerospace accidents (among others).

The girder had been under-designed by Stephenson, with the deflection under a static load of 25 tons at the foundry being 2.5ins, in agreement with the observations of Simmons.

Even to the disinterested, such a large movement of a vital structural part of a safety–critical bridge must have seemed unusual, if not dangerous and alarming. Moreover, the foundry test did not replicate the service conditions by loading the flange, a fact that emerged from evidence given to the inquest by the manager of the Horsley ironworks, where the castings had been made. It may have detected grossly faulty castings, but was in no way a test which could be relied upon as confirmation that the assembled castings would support similar weights on a girder bridge. The only way in which the structure could have been tested reliably was by constructing two girders, placing them side by side, and then loading the inner flanges, just as in the actual bridge. Even placing two castings side by side and loading the flanges would probably have shown the weakness of the design.

Walker and Simmons noted that the bridge had experienced much heavier loading than the train which fell, for example when three locos linked together passed over the bridge in October/November 1846 in proof-testing the structure. It had also experienced heavy loading since opening. So what had caused the failure? Their inspection of both types of ironwork showed that the cast iron was apparently sound. Likewise, the wrought iron was apparently of good quality. However, they thought that the vibrations induced by trains could weaken the structure:

> ... *the fact that when a weight, partly permanent and partly passing, but together forming a very considerable proportion of the breaking weight of the girder, is in continuing operation, flat girders of cast iron suffer injury, and their strength becomes reduced...*

This comment by Simmons is one of the earliest references to the problem of metal fatigue, where a component fails well below its rated strength owing to crack formation and growth by repeated loading cycles. Adding the extra load of ballast just before the accident must have contributed to the failure by increasing the static load supported by the girders.

In their report, both authors admit they had not examined the many other bridges which used trussed cast iron. This is hardly surprising given the very short time scale under which they produced their report; however, it was an omission that would be rectified after the jury decision, not so much by the railway inspectors but by the engineers employed by the railway companies themselves.

Summing Up

Although the final report from Simmons and Walker was not officially published until 30 June, they presented it (presumably in handwritten form) to the inquest on 18 June 1846. It bore the date of 15 June. Captain Simmons gave an abstract of their main conclusions directly to the court. He was not questioned by anyone in the court on the results, which clearly and unequivocally condemned the design and structure of trussed cast-iron girders.

In his summing up for the jury, the coroner went out of his way to exclude the possibility of negligence by Stephenson, let alone the possibility of manslaughter. However, he intimated that the results of the inquest would be important for railway construction:

With respect to so much of the enquiry as related to the bridge, it could not be profitless, in as much as the opinions of eminent engineers had been elicited, including the eminent gentlemen sent down by the government authorities, and there could be no doubt, but that the eminent engineers who were concerned in building railways would feel the effect of the enquiry, and no doubt if the principle was faulty it would be abandoned or modified.

Here was an explicit hint of the way the coroner was thinking. He went on to discuss the various theories of the disaster:

With respect to the theory of the accident being caused by a lateral blow the evidence materially rebutted that. One point that the paint was proved not to have been paint at all, consequently one link of the theory was gone.

There were other reasons why the theory was not credible, but that was a question for the jury to decide. He went on to give strong advice for the jury:

After the evidence of General Pasley, and the government commissioners that the bridge was not safe, it would be well if the opinion of the jury also went forth to the public. This bridge was erected by the most eminent engineer in the country, and who had examined this bridge on the morning of the accident; and unless an opinion was given on this bridge whether it was safe or not, this enquiry could have no practical result.

If they so wished, then the jury should comment on the design of the bridge.

Jury Decision

The jury returned after retiring for about an hour. They were unequivocal in their own view of the causes of the accident, stating first that all of the victims had died accidentally. The jury, presumably in the person of their foreman, the irrepressible Sir Edward Walker, first gave their verdict on the victims:

We find that George Roberts, John Matthews, and Chas Nevitt were accidentally killed on the evening of 24th of May last, in the parish of St Mary-on-the-hill, in the city of Chester, by being precipitated along with a train of carriages on the bank or bed of the river Dee, from the breakage of one of the twelve cast iron girders constituting the bridge over that river.

They also found that Isaac Roberts and Thomas Anderson died from the same cause. They commented on the Stephenson defence:

We are further unanimously of opinion, that the aforesaid girder did not break from any lateral blow of the engine, tender or carriage, or van, or from any fault or defect in the masonry of the piers or abutments; but from its being made of a strength insufficient to bear the pressure of quick trains passing over it.

The design was faulty, as they expressed it:

> *We feel that the eleven remaining girders having been cast from the same pattern, and of the same strength, are equally weak, and consequently equally dangerous for quick or passenger trains, as the broken one.*

But they went much further, bearing in mind their duty to the travelling public:

> *We consider we should not be doing our duty towards the public if we separated without expressing our unanimous opinion, that no girder bridge in future should be made of so brittle and treacherous a metal as cast iron alone. Even though trussed with wrought-iron rods, is not safe for quick or passenger trains. And we have in evidence that there are upwards of one hundred bridges similar in principle and form to the late one over the river Dee, either in use, or in the course of being constructed on various lines of railway. We consider all these unsafe more or less in proportion to the span; still all unsafe.*

They then made their clarion call:

> *We, therefore, call upon Her Majesty's Government, as Guardians of the public safety, to institute such an enquiry into the merits or demerits of these bridges, as shall either condemn the principle or establish their safety to such a degree, that passengers may rest fully satisfied there is no danger; although they deflect from 1½ to 5 inches.*

The coroner called for the gentlemen of the press to publicise the need for a public enquiry of some kind, although he would be forwarding the verdict directly to the Board of Trade. At a later session, where they all signed the legal documents, the jury foreswore their allowance of £32 for their time, directing that it be returned to the borough fund.

Parliamentary Interest

The problem of the spate of recent railway accidents was raised in a Parliamentary question on 24 June 1847 by a Mr Rice, who referred specifically to the Nutbourne accident in his question. He wanted to know whether the powers of the Railway Commissioners were sufficient to protect the public from accidents. The Minister, Mr Strutt, mentioned in his reply the Dee bridge along with the Wolverton and Nutbourne accidents. Following the highly critical decision of the Chester jury, the minister showed the concern of the government in the use of cast iron in railway structures:

> *The commissioners have since taken the report [by Simmons and Walker] into consideration, and the conclusion they have drawn from it is, that further experiment and examination are necessary with regard to the use of cast iron in the construction of railway bridges. The commissioners have reason to believe, that though there has been sufficient experience to regulate the use of cast iron where it is subjected to*

steady pressure, additional experiments and further information are required as to those cases where, as in railway bridges, it is liable to the passing of heavy weights at great velocities, and where the vibrations are caused under different circumstances. Taking this into account, the board has recommended the government to appoint a commission to investigate the subject, with power to make experiments upon it; that commission to will be constituted partly of gentlemen of eminent scientific experience, and partly of practical engineers.

He went on to outline the immediate practical steps taken by the government:

In the meantime, circulars have been issued to all the railway companies … requesting them to make a return of all the cast iron bridges they have on their lines, their dimensions and other particulars; they are also recommended, in case there is the slightest doubts of the stability of any bridge, at once to give it additional temporary support, and, till the report of the experimental commission is made to me, to run the trains over it with great caution, and only at low rates of speed.

Strutt then turned to the other recent accidents, at Wolverton and Nutbourne, where new regulations would be brought forward on braking. But it was clearly the Dee accident which raised the greatest concern given the sheer number of bridges of the same design either planned or actually in use on many lines across the country at the time; this was what made the Dee accident so significant, despite the smaller number of fatalities than at Wolverton.

The Board of Trade also issued a circular to all railway companies requesting details of the many trussed bridges still in use, or planned to be opened on new lines.

Modern Analysis

What can be said today about the causes of the disaster? Modern interpretations of the Dee disaster are few and far between, but one eminent railway historian has presented an explanation not strongly supported by the original evidence. L.T.C. Rolt suggested, in his classic biography of the Stephensons, that the examination of the broken cast-iron girder

… proved that the fracture had begun in the top flange, which had failed in compression…

Walker and Simmons did not draw this conclusion at all, and the suggestion was in fact made by Henry Robertson, engineer to the Shrewsbury & Chester Railroad Co. During the final session of the inquest, he claimed that the top flange had broken in compression, although this interpretation contradicted the eye-witness evidence. Moreover, Robertson did not support his claim with any comments on the exact nature of the break.

Other more recent analysts have said that the bridge failed through 'torsional instability'. However, this is not a failure mode, but rather a symptom of an underlying problem involving design. When something cracks and breaks apart, it necessarily involves crack initiation and growth, which may or may not be related to torsional instability.

The subject is best approached by looking first at the limitations of the official report, as seen from a twenty-first-century perspective.

Limitations of Simmons Report

The official report was clearly constrained by the political pressure to have some conclusions to present to a worried public. The report was completed in only about three weeks, with, of necessity, only limited access to all the remains. Although comparison with modern practice is perhaps unfair, it can point to gaps in the information which may indicate how failure actually occurred in the girder. On the other hand, the Simmons report suffers from some deficiencies which would have been clear to other engineers of the time.

After all, considerable knowledge of the problems of large cast-iron girders had been gained during the investigations of building collapses, principally by de la Beche and Cubbitt in their report of 1844, as well as the research of William Fairbairn. He had personally warned Robert Stephenson of the problem in late 1846, and actually offered to design a wrought-iron girder bridge to cross the Dee. De la Beche and Cubbitt had explored the problem of casting practice, after they found small brittle cracks in the failure beam. It pointed to premature removal of the new castings from the sand mould, causing uneven rates of cooling and, as we know now, formation of residual tensile stresses within the beams. One symptom of the residual stress is the formation of small cracks, especially where a tension zone impinges on the exterior surfaces of the product, perhaps encouraged by other defects such as inclusions or blowholes there.

But there was very little reported about the way the Dee castings had been made at the Horsley foundry. The only comment made by Simmons concerned the slight axial deformation found in some castings still presumably on the bridge, by about 3in off true in one case. Such measurements would have come naturally in the inspection of the intact part of the bridge, when Simmons was conducting his dynamic experiments on vibrations caused by his running trains over it. There was an opportunity to cross-examine the manager of the Horsley foundry who attended the inquest, but this was not taken, so the trail runs cold.

There were further limitations to the work done by Simmons and Walker, especially when they examined the broken parts, and the fractures themselves.

Fracture of Castings

We know from the report in the *Illustrated London News* that by the time the reporters appeared on the scene at some time, probably several days, prior to 12 June (the date of the publication of their article), some of the debris had already been removed. Goods trains had resumed on the intact line, presumably to supply the further work on the C&H railway line, but they were running without locomotives, so we are told by the intrepid

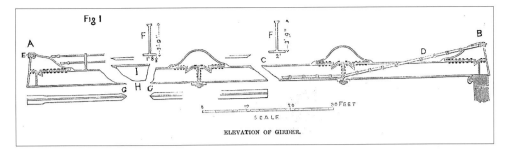

(6.2) Broken girder as shown in the Illustrated London News.

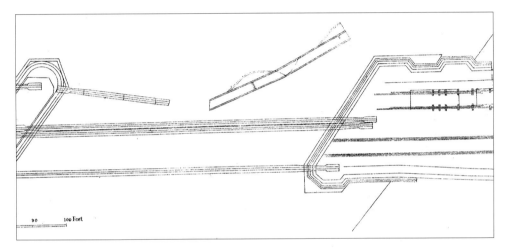

(6.3) Plan of the fallen Dee bridge girder showing positions of castings.

reporters. They saw no substantial deflection of the remaining girders, but then the imposed load will have been much lower than if a locomotive had been used. Presumably the wagons were being hauled by a fixed engine and rope.

The authors of the article provided several diagrams including a long section of the broken girder *(6.2)*, which shows the two breaks, one at the centre of the abutment casting, the other in the middle of the centre casting. There is much greater detail shown of the abutment fracture, suggesting that the parts had been taken from the river and reassembled on dry ground. The drawing shows two oblique ends to the girder enclosing a large triangular fragment (I) and the fracture ends at the lower flange (GG). The two small sections of the girder show it to have a smaller lower flange at the side of the girder compared with the centre. The drawing is interesting when compared with the official drawings of the same structure, firstly because the centre crack of the middle casting shows just a simple oblique crack, probably because the remains of the middle girder had not then been removed from the river. The official drawing shows the same break as being much more complex, and indeed, somewhat similar to that of the abutment break, comprising two oblique ends enclosing a truncated triangular part. Simmons admitted in the report that fractured parts from the centre casting had been lost in the river, and neither he nor Walker identified exactly where the crack started, either in this or the abutment casting. *(6.3)*

Part of the lower flange appears to be missing in the *Illustrated London News* diagram, presumably lost in the river, and the profile is consistent with fracture starting in the lower flange, and then growing into the upright web so as to eject the large fragment I. However, it is likely that the abutment casting was still in one piece when it was found in the river, as shown by the Simmons's drawing *(6.3)*. The plan shows one length of the girder (about one and a half castings) bent slightly about the fracture. It is therefore likely that the fracture had not grown to completion when found, but it soon expanded, probably when being retrieved from the river bed. The *Illustrated London News* illustration of the accident scene shows one of the hemi-spherical joints rising above the water level, so it should have been easy to retrieve when the tide went out. It is a pity that there are no further details of the crack apart from the *Illustrated London News* section, especially as this part was to form the basis of Stephenson's case for lateral impact.

Cast Iron

Cast iron is much weaker in tension or bending than in compression, which is why the arch is the optimum structural form for bridges, or columns which support only vertical loads. At the Tay bridge inquiry over thirty years later, the measured compressive strength of the cast iron was about 34.6 tons psi, and the tensile strength only about 9.1 tons psi, nearly four times smaller. The abutment fracture was incomplete, because Simmons shows the casting intact in his plan of the accident scene.

The inquest found that the bridge failed by fracture of the centre of the middle casting under load from the train, and in my view this is the likely way in which the disaster occurred. The girder deflected downwards and was also twisted slightly by the asymmetric loading conditions, with the weight of the train being supported by the inner flange only. The lower part of the beam will have been in tension, the upper part compressed. Since cast iron is much weaker in tension, it is thus most likely that the fracture started at the lower flange, and grew upwards until it met the free upper surface. It is also clear from the sketch of the break that there were two separate cracks growing simultaneously, since a large trapezoidal fragment was created *(6.3)*. So what was the most probable origin of the failure? Without sketches of the fracture surfaces, it is difficult to be specific, but there are some obvious zones of weakness in the section profile as provided by Walker and Simmons *(6.4)*.

Stress Concentrations

The inner corners of the girder were not smoothly rounded out, but were in fact given a curious shape more like that widely adopted by carpenters working with wooden beams. The section is known as a cavetto moulding, two sharp corners (fillets) next to the web

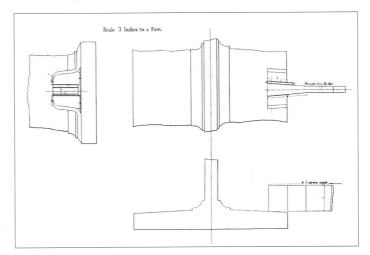

Scale. 3 Inches to a Foot.

(6.4) Plan and section of lower flange of girder.

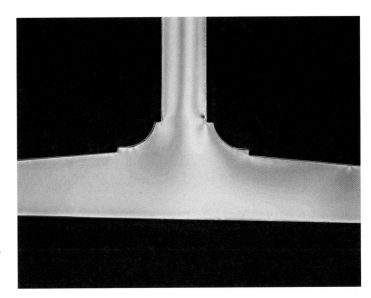

(6.5) Strain birefringence of plastic model of girder section showing upper corner of cavetto moulding to be a serious stress raiser.

and flange parts, with a concave surface in between (*(6.4)* lower section). The diagram of the cavetto moulding shown in the figure is not exactly comparable with that used on the castings, having only one corner and an ellipsoidal curve, but there was a considerable degree of choice when using this architectural feature. The feature ran along the entire length of the girder both on the inner and outer sides. It was part of the aesthetic detail presented by the girder when in full view, and was a common architectural motif adopted at the time for large railway girders (such as the old and current Water Street bridges in Manchester).

However, such details can give rise to serious structural problems, especially in a very brittle material like cast iron which will be stressed heavily in service. The fillets or corners are very serious stress raisers, and the load imposed by the track and train will have been concentrated at the corners of the cavetto of the lower flange. Another zone of weakness is present in the lower flange at the points where the horizontal tie bars were attached *(6.5)*.

Design defects like corners are known as stress concentrations, because the stress at those points or zones is much greater than elsewhere in the loaded product. A common example of a corner which weakens a product is a scratch on a sheet of glass. When loaded, the sheet will inevitably fail from that scratch because the stress there is much greater than anywhere else. Hardware stores that supply glass sheet to the consumer use this fact to cut glass to shape, by scribing the surface with a diamond knife, for example. They then bend the sheet over a straight edge and the glass cracks neatly along the scribed line. Many disasters have been caused by stress concentrations, for example the Comet disasters in the early 1950s, when brittle cracks grew in the fuselage from corners and microcracks at windows and portholes in the aircraft. The worst aerospace disaster in history occurred when the tail of a jumbo jet fell off an aircraft in flight in Japan in 1976. A brittle crack had grown slowly from a botched repair job involving a rivet hole and a corner in the pressurised fuselage.

The brittle cast iron in the Dee beam will have been most vulnerable at these corners, and the corners on the cavetto moulding are the most likely origin of the brittle crack which caused the beam to fail. The crack will have run along one of the corners under tension and a small shear component, before running up the web to the top free surface of the girder. In fact, looking at the crack profile, it is easy to see that such a crack along the line of one of the two corners would have run in two directions, and then branched or diverted into the very thin web of the casting. The two crack ends will have grown fast through the web until they met the free upper surface of the girder, so producing a large triangular fragment as found in both fractures.

But which of the two corners represents the most serious stress raiser? A direct experiment was attempted using polaroscopy. It has been a standard way of assessing the way specific designs respond to load for many years, although it is now less well-used than computer-aided analysis. A scale section of the casting was machined from 4mm-thick polycarbonate sheet, a polymer with a high stress-optical coefficient. The right-hand flange was bent downwards in a polariscope, producing the birefringence shown in *(6.5)*. The upper corner of the cavetto section is where most of the applied stress is concentrated, and therefore where fracture will have started in the cast-iron beam.

By adding such a decorative feature to a structural beam, the designer unwittingly catastrophically weakened it. Aesthetic features may have been suitable for plinths for statues, but were totally inappropriate for structural components.

Fracture Mechanism

So, if one of these corners was the source of the brittle crack that destroyed the bridge, was it produced by overload or fatigue? The static load on the structure was increased greatly by the addition of ballast just before the accident, but the load was distributed evenly over the whole bridge, so this does not explain why just one of the three spans failed. Clayton drove the train across four girders before reaching the critical one, and drove back across the intact track on the bridge safely when he raised the alarm at Chester. The most credible explanation is that the fatal girder had been weakened by a fatigue crack which had grown progressively with use by passing trains. On the day of the accident, the previous six trains and the load of ballast allowed the crack to grow to a critical length, and it grew catastrophically when the 6.15 p.m. train entered the span. A small blowhole or casting crack near the centre of the beam will have been enough to start the crack growing with passing trains. It is interesting to note that one of the painters (William Clarke) who worked on a girder which cracked before the accident, actually measured a very large deflection of 5½in at the centre of this span when a train was passing. If there was a growing fatigue crack, then this is just what would be expected: the remaining iron would be more greatly strained and therefore show a much greater deflection than for the unaffected girders. It is thus entirely possible that a similar effect occurred on the fatal girder and gave a warning of what was to come.

Fatigue Failure

As many forensic investigators will say, most, if not a majority of failures, in a wide range of products, are caused by fatigue. So what is the problem, and how does the problem appear in failed products? Fatigue occurs simply by the initiation of a crack, usually at a defect on a surface, followed by progressive crack growth until the section of solid material left can no longer support the applied load. A varying load is implicit in this definition of the problem, or in other words, a cyclical load. But this simple statement does not really give a true perspective of the problem. It is often thought, for example, that fatigue is a problem of ageing products, and that cracks take a very long time to grow to a critical state. Not so: cracks can grow very fast indeed, with just a handful of cycles of load to failure. It really depends on the severity of the applied load, the greater it is, the sooner the crack will grow to completion. So new products can fail by fatigue, depending on their design and response to the load. Examples include a new power tool (angle grinder) where the plastic handle breaks suddenly, and the user nearly severs a leg when the revolving disc moves freely with no control.

A common feature of fatigue failure is the sudden loss of a critical part of a product, when the crack reaches a critical size, and the component breaks into two or more fragments. Sudden failure of a range of products is, unfortunately, not uncommon, as aerospace vehicles and the continuing loss of life in aircraft accidents so visibly demonstrates. Fatigue failure is a common suspect in such terrible accidents. Of course, it is not the only cause of sudden failures, but it ranks high when it comes to investigation. It is usually observed that the product which suddenly failed bore higher loads at the beginning of its life in service than when it fractured. This must be true because a crack may not have existed initially, so the product will have been able to bear the full load easily. However, with progressive crack growth (cracks always grow larger), the section area available to support the load will diminish until the product can no longer support the applied load.

Fatigue cracks can be very difficult to detect because they are present as hairline features in external surfaces, so they are easily overlooked during inspection. They may be concealed by contamination of the surfaces, and do not appear dangerous until a load is applied, when they open slightly. In other cases, they may be totally concealed from view. This would certainly be the case if the fatigue cracks grew from the inside corner of the lower flange, as suggested above.

So, a railway bridge which supported very high loads at the outset, may fail at much lower loads as the crack or cracks grow with time and repeated flexing. This appears to have been the case with the Dee bridge, which supported coupled engines of 100 tons at proof testing, but then failed under an engine and tender of 30 tons. Indeed, heavier loads used during proof testing can actually initiate cracks, and start the process going.

Finite Element Analysis

More recently, a finite element analysis (FEA) has been performed by Bob Burt of Lockheed Martin aerospace company in Dallas, Texas, of the Dee bridge. The method uses the power of computers to determine how the stress is distributed within a loaded component. It is used widely in product development to assess structural integrity of new designs without the need to test the component itself, although prototype testing is usually needed to corroborate the results of FEA. Bob Burt has confirmed the lateral instability of the girder, his animation showed torsional oscillations of the kind described by Simmons.

Sequence of Events

Using the results of the new reinterpretation of all the evidence, it is possible to reconstruct the probable sequence of events at the Dee bridge.

The design of the trussed cast-iron girder had been developed following earlier use of the principle at the Minories station (1840), Stockton (1844) and elsewhere on the new railway system. The design was developed in the rush to complete new railway lines crossing large spans, despite the well-known brittle properties of cast iron. It was thought that the wrought-iron reinforcement would provide good security against failure by sharing the loads on the bridges. However, there were alternative designs, such as arched cast-iron and wooden trestle bridges. Other trussed bridges may have been used even earlier, and are said to have been developed by Vignoles or Bidder. They appeared to be able to support trains successfully, but relatively little is known about their performance in service. The trussed bridge at the Minories would be relatively lightly loaded, for example, since motive power was provided by fixed engines and ropes rather than by heavy locomotives. It is not known what tests were performed on trussed bridges, if any, although there is some anecdotal evidence from the Dee inquest that some tests were done. On the other hand, the fact that the Dee bridge failed catastrophically took a number of engineers by surprise, and it is most likely that very little systematic testing was performed at all on trussed bridges. However, a trussed girder fitted to a mill in Manchester did fail suddenly, perhaps in 1845 or 1846, and was well publicised, especially by William Farbairn, so the principle should have been used very cautiously in heavily loaded safety-critical railway bridges. A cracked casting had been found in the Stockton bridge and replaced.

The castings for the very long Dee bridge spans, the longest so far to be used, were supplied by the Horsley foundry in 1846, one of which was definitely flawed, because it cracked, was discovered and replaced, possibly after November 1846. The castings varied in quality, some showed signs of permanent distortion when Simmons surveyed the bridge in May/June 1847, after the accident. Every casting had apparently been tested by a central load of up to 50 tons at the foundry, a test which could not reveal the state of the lower flanges. Each casting weighed about 30 tons, and they were probably pre-assembled into girders before being hoisted into position on the masonry piers. It is likely that the wrought-iron tie bars were fitted before hoisting, and tensioned so as to tighten the joints and stabilise the girders. This could be achieved by screws fitted under the joints. They could then be inserted into the spans, probably using supports buried in the river bed, and ropes from block-and-tackles fitted to tripods above the level of the bridge. Further adjustment of the girders using the screws may have been undertaken, given the large self-load over the clear spans.

Wrought-iron tie bars with dovetail ends were inserted into the lower flanges of the girders to provide lateral stability. The massive oak joists were placed in position across the space between the girders as the base for the track platform. Some of the joists were fitted with iron shoes, but all were laid with their ends resting on the lower flange of the girders. The sleepers were laid on top of the oak platform, and the wrought-iron tracks then fitted, increasing the dead load on the lower inner flanges of the girders. The girders were designed with architectural features, including a cavetto moulding between the flanges and webs, with two sharp fillets at their edges. Model experiments have shown that the stress from the platform will have been concentrated most severely at the upper corner of the moulding on the lower flange. The bridge was inspected and approved by General Pasley in October 1846, and, if not proof tested by three coupled engines and tenders at the time, then, definitely at a later date. They weighed in total about 100 tons, well in excess of the normal load of a train.

Passenger trains of the Shrewsbury & Chester Railway were run over the new bridge at an unknown frequency, but we can estimate that towards the spring of 1847 there were probably a minimum of about six per day. In addition, the bridge was used to supply materials and equipment at the growing end of the line beyond Saltney on the far side of the river bank from Chester. Motive power came from locomotives as well as fixed engines, at least according to the reporters of the *Illustrated London News*.

The bridge was painted in the early spring of 1847, and at least two of the painters noticed large deflections of up to 5in at the centre of the girders when passenger trains passed over the bridge. Robert Stephenson may or may not have been informed of the deflections. On 24 May 1847, he requested that all the track be covered with a layer of sandstone ballast in order to fire-proof the structural timbers of the platform. A recent fire on the GWR had destroyed a large bridge, so it was a precautionary step taken to protect the Dee bridge from a similar fate. The ballast was about 5in deep, and weighed about 18–25 tons per pair of girders, so increasing the dead load on the inner lower flanges of the girders. Using Robertson's estimates, the dead load on the flange was roughly doubled. As in all beams, the greatest load will have been at the centre. Six trains had passed safely over the bridge on the morning of 24 May, before the ballast was laid in the afternoon.

The 6.15 a.m. passenger train from Chester was travelling towards the bridge at 20–30mph, and proceeded safely over the first two spans, but fell through the last span when the outer girder suddenly fractured. The coupling between the tender and carriages broke, and they fell into the water, killing five passengers and crew. The engine broke away from the tender, which derailed and hit the masonry abutment, causing damage to the stonework. The evidence showed that the train was in the centre of the middle casting when the break occurred. Stephenson defended the design of the bridge by suggesting that the tender of one of the carriages had derailed, hit the girder laterally, and broken it, so causing the disaster. However, all the evidence pointed to the centre casting having broken before another break in the abutment casting, the theory being corroborated by the fact that the abutment casting is shown in almost one piece on Simmons plan of the remains. Most of the eye witnesses, and many of the experts, also dismissed the theory. Paint traces said by Stephenson to prove the sideways impact theory proved to be unsubstantiated when inspected by the jury. A broken carriage wheel was said to have been broken during the subsequent rescue operation. Simmons's plan shows that the tender derailed where the guard rail ended.

The girder broke in two places, at the middle of the centre casting, and near the middle of the abutment casting, producing a trapezoidal and a triangular fragment respectively. Most witnesses at the inquest and Simmons favoured first fracture at the geometric centre of the girder, followed by the abutment fracture. The ejected fragment from the first break was about twice the size of the second fragment, and had roughly equal sloping sides angled at about 45 degrees to the horizontal, with the interpolated centre almost precisely at the geometric centre of the girder, where the load would be at a maximum. The second break occurred off centre, further from the abutment, corresponding to loading of a free cantilever.

Fracture of the girder probably occurred from a stress concentration in the lower flange, the sharp corner of a cavetto moulding between the flange and the rib of the girder. Alternatively, the break was initiated at one of the dovetail sockets in the lower flange. The critical crack branched from the corner into the web, and produced separation of a trapezoidal part. It was symmetrical because the crack was moving at a constant speed from the putative centre, where initiation occurred. Although fracture will have been extremely fast, there will have been some delay on fall of the parts. All of the instantaneous load will have been immediately transferred to the wrought-iron tension bars and tie bars, as well as the double rail. Since both tie bars and rails were made of tough material, wrought iron, fall of the girder parts will have been delayed momentarily, the broken parts being held together very briefly before they broke by overload.

Simmons estimated that the locomotive was travelling at about 30mph (44ft per second), rather than the 20mph claimed by Clayton, so it will have been over the centre of the last casting in about 0.5 secs, when it too cracked in a similar way to the primary fracture *(6.1)*, *(6.2)*. As the track sank behind the engine, its momentum carried it to the further bank. However, the carriages behind were pulled backwards, and the coupling with the tender broke, allowing the carriages to fall into the river below. It is at this point that the second fracture occurred, due to asymmetric loading of the cantilever beam. The wrench derailed the tender, and its coupling to the locomotive broke, the tender then striking the abutment and causing substantial damage. Clayton, the driver of the engine, drove on to Saltney junction and reversed the locomotive, driving back across the intact spans to Chester to raise the alarm.

In detailed tests done after the disaster, Simmons subjected the intact spans to dynamic loads from a 30-ton locomotive and tender. He confirmed that the centre of the girders did indeed sag beneath the load by several inches, and the speed of the engine influenced the sag. He saw violent lateral oscillations in the girders when trains crossed, and attributed the failure to progressive deterioration in the strength of the cast iron, a phenomenon now known as fatigue.

Mystery of the Missing Eagles

There was, as might be expected for such a traumatic accident, much discussion of the disaster, not just in the popular press, but also in the technical journals of the period. An unsigned article in the *Civil Engineer and Architect's Journal* of July 1847, for example, devoted four pages to an extensive discussion of the causes. After summarising the witness evidence, they presented several diagrams of the bridge, partly based on the Simmons drawings, partly from the *Illustrated London News*, and some from their own original contributions. Although they made the same mistake as the *Illustrated London News* in showing the primary fracture as involving only a single crack, they did show a section of the casting at the fracture which introduced a new factor into the argument *(6.6)*.

The top flange of the abutment casting had apparently been drilled with two vertical bolt holes, intended, so they said, to carry a decorative eagle on the bridge. This extra ornamental element cannot have been fitted, and is not mentioned by any authors at all, and it is strange that it would have been off-centre, unless other eagles were planned for all the girders. Nevertheless, they say that the flange was 'much crushed' here, presumably implying that it may actually have initiated the crack. This is unlikely since everyone concluded that the primary fracture was at the centre of the bridge. It illustrates the confused thinking of the time in matters pertaining to crack initiation and growth, but also shows that there were other details which did not emerge at the inquest, or from Simmons's inquiry. In any case, the article condemned the bridge as being very badly designed for the loads it would carry, a conclusion shared by most experts at the time, and ultimately the travelling public.

The theory received a new boost from Paul Sibley in 1976 when he published his research thesis, which studied the disaster in detail. He also spotted the 'eagle holes' drilled

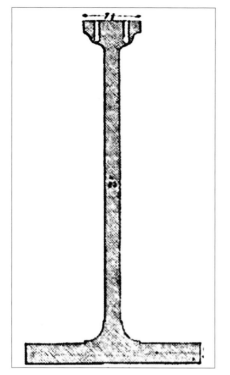

A DANGEROUS CHARACTER.

Policeman Sibthorpe. "COME, IT'S HIGH TIME YOU WERE TAKEN TO THE HOUSE; YOU'VE DONE QUITE MISCHIEF ENOUGH."

Above left: (6.6) Bolt holes for ornamental cast-iron eagles.

Above right: (6.7) Punch cartoon lampooning the 'guilty' locomotive.

(or perhaps cast) into the top of the castings. He believes that the beam broke by torsional failure from the holes, essentially by lateral buckling of the girder when the train passed. The eagle holes do represent serious stress concentrations, but it is unclear whether or not they are oriented at the appropriate angle to the loads to be effective stress raisers. The proposed failure mechanism, however, does not explain why the bridge fell in May and not earlier when heavier trains passed over. Nor does it explain why the ballast enhanced the likelihood of collapse. If anything, rotation of the web when the train entered the bridge would be lower than before, with the extra load on the lower flange. Fatigue of the flange remains the most likely explanation of the sudden failure of the Dee bridge, just as Simmons and Walker implied.

The final word came in a *Punch* cartoon printed after the disaster *(6.7)* showing a recalcitrant locomotive being dragged off to the House of Commons in chains. Colonel Sibthorpe was the Tory member for Lincoln, and a vociferous critic of the new railways, forever raising the problem of railway accidents in the Commons. The irony is directed at Robert Stephenson, who infamously blamed the engine for derailing, and so bringing the bridge down. The face of the loco is one of suitably injured innocence.

7

Aftermath

The accident was to have long-lasting effects on engineering practice in Britain. The decision of the jury to request a government enquiry resulted in a Royal Commission on the use of iron in railway bridges, and a programme of testing of iron structures started. In the meantime, there were many existing trussed bridges which would need inspecting and reinforcement. The proceedings of the Chester inquest were publicised widely, both in the local and national press such as *The Times*. There was a crisis of confidence in cast-iron bridge structures and the railways, with many judging the risks of travelling by train to be too great. It was also an interesting period politically, with several other major crises developing, such as the famine in Ireland, revolutionary movements in Europe, and an impending General Election in Britain.

And yet there was a sense of optimism, a belief that though there had been serious problems with the new railways, all would be well in the end. And the same engineers were already working on an idea which would come to fulfillment in 1851: the Great Exhibition, and the palace of cast and wrought iron, glass and wood which would house the exhibition. Cast iron would come good for this gigantic structure, where Britain would show the world (and her own citizens) what she could make with all her new machines, as well as display the products of her vast empire. Growing industrial economies, especially those of mainland Europe and the USA would also display their goods and manufactures.

For the longer term, a Royal Commission was set up from the great and the good to report on the design of railway bridges, especially those made of cast iron, but also including wholly wrought-iron bridges. The effects of heavy fast trains on those structures would be an important issue to explore, both from direct experiment and by interrogation of the major engineers of the day, including Stephenson, Locke, and Brunel. Many existing cast-iron bridges were examined, including trussed bridges like that at the Dee, and many others which tried to combine the two types of material. The Commission would expose many problems, and a divergence of opinions concerning the integrity of such structures.

Dee Bridge Repairs

The immediate need was to support the Dee bridge by underpinning the girders, probably by reusing the poles and beams which had survived from the initial building phase a few months before, as well as adding more substantial props. The bridge was needed very urgently to transport materials needed for extending the line into Wales. Whether they continued to use the fixed engine as a precaution to haul the goods wagons is unknown. The Dee bridge was rebuilt by creating shallow arches below the girders, so relieving the girders of much of the load. More castings were added to the superstructure as well. However, further failures of the surviving girders occurred during the first rebuilding phase after the disaster. Each of the original girders was tested in a bend test, and another girder failed by brittle cracking well below its design strength. This test was probably no more than a centre suspension test, just like those used to test castings at the foundry, although Stephenson later claimed at the Royal Commission hearings that he now suspended weights from the lower flanges by a double hook. According to Sibley, the girder failed at just 32 tons, a value well below the combined weight of the platform and ballast of about 40 tons. Yet a fifth cast-iron girder was cracked by a workman in 1848 when driving a pin, requiring yet another replacement. It must have destroyed whatever confidence remained in cast-iron girder bridges, and confirmed the worst conclusions made by the jury and the Railway Inspectorate. Why they were still attempting to replace the castings with others of the same design remains a mystery, although Stephenson continued to defend the integrity of the design, suggesting that he had been a prime mover in their design and application in many other railway lines. And it would suggest that his defence at the inquest was not a 'put-up' job by his solicitor (as some have suggested), but rather a genuinely held belief. The Dee bridge was rebuilt yet again in 1870–71 using wrought iron, according to John Rapley, over twenty years since William Fairbairn had first suggested it personally to Robert Stephenson.

There were some personal repercussions too. General Pasley left his job as Inspector General, whether he jumped or was pushed out by the government is unclear. One newspaper report said quite clearly that he had been sacked, but, whatever the truth of the matter, it did not prevent him being honoured by the state in other ways. He was knighted after leaving the railways, and was promoted to lieutenant-general in 1851. He became a colonel commandant of the Royal Engineers in 1853, and was appointed full general in 1860. He died in London in April 1861, after a long and very distinguished career. Captain Simmons continued his work with the Inspectorate for several years, before returning to the Army and fighting with distinction in the Crimea, ultimately being promoted to general.

Other Trussed Bridges

All of the other bridges built to the same design were apparently either replaced by wrought-iron designs or strengthened and reinforced like the Dee bridge. The props are shown on a contemporary engraving of the Stockton bridge, for example *(7.1)*, which, nearly as long as the Dee bridge, would have been most at risk of sudden failure. As at the Dee, there would have been immediate action to stop traffic entirely, or use only the most lightly loaded goods trains. As the results of the Dee inquest were broadcast very widely, passengers would simply have refused to cross any truss bridges whatsoever for

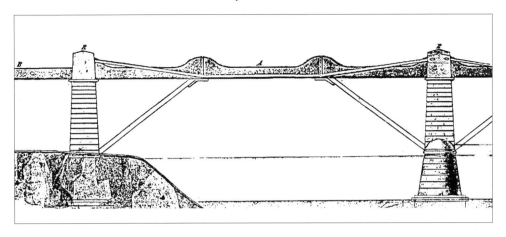

(7.1) Stockton trussed girder bridge propped to prevent premature fracture.

fear of their lives. The railway companies would have had to act very quickly to reassure the travelling public.

The Board of Trade circulated all the railway companies to elicit information on the use of trussed bridges, and the current state of those structures. A large number were discovered in use in addition to those mentioned at the Dee inquest. A survey by Paul Sibley in 1976 summarised the extent of the problem, with nearly sixty trussed bridges mentioned by the Board of Trade survey. The earliest examples shown at the date of the start of building (so they were not complete at the dates shown) included:

Three bridges on the North Union Railway in Lancashire (Wigan)	1831
One bridge at Lutterworth on the L&BR	1836
Three bridges on the Eastern Counties Railway	1836
Minories bridge on the Blackwall Railway	1837

The first set were built by Vignoles, the remainder by Robert Stephenson and were all early examples of the concept. Most of the trussed bridges were of more recent origin, however. They included:

Four bridges on the York & Newcastle Railway	1841
Two bridges on the Dublin & Drogheda Railway	1841
One bridge on the Macclesfield branch of the L&BR	1843
Two bridges on the East Lancashire Railway	1844
Two bridges on the York & North Midland Railway	1844
Two bridges on the Stockton & Darlington Railway	1844

Apart from anything else, the list shows the growth in railway building; a veritable explosion of construction following the first successes, and the positive public reception and growth in profits. But even these years were eclipsed by the numbers of trussed bridges in 1845:

One bridge on the Bury St Edmunds Railway
One bridge on the Huddersfield Railway (Ramsbottom Street)
Seven bridges on the Lancashire & Yorkshire Railway (Wakefield, Pontefract & Goole Division)
Twelve bridges on the Manchester South Junction & Altrincham Railway
Six bridges on the Trent Valley Railway
Three bridges on the York & North Midlands Railway

The bridges on the Trent had been engineered by Thomas Gooch, and none were used since the railway had not been opened to the public; they were investigated after the Dee inquest. John Hawkshaw was the engineer of the Lancashire & Yorkshire Railway, and later collaborated with James Brunlees in the first attempt to design a tunnel under the channel to France. While that project failed, he did succeed in building a long tunnel under the river Severn, although with great difficulty. Robert Stephenson was in charge of the York & North Midland line.

The year before the Dee accident, in 1846, only three trussed bridges had been built, and included a bridge on the Shrewsbury & Birmingham Railway (at Hadley Road) and the Dee bridge itself. Such was the level of confidence in the design, however, that no less than six bridges were being built in 1847, three by a young engineer (W.H. Barlow) on the Midland Railway. Robert Stephenson himself was building two very long trussed bridges on the Leopold Railway in Italy, and another trussed structure was being designed by John Fowler. Both Barlow and Fowler were a new generation of railway engineers, both of whom were destined for fame in the future, Barlow for his magnificent railway shed at St Pancras, and Fowler for the iconic Forth Railway Bridge (with Benjamin Baker). But at this stage in their careers, they were both unwisely imitating Stephenson.

The designs were very variable, with spans much lower than that at the Dee, with the exception of the two long bridges for the Leopold Railway in Italy (just 2ft shorter than the Dee at 96ft unsupported). Stephenson changed their design after the inquest verdict. The bridge over a canal at Knottingley and Goole came next at 89ft, followed by the Stockton bridge at 84ft, both being propped while more fundamental changes were made (they were eventually demolished). The bulk of the rest had spans of 50 to 70ft, such as the lightly loaded Minories bridge at 65ft, although there were much smaller examples at 26 and 32ft, such as the three bridges on the North Union Railway in Wigan.

The bridges generally shared the concept of heavily reinforced joints, thought to be the weakest parts, often by incorporating the characteristic bulb into the girder itself rather than a separate casting (as at the Dee). The number of wrought-iron trusses varied accordingly, as did casting dimensions, especially of the web and flanges, a not unsurprising feature given the uncertainties of estimating the strength of the girders. Testing the strength of the girders, whether by calculation using misleading formulae (Hodgkinson), or by even more misleading tests performed by suspending weights from the top of the centre of the castings, was an inexact science. A greater degree of accuracy could have been ensured by running the tests from the lower flanges, where all the weight of the platform and trains would be borne. The tests of the time may have been a very crude way of finding internally flawed castings, but they were in no way an accurate test of strength of the final assembled girder. Trusses also varied in both size and number, tending to be smaller or fewer the shorter the span. But all appeared to have the tension bars or rods attached to the ends of the castings, so did not reinforce the beam when a train passed over. The ends deformed inwards under load, so they added little to the intrinsic stiffness of the structure. There are no records of any trussed structures being tested systematically, either on models or full size structures to see how they responded to heavy and fast moving loads.

In addition to the compound or trussed girders, there were a larger number of simple cast-iron bridges, amounting to about 1,400 from those companies who replied to the circular. There was a great variety of form or section, without any apparent rationale, according to Sibley. Some were, however, arched constructions, and a few bowstring, where the arch was built over the railway rather than under the track. Another small set were wrought-iron girder bridges, a design developed by William Fairbairn from his experience with riveted wrought-iron sheets in ship hulls. The straight girder cast-iron under-bridges were to cause accidents themselves from sudden failure in the future, because they were largely kept in place, while the trussed compound bridges were gradually replaced completely.

As the Royal Commission proceedings showed later, the engineers were in a very confused state, as reflected by their testimony at the inquest. The examples Stephenson had quoted to demonstrate the principle were either small, carried light loads or had not been used intensively during their short lives, so were actually poor examples to bring as proof of the principle.

Robert Stephenson and William Fairbairn

Prior to the Dee accident, Stephenson was trying to conceive ways of crossing the Conwy estuary and Menai Straits, with much longer single-span structures. According to Fairbairn, they first met and discussed the problem as early as April 1845, when Stephenson recommended some form of circular or egg-shaped tube as a way of resisting the huge stresses which would occur on a long span bridge of 450ft. Fairbairn was at that time pre-eminent in his work on wrought-iron structures, which, being made entirely of tough wrought iron, were very much stronger than any cast-iron designs. Later he recommended a wrought-iron girder bridge at the Dee, but would be ignored by Stephenson. The great stiffness of a tube would appeal to the pair of engineers, but it was Fairbairn who brought the concept to fruition. He was given an entirely free hand to develop the concept to completion. He did start his research using circular tubes, but they proved quite insufficient for the task, distorting and buckling when stressed by high loads. But why not a rectangular section of large enough size to allow trains to run within it? Fairbairn proceeded to build and then test small models using riveted wrought-iron sheets at his shipbuilding yard at Millwall in London. As was his practice, he performed his tests systematically, and to destruction, so he was able to isolate their weaknesses, and so correct the design before going on to build the real structures.

For example, the first prototypes buckled at high load not at the base of the structure, but under compression at the top. Fairbairn therefore reinforced the top first with a corrugated sheet, and then with an extra layer of material in the form of rectangular cells. They resisted the compression loads very efficiently, and a similar layer was also added to the base to resist the tension developed by the load of passing trains. In effect, he invented the box girder principle, a principle which is used very widely, not just in bridges, but also in many other engineering applications. In fact, use is so widespread as to be commonplace, the concept being used in all transport vehicles, such as cars, ships and aircraft. All such structures have thin shells of metal (or composite plastics) which bear the loads imposed by external influences, as well as carrying the internal load. Such structures are known as *monocoques*, by contrast with space frames, where the loads are carried by slender isolated members built into a three dimensional framework. Fairbairn also developed smaller wrought-iron girder bridges, and patented the concept in 1846. His work was the first substantial approach to the problem of spanning great distances, an approach repeated many times since then.

Stephenson made a report to the directors of the C&HR in February 1846, on the progress in developing new designs for the Menai and Conwy crossings. It included separate reports from Fairbairn and also Hodgkinson, who by now had joined Fairbairn in his research. An interesting point emerged in those reports; Fairbairn believed that rectangular tubes could be self-supporting, and so would need no extra means of suspension. He was opposed by both Hodgkinson and Stephenson, who thought that the tubes would need support from chains carried by the two main masonry towers which would carry the tube across the straits. This is why the bridge, when finished, still shows the tall towers with holes originally destined to carry the chains. Fairbairn was right: it was in fact far stronger than proved necessary, as other engineers, especially in the USA, were to demonstrate shortly when they pioneered lattice girder bridges. Hodgkinson subsequently stopped collaborating with Fairbairn.

However, Fairbairn was asked by the company to proceed to scaling-up his rather small initial models, and he built a 'model' some 75ft long, 4.5in high and 2ft 8in wide. It was ready for trial experiments by June 1846. He tested it destructively, and reused it several times by simply mending the damaged parts, further modifying the design entirely by experiment. By March 1847, he was ready with drawings of the final tubes ready to be made, and proceeded to arrange for the sites at Conwy and Menai to be made ready for the tubes *(7.2)*.

Conwy Bridge

The first major obstacle was the crossing of the Conwy estuary. Tidal scour would make piers in the river bed a particular problem, so the tube concept was first developed here since the required span was smaller (400ft) than at the Menai Straits (460ft). The height of the bridge above the waters was also much smaller, so it was inevitable that this tube bridge would be built first, and indeed would act as a rehearsal for the more formidable task further up the coast to the west. The structure was erected immediately next to Telford's suspension bridge carrying the road across the river, one

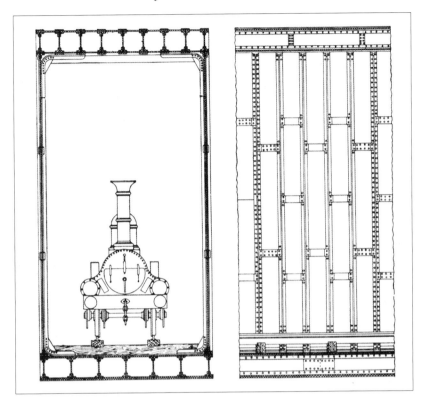

(7.2)
Sections
across the
Britannia
bridge tube.

line of communication followed earlier attempts, as was so common in this and later periods. The first tube was made very laboriously by hand, even to the beating of sheet wrought iron down to the specification thickness by sledgehammers, followed by hand riveting the sheets together during late 1847 and early 1848, well after the Dee accident.

The next step was to test the full size tube in just the same way as before, except this time non-destructively. The experiments proved that the tube passed the test loadings with flying colours, and it was now ready to jack into position from pontoons in the river. The event was not without incident, however, when a cast-iron cross head to which the lifting chains were attached suddenly cracked. The lift was achieved on cue, but the cross heads were replaced by wrought iron for the Britannia lift.

The first trains passed through the completed bridge in April 1848, justifying Fairbairn's systematic approach to the problem. However, relations between the two heroes of the hour were souring, and Fairbairn resigned in May 1848, and wrote a detailed book about his work. There had arisen a dispute between Fairbairn, Stephenson and Hodgkinson about who really invented the idea of cellular layers at top and bottom of the tube, each making a claim, although the patent of 1846 clearly establishes Fairbairn as the originator. As a legal document, it establishes his priority, and indeed, Fairbairn went on to build several smaller bridges based on the concept.

Britannia Bridge

But the major problem faced by the company was the Menai Straits, where the span needed was greater at nearly 600ft. The required length of the several tubes was reduced to 460ft by building a high pier in the channel, and the lift was very much higher. Many of the problems had already been solved by the Conwy project, but there were still issues of major concern. Since the total length of the tubes was much greater, some way of attaching the free tubes would need developing when they had been lifted to the great height needed, without excessive distortion of the tubes themselves. The first tube was completed, albeit with several problems during the lift, and opened on 5 March 1850. Robert Stephenson, ever the enthusiastic showman, drove the first train (carrying coal) through the tubes, amid much celebration. The bridge was inspected by Captain Simmons on 15 March, and approved for public use. Concern about the effect of wind on the tubes showed that its natural frequency was sixty-seven cycles per minute, or 1.117 Hertz.

Completion of the project came rather too late to help the Irish people, who in the intervening years had suffered great loss of life from the potato blight, as well as loss of population due to mass emigration. The tube bridge was extremely expensive owing to the large amounts of wrought iron needed, but was applied in Canada to the Victoria bridge crossing the St Lawrence seaway. In the interim, designers had realised that a tube was inefficient in supporting loads, and much less material was needed in lattice girder bridges, which henceforth became the norm.

Although Stephenson received most of the credit for the two bridges, it was Fairbairn who established the principle by practical experiment, a fact ignored in most biographies of Stephenson. Many biographers, such as Samuel Smiles, also either ignore the Dee disaster, or downplay the event. In fact, it was a national scandal at the time, and showed Stephenson to be most resistant to progressive engineering practice.

Royal Commission

It was well known at the time that cast iron was a very brittle material. Indeed, the world-famous bridge at Coalbrookdale built in 1789 was so designed that all structural members were in compression. The numerous road bridges built later to the same design with cast-iron arches were testimony to their integrity. Failures had been caused not so much by brittle fracture of the arches as movement of the abutments which took the lateral pressure.

However, they were unsuitable for providing the flat track needed for railways, which is why engineers attempted to use straight girders. The jury's decision was acted upon rapidly by the government. They set up a Royal Commission in August 1847, chaired by Lord Wrottesley with many distinguished commissioners. It was called to investigate 'The Application of Iron in Railway Structures' and its membership included Cubitt, Hodgkinson and George Rennie, with Douglas Galton as secretary.

It reported in July 1849 and included the results of numerous and very detailed experiments with cast and wrought iron. Full-scale tests confirmed the low strength of cast-iron girders and their decrease in strength with repeated flexing:

The results of these experiments were, that when the depression was equal to one third of the ultimate deflection, the bars were not weakened. This was ascertained by breaking them ... with stationary loads in the centre. When, however, the depressions produced by the machine were made equal to one-half of the ultimate deflection, the bars were actually broken by less than nine hundred depressions.

Although not then called 'fatigue', the experiments demonstrated the problem of low cycle fatigue as well as the idea of a fatigue limit. However, they also introduced the erroneous idea that the structure of the metal changed fundamentally, repeated flexure was held to produce:

... a peculiar crystalline fracture and loss of tenacity.

The comment was to bedevil future studies of the problem, because investigators looked for the 'peculiar crystalline texture' as a characteristic symptom of the problem. Later studies showed that fatigue produced no such changes in metal micro-structure, and the alleged effect was quite spurious. By performing experiments on two actual bridges, they confirmed that the downward deflection at the centre of the supporting beam did indeed increase with the speed of a train passing over.

Stephenson was interrogated in detail about the Dee bridge, and it emerged that he and several other distinguished engineers had used, or were planning to use, the design in many other bridges. Stephenson insisted that the design was not defective, strangely, given the accident on the Dee and problems with the castings failing suddenly. Brunel, however, refused to use cast iron at all for structural application on bridges. Still, the discovery of an original cast-iron bridge in 2004 designed by Brunel near Paddington station in 1838 clearly shows that he did use cast iron for some of his first bridges. The design of the bridge uses arches of ironwork and makes little use of bolts, the castings fit together like the famous structure at Coalbrookdale.

Fairbairn favoured his own solution of wrought-iron plates riveted together to give large bridge sections, an entirely successful solution because he and Stephenson used it in the Britannia and Conway bridges built for the same railway at roughly the same time. The toughness of this material provided a substantial degree of safety to the travelling public. Despite this wise decision, Stephenson still maintained that cast-iron girders could be used safely, and he reinforced his existing bridges by stacking yet more girders on top of existing ones (as in the bridges at Florence). He also made the strange suggestion that flexibility in the girders provided a degree of protection against impact or sudden loads from passing trains.

Stephenson's Interrogation

Stephenson had by this time been elected MP for Whitby, largely with the support of George Hudson, the Railway King and MP for York, a powerful magnate who had control of a large number of new lines in the Midlands and North. He had employed

Stephenson as engineer on many of those new lines. Shortly after, he was exposed as a fraudster who had manipulated the finances of many railway companies by illegal practices. They included paying dividends from capital, and it was clear that Hudson had deliberately bamboozled many small investors during the period of 'Railway Mania'. Despite the Reform Act of 1832, seats in Parliament could still be bought by hard cash and political corruption.

At the start of his questioning by the Commissioners on 16 March 1848, he was asked about the variable quality of iron produced, for example, from different iron ores, a topic frequently raised by this and previous investigations. It was another variable in the discussion over the properties of iron, and was not solved until much later when better methods of analysis were developed. He was then asked about wrought and cast iron, simply because the former was so much tougher than the latter, and his own attempts in using trussed bridges had failed at the Dee bridge. His was not the only attempt, however, and there were many examples of different combinations of the two materials attempting to transfer that toughness into, for example, brittle cast-iron girders. Wrought iron produced by labour-intensive 'puddling' was much more expensive than cast iron, which was simply run direct from the blast furnace into the sand moulds. One improvement in the design of the blast furnace involved pre-heating the blast of air need to reduce the ore to metal, but Stephenson thought (erroneously, as it turned out) that hot blast cast iron was actually weaker than the traditional cold blast iron.

The Commissioners asked him about the safety factor used in his bridges, a leading question if ever there was one:

831. What multiple of the greatest load do you consider the breaking weight ought to be? – A: I have generally employed about six times the working load to be the calculated strength. Will quote a case; I generally test girders with a weight equal to two trains of locomotives, one upon the other, and a train of locomotives is about one ton per foot length, and test them to 2 tons per foot length.

832. Whatever the length may be? – No. I quote the case of a number of bridges that I built on the plan of the Dee girder-bridge; the truss-girder it is called. I have added three corresponding parts on the top [to the girder], so as to correct that which I admit to have been a certain degree of oversight …

833. Are we to understand that this is an old bridge [pointing to the drawing of the Dee bridge], and these are additional pieces attached to it? – Precisely so; in order to save the metal of the girder there were ramps put up, and these joggles [describing on the drawing] were to keep the ramps in their place; this girder, which is 96 feet span, has been proved, with 56 tons in the middle, which is equal to two trains of locomotives plus the dead weight of the girder and the platform, and the deflection was an inch and three-eighths … that is the stiffest girder I have ever made use of; it is rather stiffer than I like. I always held the opinion rather strongly, that a certain amount of flexibility in a cast-iron girder is essential for resisting the suddenness of the passing-weight; and that it should be able to yield so as not to convert pressure into concussion.

So Stephenson would not concede that the principle of the truss girder was at fault, and all that was needed were extra cast-iron pieces added to the top. His was a grand example of a stubborn mindset refusing to shift in the face of the powerful views (expressed at the Dee inquest) of his engineer colleagues, who had either refused to use the trussed bridges at all or now had second thoughts about their integrity.

The questioning then looked at how he tested his castings and girders, especially after the Dee inquest had revealed so little about this crucial issue:

> 835. *What processes do you employ for proving and examining cast-iron girders? – Sometimes I employ the hydraulic press between the two girders, and sometimes dead weight, for instance, in very large girders lying on their side it will be objectionable, and you could not get anything like an average result, but with small girders the friction by lying on their sides forms so small a proportion of the gross weight that you put upon them, that it is immaterial; but in these girders when they amount to 60 or 100 feet in span; I weighted them actually with pig-iron.*

This is a confused answer to a very simple question, revealing the pressure on Stephenson to come clean about his test methods. And the Commissioners could not resist the urge to cross-examine him further:

> 836. *How do you apply the load then; at the top? – No; there are clamps of iron that lay hold of the bottom flange, and hang down and support the platform.*

> 837. *Then you have two platforms? – No, only one.*

> 838. *The weight, however, is in the centre of the girder? – Yes; it would not keep upright if it were not so.*

> 839. *When a girder is so employed in a bridge, the pressure is always on one side, and tends to produce a torsion? – A slight torsion, but very inconsiderable.*

> 840. *Do you consider that that torsion can be neglected in those large girders? – I think so.*

In this passage Stephenson has admitted that he didn't then, or now, test the cast-iron girders in such a way as to mimic the real way they were loaded in the bridge. The bottom flange was loaded asymmetrically, with all of the weight of the platform on just one wing of the flange, so tending to twist the web out of alignment. The questioner persisted, because the issue lay at the heart of the Dee failure:

> 841. *The object of my question is this, as torsion is produced when a girder is applied to railway works, should you not test it in a way to produce that torsion? – I think not, because the beams that form the platform really are made to rest upon the shoulder of the end rail over the flanges.*

> 842. *They take their bearings at the corners too? – Not if they are properly and sufficiently made; I have had many that rest principally upon the shoulder; sometimes a cast-iron shoe is put on a wooden beam*

with half an inch of projection which is put upon it to secure the bearing. I do not do that invariably, because I do not think it of much consequence.

843. The torsion is observable during the passage of a train to the amount of half an inch or three-quarters; but you consider that that is not likely to have a destructive effect upon the bridge? – No; I have often tested girders accidentally so placed, and I have never found that there was any difference. You cannot always get them vertical; when you screw two girders together to try them with the hydraulic press they are never within an inch. They may by accident be accurate; but I have observed them several times fully an inch out of the corresponding plane.

Stephenson appears to be saying that he has tried to test pairs of girders in a way simulating their final position on a bridge, but it is quite unclear whether or not he was successful, or whether the inner flanges were loaded alone, or (most crucially) whether or not he tested the girders in this way before the Dee disaster. It looked like retrospective analysis to cover up earlier omissions.

He was also asked about any permanent changes in cast iron when loaded heavily, and he gave the example of Cornish beam engines where, despite regular and repeated impacts, for many years no changes occurred. He then referred to his experiences with the Blackwall Railway, where some of the first trussed bridges had been introduced:

848. Probably a very small change might take place? – I do not venture to give any theoretical view now. A change may possibly be taking place, but so small that I only want to convey practically that it is purely visionary. Take again the Blackwall girders; there is a railway there where we have girders that are by no means strong, and something like 48 trains a day passing in opposite directions. Since the opening of the line, 120,000 trains have passed over them, with all the jar to which railway trains are subject, those trains being composed of 12 heavy carriages, and of course, as each train passes over the girder and along it, it changes the extension and compression of the different parts of the girder, and, therefore, 120,000 trains might be multiplied by 12 actually; but taking it at 120,000, there, I think it is a very good experiment ... There are some girders leading to the West India Docks, over which those trains have passed, and I think that they are either 48 or 50 feet. I examined them four or five months ago, and do not believe that any sensible change has taken place.

849. There is no locomotive of 30 tons which passes over those girders? – No; but they are made proportionately weaker. I did not make them to carry locomotive engines; but they are doing as near their ultimate duty as the locomotive girders are doing. I may say that we are experimenting every day to such an extent that, if we only cast our eyes about us, we might obtain such practical facts as to make the question unnecessary. I think the connecting rod of a locomotive is an instance, and this is more particularly as regards wrought iron; ...one I know has just come into the shop from the Norfolk line, which has run 50,000 miles, and it is an exceedingly violent jar eight times in a second ... it shows that the rod has vibrated 25,000,000 of times, and yet to all appearance no change has taken place which can be detected.

851. The same remark does not apply with respect of railway axles; they frequently break, and indicate considerable crystals, do they not? – Yes. I take of course cases which have come within my own experience, and I have never been able to come to a just conclusion as to whether the axle was fibrous to begin with after fracture had taken place, and there is always some link of that kind wanting.

Here there is a reference to the opinion about crystalline textures developing in fatigued iron, an entirely spurious idea, which was widespread at the time (but was questioned by Stephenson). It is interesting that he brings wrought-iron products into the argument, which is really about cast and not wrought iron.

But it seems clear from further testimony that he prefers wrought iron for long girders, so Fairbairn's ideas have had some influence on his thinking:

867. What is the greatest length between the supports to which you would limit the use of simple cast iron girders? - I have increased them up to 50 feet, but have recently, since the introduction of wrought-iron girders, made it a rule not to go beyond 40 feet, and at 40 feet to begin with wrought iron…

But he persisted in defending the concept of the trussed bridge, as the following answer shows:

880. In bridges then of more than a certain span where simple cast iron girders are not applicable, what mode of construction do you prefer? – I should adopt the modification which I have made in the Dee bridge, and I do not think that the material can be brought into a better shape.

The contradiction between the two answers is stark. Either he prefers wrought-iron box girders of the kind developed and used by Fairbairn, or he does not. There then followed yet more questioning on why the trussed cast-iron girder was preferable, without a reasonably logical reply. Did Stephenson have a contract with a supplier of cast iron, or had his arguments with Fairbairn clouded his judgment? Stephenson had not yet put the first Conwy tube in position, and, by all accounts, was nervous about the final lift into place. It was duly completed on 16 April, exactly a month later, and the first train was driven through by Stephenson himself on 18 April 1848, so he may have changed his opinion by then. In fact, he did refer to the tube bridges later in the questioning:

920. What is your opinion of the box-girders? – I think highly of them; I mean to apply them in all cases where I have to apply girders and where the span exceeds 40 feet.

921. What advantages do you think these box-girders have over cast-iron girders? – They are a little cheaper, and I consider them more elastic. When wrought iron can be employed at the same price as cast iron, then I prefer wrought iron.

923. The girders on the Britannia and Conway bridges are only of wrought iron; but in many cases you would use cast iron in conjunction with wrought iron to assist compression? – Yes; and I am doing that in the Newcastle bridge, and in the Chalk Farm bridge it was so used; there was a cast iron girder put in as a top piece. The effect was very marked indeed.

But, like all engineers then, he would not like to be hindered by government regulation, and tied down by preconceived rules.

Joseph Locke

The questioning of other eminent engineers continued. Joseph Locke was also an MP by now, and had built many new lines. He was asked about testing girders, and thought that tests were done on the inner flanges where the platform rested, but gave no further details. As he had said at the Dee inquest, he did not like trussed bridges, and had not used any on his lines. The outcome of the inquest did worry him considerably, however, and he had been testing his bridges by running heavy locomotives over them at high speeds. No doubt many other engineers were doing the same. Asked about apparent changes in crystal structure, he demurred, saying that all his broken axles and other parts looked similar, and did not show any obvious change in structure. He approved of wrought-iron box girders, and planned to use some himself on new lines. He thought that cast iron should only be used in arch bridges, never as flat girders.

Brunel's Testimony

Isambard Kingdom Brunel had not appeared at the Dee inquest, but was questioned extensively by the Commissioners. He had made little use of cast iron at all in bridges, preferring wood and wrought iron for long spans, and occasionally cast-iron girders for very short spans:

1189. Supposing you have got to deal with a case where you cannot employ these simple girders, what mode of construction would you prefer for the girder? – I should prefer not using cast iron at all.

1190. By which you mean to condemn the whole race of compound girders? – By no means. But I should observe generally … that I avoid the use of cast iron whenever I can, and that in my experience, therefore, is more limited than that of any other engineer probably. In all cases, where it is beyond a certain span of from about 35 to 40 feet, I should prefer using timber or wrought iron, or the two combined.

He thought very highly of box girder construction, especially with his own experiences of shipbuilding. He paid especial attention to the quality of the riveting, which could produce a joint as strong as the material itself. On alleged changes in the metal itself from repeated blows, he was sceptical of any changes apparently produced. Indeed, he had brought various samples of broken iron products which exhibited both crystalline and fibrous structure, but the texture seen depended on the type of stress applied to the samples. He then produced an iron bar which showed different types of fracture surface, depending on how it had broken. The bar had been notched and then broken by a fast blow, the other by slow pressure, one showing a crystalline texture, the other a fibrous texture. Since the material of the bar was the same, it was thus easy to show that the fracture surface depended on the way it had broken rather than by any changes in the material itself.

Brunel also brought a rather more urgent matter to the attention of the Commissioners: the increasing weight of locomotives. This had to be worrying, because if there were basic design flaws in some bridges, then increasing the moving load could only enhance the likelihood of yet more serious accidents in the future:

> *1215. What do you consider to be the amount of the greatest weights which now pass over railways, and what are the limits of such weights? – The greatest weights which now pass over the railways are the locomotive engines.. and those will shortly weigh … 35 tons … I don't think we have anything which limits us.*

Although the weight of locomotives on the GWR would always be higher than the standard gauge, the trend would increase wear and tear of rails and many other track structures. Understanding the mechanism of failure would be vital in controlling, if not reducing, the risk of serious accidents.

W.H. Barlow

The young engineer, who had built or was in the process of building three trussed bridges, was also questioned about his attitudes to the various issues raised with his older colleagues. Unlike many of them, he averred that he left choice of the iron to the founder, and relied on girder dimensions and testing alone to judge quality. He could not distinguish between hot and cold blast iron. He used hydraulic pressure to test to half the strength of a girder, and used a safety factor of four, just like others. Although he did not think that impact or vibration affected girders, he thought that increasing the safety factor to five would be appropriate. He did not test the inner lower flange, and had not noticed any twisting in his girders, although they were shorter than the larger ones at the Dee. He was concerned (unlike Stephenson) about deflection of girders under fast trains, and removed any girders from bridges where excessive movement was found. He went on to relate a problem he had encountered personally:

> *737. But may not the rapid way in which the load is brought upon the bridge introduce a new species of failure? – Yes. I noticed one case not in an iron bridge but a timber bridge. I was sent for in consequence of weakness in the bridge; it was a viaduct, and I stood under the viaduct while a*

heavy goods train passed over it; it produced a certain amount of deflection; but it was so little, that we were leaving the bridge under the impression that it was sound; but just before that, we heard an express train coming, and we waited, and when it came, it produced quite a different effect, though a much lighter engine; it seemed to produce a wave through the bridge, and it became evident that the express train produced a much worse effect than the heavy goods train, and we strengthened the bridge accordingly.

738. In truth, it ought to be so from the ordinary principles of dynamics. This load was passing over the bridge in a very few seconds, and therefore the total deflection is performed by the weight in a few seconds, and it therefore becomes a kind of blow; the descent of a heavy weight; and the bridge has not time to accommodate itself to the deflection required of it. Perhaps, as you justly observe, they are originated and propagated throughout the structure, and may prove exceedingly dangerous and disagreeable? – The point of maximum effect would not be when the load was in the centre of the bridge.

The admission of dynamic effects being of some importance was to prove critical many years later in the Tay bridge disaster, especially for Barlow, who sat in judgment at the inquiry of 1880. His answer also showed that timber bridges were widespread on the new railways.

William Fairbairn

The experimental engineer was actually questioned very early in the proceedings by the Commissioners, and he gave comprehensive and extensive evidence of the problem of the structural integrity of bridges, thus setting the tone for the rest of the questioning. His testimony was liberally illustrated by tables of data and numerous explanatory diagrams. Unlike many others questioned, he presented tables of iron composition, showing the improvement in strength caused by adding wrought to cast iron. He also produced tables to demonstrate that hot and cold blast iron were equivalent in terms of their properties. The critical variables he pointed to included the carbon and sulphur contents, perfectly correct by modern standards. He preferred a safety factor of four with girders, and never exceeded a half of the breaking strength when proofing them, but preferred one third for fear of damaging the structure. He tested girders with suspended weights *(7.3)* and went on:

545. A girder is often intended to sustain the load on one of its bottom flanges, and out of its central vertical plane, do you consider that the same amount of pressure can be borne that way as if applied at the top? – Supporting the load on one side of the flange is wrong in principle, and to a certain extent, injurious in practice: but that method has many conveniences, and in practice we are frequently called upon to abandon self-evident principles, in order to meet the requirements of different structures. Under such circumstances … the flange should be carefully constructed in order to bring the cross-beam as much as possible into the centre or vertical plane of the girder.

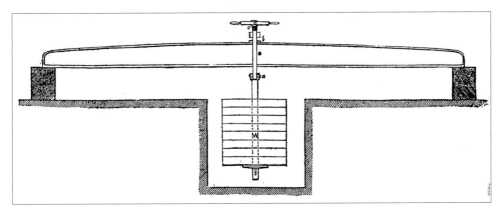

(7.3) Fairbairn's rig for testing girders.

He showed two ways in which this could be done, exhibiting small diagrams of his proposals *(7.4)*. The first suggestion involved cutting a hole in the web of the girder, to which the cross-beam could be attached, and so prevent twisting of the girder. He went on to elaborate on some of the new problems his proposals might introduce:

> *546. …do you think the remedy, by perforating the middle portion of the beam, and strengthening around the hole … effectual? – I am of the opinion that in cast iron girders such a process, if not fatal, would be … exceedingly injurious. I have decided objections to anything like perforations in cast-iron girders, and it is even with some reluctance I would have a bolt-hole through the neutral axis unless thickened so as to compensate for the part taken out; besides, it is exceedingly objectionable to cut off the connection between the two resisting flanges of a girder, or to damage in any other way a casting of this description …*

> *547. Is it from fear of causing a bad casting? – Certainly not, but from considerations of more importance, namely, the complexity of such a girder, and the additional material you would require to give it the same security as regards strength. Again, I am a strong advocate for <u>simplicity of construction in everything</u>, and would on no account allow a distortion of form unless other circumstances which were inevitable.*

> *548. How would you propose to remedy this? – Either by placing the cross-beams entirely on the top, or suspending them from the bottom flange … In suspending the cross-beams from the bottom flange, the greatest care must be observed not to perforate the bottom flange, but to suspend the cross-beam by hook-bolts as per sketch. I have adopted this plan for many years with great success, and have never found it fail.*

His sketch is shown in *(7.5)*. Fairbairn is describing the problem of stress concentration at the edge of a hole, now known to raise the stress by no less than a factor of three. He would not have approved of the dovetail holes cast by Stephenson in the lower inner flange, nor the sharp corners left by the cavetto moulding. He preferred loading the top of the beam, just as Stephenson had done many times, but only in the shorter spans, such

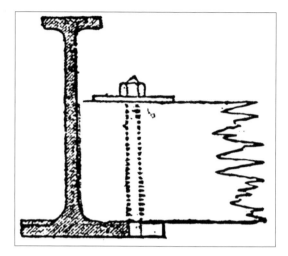 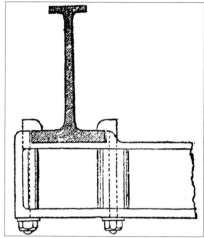

Above left: *(7.4)* One of Fairbairn's proposals to improve girder flanges.

Above right: *(7.5)* Fairbairn's preferred design for the lower flange.

as at Wolverton station, and he and George Stephenson had done at Water Street station on the L&MR.

He also gave full details of experiments on the effect of temperature on the strength of cast iron, showing that the strength of the material fell when its temperature rose above about 220 degrees Fahrenheit (104 degrees Celsius), and strength was also lost when the cast iron was exposed to temperatures of 32 degrees Fahrenheit (0 degrees Celsius) or below. He would never use a girder above a span of 40ft and simply refused to use a compound trussed girder at all. He advocated the wrought-iron box girder, and the very first had been erected on the Blackburn & Bolton Railway, at Blackburn in Lancashire, by Vignoles. He was quite adamant about the trussed compound girder:

> *577. What objections do you have about their use? – In trussing a cast iron girder, I would much rather give the strength to the girder itself, than depend on a malleable iron truss. The two materials are widely different in character, the one being ductile and subject to elongation under a severe tensile strain, and the other rigid and firm under compression; they seldom if ever agree well together, and during the whole of my experience I have found it safer to keep them separate.*

Asked about the supposed change in texture brought about by repeated flexing, he demurred:

> *581. Have you had any opportunity of observing whether the internal structure of an iron beam becomes altered by being subjected to a succession of slight blows at a low temperature, as in rails long used, railway axles or springs of carriages; and if so, to what cause do you attribute this change? – ... instead of supposing any material change in the internal structure ... I conceive the change to arise from the weight of the blow and not from the vibrations. A very small inequality of the road will cause*

a severe shock; and assuming that each percussion has a tendency to bend one or more of the axles, it then appears obvious from this bending, if continued for many thousands [of] similar bendings, that time alone determines when fracture takes place.

Fairbairn thus dismissed the idea that iron could change its structure by cyclical loading at all, a common sense approach to the problem of fatigue. His philosophy did much to clarify the situation, and thus open the way to detailed experimental investigation of the problem (much of which he did himself).

Testing Programme

The many appendices to the report include much detail about the equipment used to test for dynamic loads on materials, especially from Fairbairn, who had pioneered the subject at an experimental and practical level. He described a range of machines to examine impact loading and repeated impact, as well as other loading patterns. His work established a very firm scientific base, which developed in leaps and bounds after the Commission's final report.

There were also many full-scale tests on bridges to check the effects of vibration and impact on the integrity of the structure. G.G. Stokes of Cambridge University performed theoretical work, as well as dynamic studies on the deformation of girders under load.

Materials of Construction

All types of material were used in structures, but especially timber of various types (such as oak and pine), and the two types of iron: cast and wrought. Wood varies enormously in its structure, depending on its species, source and treatment, and much skill will have been needed to make good selection of the best timbers for structural application. The grain is important in establishing uniformity of properties, and knots (the vestiges of branches within the structure) carefully eliminated for their stress concentrating effects on the strength of the final product. In the same way, both cast and wrought iron could be provided by numerous foundries throughout the country, and there appeared to be significant differences between samples from different factories.

Indeed, a great deal of space was devoted to extensive tabulations of analytical data on the two materials, but it could not be rationalised to give any clear conclusions. Understanding of the significance of carbon, its sulphur and phosphorus content in particular, had to be related to the constituents or compounds in which they were present, a task beyond scientific capabilities at that time. We now know that carbon occurs in solution in the iron, as well as the carbide cementite (Fe_3C). The latter is hard but brittle, and in steel occurs as plates or lamellae in a composite microstructure in a softer iron matrix. Sulphides and phosphides deleteriously affect the properties of iron, as was to be discovered when Bessemer invented a way of mass manufacturing steel in the 1860s.

Later research established that grey cast iron possessed a high carbon content above about 4 per cent, while wrought iron has less than 0.4 per cent carbon. Thus, to make tough steel demands that the carbon content be lowered substantially. Up till Bessemer's invention making steel was costly and slow, and certainly not capable of supplying the large amounts needed for bridge castings, railway lines or other large products.

Humber's Bridges

The final proof of the defective state of many cast-iron girders is presented in a treatise published by William Humber just ten years after the disaster. The introduction to the book makes some pertinent comments about the use of cast-iron girders. They should always be tested before use, but never more than twice the design load. He then says that it is:

> ... desirable that a girder should always be loaded in the direction of the centre line, instead of the load being supported by the bottom flange only, especially on one side...

It is a clear reference to the Dee disaster, and the way the girder was asymmetrically loaded by Stephenson. The author goes on to talk about defects in castings, and makes very specific reference to inner corners. Indeed, his very first diagram is of the lower corners of a cast girder *(7.6)*. The figure shows the excessive shrinkage which occurs here, and the sharp corner produced:

> Not only is the beam weakened by this, but the grain will be found to be much closer in the angles than in the other parts of the ribs, and an unequal strain in the material itself must be the consequence.

He then recommends a corner shape as shown in *(7.6)*, where the corners have been rounded to counteract the shrinkage. He says that this design modification has been proved by numerous experiments. Humber was obviously unaware that the most important effect of rounding sharp corners is to reduce the stress concentration, and so strengthen the final product.

The rest of his book is devoted to detailed descriptions of the many iron bridges then built for the rail network, including many using cast-iron girders. Some also show trusses, or other forms of cast and wrought iron supposedly working together to make a stronger structure. Most of the trussed girder under-bridges were phased out in time, although some strange survivals still exist, albeit in non-critical applications such as canal viaducts.

Recognition of Fatigue

Following Simmons and Walker's investigation, the idea that products could suffer sudden failure from repeated loading gained gradually wider acceptance, not just for

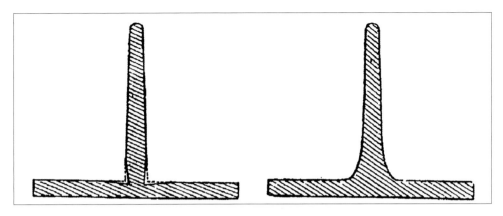

(7.6) Effect of shrinkage on girder section (left) and preferred section (right).

railway bridges but for a wide range of other products too. A pioneer in the task of studying metal fatigue was William Fairbairn, although Rankine had identified the nature of the phenomenon in railway axles as early as 1843. Fairbairn's interest lay in the integrity of the bridges he had either designed or built. Yet other engineers would recognise the problem in a wide variety of artefacts. Braithwaite, for example, read a paper at the Civil Engineers dealing with the problem, prefacing his paper with the comment:

> *There are reasons for believing, that many of the appalling, and apparently unaccountable accidents on railways and elsewhere, are to be ascribed to that progressive action which may be termed 'the fatigue of metals'. This fatigue may arise from a variety of causes, such as repeated strain, blows, concussions, jerks, torsion or tension, etc...*

He described the problem of sudden, unexpected and therefore mysterious failures of a range of products, such as brewer's vats:

> *Some years ago, at a large brewery in London, a vat was erected on cast-iron girders; they stood firmly for several years, but at length, the girders broke, when one man was killed, and another was dangerously wounded. The accident was, at the time, and is still, to the present moment, considered very mysterious. The probable solution is that the iron girders were never strong enough to withstand the fatigue caused by the intermittent loading of the vessel; it sometimes being full, sometimes partly full, and sometimes empty. When it was full, the girders were too much deflected, and when empty, or partly so, the state of rest was disturbed, by the natural attempt of the metal to regain its original position; the repeated action of deflection and of rising to its original position, imperceptibly slow, but none the less insidious, and dangerous, deteriorated the metal, and, ultimately, the girders broke.*

The failure bears comparison with the failure of the trussed girder at the mill in Manchester studied by Fairbairn in 1846, where the intermittent load was caused there by the reservoir on the roof of the building. He went on to describe failures of soldered pipe joints in another brewery, initially ascribed to corrosion by the wort in the tank.

The pipes were used for passing cooling water through the wort. The problem was in fact caused by fatigue of the joints, from the internal pressure of the cooling water together with the pressure fluctuations from the pumping system. The problems of locomotive boilers also deserved closer attention, especially when the cause of sudden explosions might not just be corrosion but also by mechanical action from repeated pressurisation, as in the problem of groove cracking. Fatigue could arise in cast-iron cranks on pumps when the pressure was increased, so putting extra loads on the cranks. And it also caused the sudden failure of crank-pins, levers, cranes, crane-chains and crane hooks. Clearly the problem was generic and caused by load repetition, sometimes when the parts were under-designed, or when the load exceeded the design loads normally expected. What he failed to mention was the point raised by Rankine in the oral discussion of the paper: that brittle cracks caused fatigue. That simple but vital message was the clue to the development of ways of detecting cracks before they grew to a critical size. However, the paper effectively raised the issue of making engineers much more aware of product failure, and encouraging them to publicise their own experiences. Then as now, there was considerable reluctance to publish case studies for fear of revealing trade secrets or breaking commercial confidentiality.

Willam Fairbairn, however, published his experimental studies in prestigious journals, as a paper from 1864 demonstrates. In that paper (Proc Roy Soc), he describes various studies of the fatigue of wrought-iron tubes, a problem raised by the increasing use of such structures to replace cast-iron railway bridges.

However, when failures result in fatalities on public facilities, such as the railways, investigations were published and widely disseminated. Recommendations by the Inspectorate were not always initiated by the many different railway companies, but pressure could be applied by others, especially the travelling public through the medium of the press, their elected representatives, or even by the shareholders in the railways. The lack of power to insist on compliance remained a sore point for many years, and is still a problem if the costs of implementation are high, such as automatic systems for stopping a train when it passes a red light.

8

Railways Supreme

After the Great Exhibition, the railways grew rapidly to cover much of the country, and indeed the work of this period remains the basis of today's national network. However, engineering structures have changed as a result of improvements in both the understanding of engineering principles and the materials available for structural application.

While many of the trussed bridges were replaced in the light of the conclusions of the Royal Commission, other cast-iron bridges remained firmly in place. Cast iron was to cause some unfortunate accidents as time passed, not just on the railways, but in buildings, where, amongst other functions, it was used widely for structural support of floors. It is on the railways where the best records survive, simply because accidents were investigated by a skilled group of inspectors. As traffic grew throughout the 1850s and '60s, accidents increased proportionally, as did the number of casualties. It is true that the majority of the accidents were collisions between trains, usually exacerbated by poor and inconsistent standards of signalling, and communication between signalmen. Just as importantly, there was a lack of control of trains, especially on heavily used tracks. Trains were controlled by the so-called 'time interval' system, where it was stipulated that trains moving on track in the same direction had to be separated by at least five minutes. Some accidents were caused when, for reasons of expediency, that time interval decreased. A train could then catch the one ahead, and if visual contact was obscured, collisions occurred, sometimes with horrific results. For this very reason tunnels were for some time a cause of major accidents.

The fragility of cast-iron girders gave rise to ongoing concern. Bridges of all kinds were to be the scenes of many spectacular accidents and disasters, from a variety of causes. And they were not the only worry. Many highly loaded parts of the engines and carriages could fail suddenly, for no apparent reason. They included wheels and tyres, axles, crankshafts, connecting rods, couplings between vehicles and a host of other components. Boilers were especially susceptible to sudden failure, usually by a devastating explosion as high pressure steam was suddenly released. They were to remain a serious problem for many years before solutions were found to the problem. And the 'permanent' way often proved less than permanent, especially if the rail was itself cracked, or out of position as a result of failure of the cast-iron blocks which held it in place.

The rather more permanent records of the Railway Inspectorate reveal a developing pattern of failure as the railway network expanded, a record unparalleled and unique in its national coverage of railway accidents. The dedicated staff of investigators provide a justly renowned source of information on the way the railways were actually worked, rather than the often idealised accounts of economic historians or railway enthusiasts.

Boiler Explosions

Ever since Richard Trevithick introduced high-pressure steam engines, there existed the possibility of catastrophic failure of the boiler in which the steam was raised. The great advantage of the new machines lay in their smaller size, reflecting the greater energy available from a smaller fixed volume of steam. It meant that they could be applied to move vehicles not just on land, but also on water. While cast iron could be used effectively in low pressure boilers, the same was not true of high pressure boilers. There were many disastrous explosions caused by the sudden explosion of such boilers, which, in one instance led to a Parliamentary Select Committee investigating the problem in 1817. It found that some boilers possessed wrought or ductile iron cylinders but were fitted with cast-iron end caps. Although cast iron might have been a useful material for low pressure boilers, it was clearly quite unsuitable for high pressure steam. The cast iron could fail suddenly from the internal pressure with devastating results. There were many accidents before engineers realised that cast-iron boilers were quite unreliable, an observation that they should have followed through with other structures.

Boiler explosions on locomotives were just as serious as those on marine or fixed engines, and the archive reports of the Railway Inspectorate include numerous examples. In the early days, when safety valves were under the control of the user, there were examples of deliberate manipulation of the valves to increase pressure, and hence engine speed. But later, when valves were removed from driver control, it could no longer be claimed that this was a problem. Yet explosions still kept occurring. The driver and fireman were most at risk of death or severe injury but anyone near the boiler was in danger. Structural damage to both the train and any buildings nearby could be extensive.

Wrought iron was much more sensitive to corrosive attack than the cast iron or copper used in boiler construction. Rusting occurs naturally with most iron products, but the rate of attack varies with the nature of the environment and the nature of the iron. More acidic water, for example, will attack iron faster than neutral water. Salt water will also act deleteriously. And there were special problems at riveted lap seams which were commonplace on early locomotives.

Longsight Explosion, 1853

Locomotives were costly items for the railway companies, and were kept working as long as possible before essential maintenance was carried out. A complete overhaul was expensive because the engine was completely out of action, and thus not earning its keep. And not all necessary inspection and repairs were finished before they resumed work. Inspecting the boiler should mean disassembly of the firebox to gain access to the innards of the boiler for detection of any corrosion. The wrought-iron boiler plates were especially susceptible to attack from hot, high pressure water and steam, especially if there were contaminants in the water. Detection of defects such as cracks or pits was essential to ensure the safety of not just the driver and fireman, but also any bystanders or staff who happened to be too close if a boiler exploded. The ageing fleet of engines was to keep the Inspectorate busy during the 1850s.

One of the worst explosions occurred at Longsight, Manchester, in the repair shop of the LNWR on 6 March 1853. It killed six people. It was commonly believed that boiler explosions were caused either by tampering with the safety valves, or by excessive build-up of pressure. The two were not mutually exclusive because, of course, deliberately holding down a safety valve would lead to an increase in steam pressure. Captain Wynne starts his report with that general assertion, and then proceeds to demolish it, step by step in direct relation to this incident.

It exploded at 8.55 a.m. after repairs on it had apparently been completed, and it was about to start a new working day. The driver was oiling the machine, and the fireman in the ashpit below. Large pieces of the shell were thrown out with great violence. One of the drive wheels was blown off, and the axle fractured, the breakage occurring from a defect in the crank. The fragments ejected were large, and did considerable damage to the shed. About a sixth of the roof was destroyed and the evidence showed that the whole roof had been lifted bodily by the blast. All of the eighteen windows were blown out. At the inquest afterwards, it emerged that the fire had been lit at 5 a.m. Just before the accident, steam was seen blowing from the fire box valve as well as the dome safety valve. One witness said that the valves had been screwed down by the driver before the accident, and indeed, the dome valve was found in this state afterwards. However, how could this happen if steam was seen blowing off the valves? If they had been screwed down, then steam would have been contained, and the pressure would have correspondingly built up (and eventually produce the explosion).

But when Wynne examined the boiler remains, he found extensive corrosion of the stays which held the boiler and firebox together. They were thickly encrusted with oxide and their sections had been eaten away. The boiler plate at their fixing points had also been eaten away, so providing weak points in the shell. He recounts the many previous boiler explosions, where there was little evidence to show that excessive pressures or tampering with the safety valves was the cause of the accidents. On the contrary, he commented:

> In most of theses cases … it will be observed that the engines were old or faulty in construction or material; and the effects … have all been produced … by steam much under 100 lbs of pressure…

William Fairbairn had opined that the boiler plate was good, and it took some courage for Wynne to oppose this eminent expert.

It was to be some time before more thorough investigation of the origins of the critical cracks in locomotive boilers was to lead to their precise explanation, and the solution to the problems of these devastating explosions. In the meantime, there were many other stressed parts on locomotives which could fail suddenly.

Tilbury Accident, 1859

There were often problems in sorting through the (usually large) piles of debris to find the critical part which failed after a serious accident. As experience developed, they were able to focus more closely on the key components under greatest stress. They were also aided by witness evidence about the sequence of events during an accident. The inspectors were careful to examine those components, especially to see if there were any hidden defects within. Some information could also be gleaned from the appearance of the fracture surface.

Just this occurred in an accident at Tilbury junction on 17 August 1859 on the London, Tilbury & Southend Railway. Tilbury is about twenty-two miles due east of London near the river Thames, and the line was worked by engines of the Eastern Railway Co. Tilbury station itself is bypassed by a loop with two junctions to give access. A passenger train was passing on the loop when it suddenly left the rails and ploughed into the earth at the side of the line. The sudden stop crushed the foremost carriage, with the second carriage severely damaged and the rest upright or on the line. Eight passengers were injured to varying degrees of seriousness, of which one died shortly after. The immediate cause was failure of the front axle of the locomotive.

After describing the extensive damage to the track and equipment, Captain Tyler focuses down onto the broken front axle of the locomotive. In his own words:

> *The broken axle showed extensive defects. Some of these which were of less importance, had occurred in the original manufacture, from imperfect welding. The more serious defects were the result of wear and tear, and were caused by the strains and concussions by which axles are severely tried in the ordinary course of railway traffic. It was evident that only one third or so of the section had been doing duty at the one end, and but little more at the other, previous to the fracture on this occasion; and the smooth appearance of the surfaces which surrounded the recently fractured portion, appeared to indicate that the mischief had been going on for some little time.*

Tyler is here describing a classic fatigue failure in wrought iron, especially by his reference to the smooth area on the fracture surface. This represents the slow growth region as the crack grew incrementally to a critical level. He then describes the previous history of this particular axle.

It had been examined only two weeks before the accident, when the engine was at the repair shop. The driver had reported that the:

> *… wheels wanted changing.*

and so they had been inspected carefully at the depot. The journal bearings had been seen by three different people and one said that he:

> *… found them quite right.*

Another said the bearings were:

> *… very bright and clear.*

and he could not find any defects in them. On the contrary, and referring to the driver, he remarked that:

> *… Jack will have a good pair of journals here.*

Captain Tyler found it difficult to reconcile his observation of the very poor state of the axle with the comments made by the fitters only two weeks before. The surface of the shaft had been worn smooth near both the fractures, damage that would take longer to have been produced than just two weeks. He comments further:

> *When once the mischief commenced, the flaws in the axle would, of course, go on getting worse and worse, in the course of traffic; and strains in torsion which it would face with in travelling around the curves between London and Southend, would, no doubt, accelerate the action thus set up, to a greater extent than if the engine had been travelling in a straight line. The axle does not appear to have been a very good one originally; but the metal of which it was composed may have become deteriorated by the blows and strains received in the course, probably of a long service. The external surface of the journals would have been the first to yield in a case of this description, and the flaw would, therefore, have been first caused at, and at once discoverable from, the exterior.*

He notes that the axle was not of a standard diameter (being ½in narrower than normal) and recommends that only standard axles should be used in future. He also thought that a register should be kept recording the history of every axle in use, and any old axles be discarded even if apparently undamaged. He bemoans the lack of records for many other safety-critical components of engines, a very general point, which in fact also covered parts like wheels and tyres, as well as that highly stressed part, the boiler.

The report does not indicate what disciplinary action was taken against the workshop fitters, who had passed the axle for service only two weeks before it failed catastrophically. Sometimes the inspectors do attribute blame to named individuals, although in this case there was no need to be specific, the implication was enough. The example is a classic fatigue failure, and of a type very common on the early railways. The first major disaster on the French railway system, at Versailles in 1842, was caused in a very similar way, by fatigue of a front axle. In that case, the brittle crack had started at a sharp corner on the shoulder of the axle, and grew slowly to a critical level in just the same way as at Tilbury.

The much larger girders fitted to bridges also gave rise to many accidents during this period, as the following examples show. The cast-iron girders had been used very widely during the hectic building phase of the 1840s, although most of the trussed girders had by now been removed. It also emerges that bridges could come in a very wide variety of different designs, using several different materials.

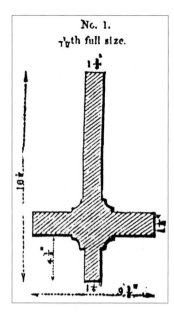

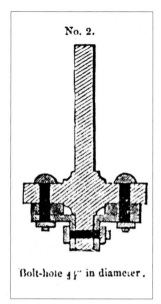

Far left: (8.1) Cast-iron girder section at Wooton bridge.

Left: (8.2) Repaired girder.

Wootton Bridge, 1860

After the Dee bridge accident, inspectors were particularly conscious of the danger of structural failure on the rail network, especially from weak bridges. Hundreds of bridges had been built on the new lines, often in wood or wood 'strengthened' by cast iron. Most of Brunel's bridges in Devon and Cornwall were built from wood alone, although all have now been replaced by more durable materials. One bridge of a composite construction was at Wootton on the London & North-Western Railway Co. line between Kenilworth and Leamington. It was a 50ft-span bridge over the junction of two roads, and consisted of two timber trusses bridging the span. They were connected together laterally by five cast-iron girders, on top of which was laid the planking which supported the track itself. A section of one of the girders is shown in *(8.1)*. The ends of the iron girders were attached by wrought-iron bolts to the timber beams. The bridge had been built in 1844, three years before the Dee bridge accident. However, the bridge was renovated in 1853 when some of the timbers were replaced and one of the cast-iron girders was reinforced. A defect had been discovered in the centre and had been patched with a 3ft-long angle iron either side of the web below the flange *(8.2)*. It was attached to the cast iron by bolts through holes drilled in the girder.

On 12 June 1860, a mineral train (with a 30-ton engine) had passed over the bridge with a full load from Kenilworth, and was returning empty later that morning. It was travelling at 7 or 8mph over the bridge, but the track suddenly gave way, and the locomotive dropped into the road below. The tender crashed into the cab, killing both the driver and fireman instantly. *(8.3)*

Captain H.W. Tyler of the Railway Inspectorate was sent to investigate the remains (preserved intact by the coroner), and determine the cause of the accident. The main timber beams had hardly been affected, but all the transverse cast-iron girders had cracked

(8.3) The broken mended girder at the top of the ladder.

near their centres, allowing the locomotive to fall through the gap. The broken ends were swinging freely on the timber beams across the span. Six of the empty wagons had fallen into the hole, forming an entangled mass of debris, but the rear wagons were still on the track, so saving the lives of the guard and a porter. Tyler then examined the fracture surfaces exposed on the broken girders. Two of the five girders showed internal defects in the form of blowholes about 1½in by ½in in size, with the mended girder showing the most serious defects of all. *(8.3)*

The girder showed serious cracks extending either side of one of the bolt holes used to attach the angle iron. The cracks could not be seen externally because they were hidden by the angle iron, although they would have been seen when a train passed over the bridge, by opening up under the load. Tyler clearly thought that this was the girder which initiated the collapse of the entire platform of the bridge. He estimated that each girder would experience at its centre a load from a 30-ton train of 11 tons, compared with a design strength of 40 tons in the centre (or 80 tons distributed). This gave a safety factor between three and four, rather than six as recommended by the Royal Commission.

Tyler went on to criticise the form of the girders, such as the position of the flange, not at the base, but rather 4.5in above. He also drew attention to the heavier locomotives in use compared with those of 1844, further criticising the railway companies for not strengthening bridges to allow for the increased weight of locomotives. In his own words:

Instead of splicing that defective girder at that time, it would have been better to have taken out all the five girders, and to have substituted in their places new transverse girders of a better description and more suitable material. That this should have been allowed to remain, and that this girder had been so patched, and retained until failure occurred, is too much in accordance with ordinary railway practice, which does not take sufficient account of the increased weight, and I may add, increasing weight, of the engines of the present day. Those engines are permitted daily to run in too many instances over bridges which were never designed to carry much more than half their weight; and sufficient attention is not as a general rule paid, upon lines which have been opened for a number of years, to the necessity of strengthening the bridges in proportion to this increased weight of the engines employed, so as to ensure the margin of strength that it is desirable to interpose between a reasonable degree of safety and actual failure.

In the light of the Dee bridge disaster, it is surprising that many cast-iron bridges were left unstrengthened. However, many were replaced entirely by structures of wrought iron of the kind pioneered by William Fairbairn. They were riveted structures made from a far tougher material, more capable of resisting repeated dynamic loads. So what comment can be made today about the Wootton bridge accident? The symptoms indicate that fatigue cracks were growing from the edges of the bolt hole, so that the brittle cracks grew a tiny amount at every train which passed over. Eventually those cracks reached a critical size and the bridge collapsed. The effect of a circular bolt hole is to raise the stress at the edges of the hole by three: in other words, the local stress there is three times the nominal stress over uniform girder material. This is why a factor of three to four comes into play, as mentioned by Tyler.

This is the most credible modern explanation of the accident, and explains why the fully laden train did not break the girders on the morning of the accident. The cracks were simply just short of a critical size. But that first trip would extend the cracks by a minuscule amount to reach a critical level, so that the next time the train went over the bridge, on its return journey with empty wagons, the bridge collapsed.

Bull Bridge, Ambergate 1860

Later that year, a cast-iron girder fractured under a passing goods train, but fortunately with no casualties. This time it involved a 29ft-wide bridge covering a clear span of 23ft, where the track was again supported by baulks on the inner flanges of the girder. It happened on the Midland track between Derby and Chesterfield, on the dark and foggy night of 26 September 1860. With visibility only about 10 yards, the train was proceeding north at only 14mph. It was a long train, with twenty-seven wagons loaded with salt, two loaded goods vans, engine, tender and brake van. The heavy load was causing some slippage on the rail. Half a mile beyond Ambergate station, the driver suddenly noticed that his rear wheels were no longer on the rails. He shut off steam, stopped the engine and went to investigate.

His tender was attached to only two wagons, and they were all off the rails too. There were two more wagons about 10 yards behind, close to Bull bridge, a small viaduct over a local road. The next nine wagons behind were piled in a heap about 25ft high from the bottom of the road, reaching up to the telegraph wires by the side of the track. The guard in the brake van had been thrown head first against the front panel when the accident occurred, but was not seriously hurt. All the wagons behind the bridge were still on the line.

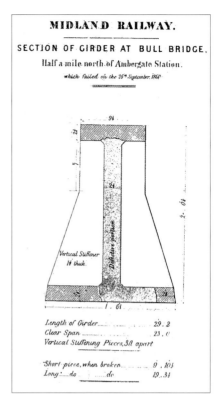

MIDLAND RAILWAY.

SECTION OF GIRDER AT BULL BRIDGE,

Half a mile north of Ambergate Station.

which failed on the 26ᵗʰ September 1860

Length of Girder............................ 29 . 2
Clear Span.............................. 23 . 0
Vertical Stiffening Pieces, 3ft apart

Short piece, when broken............... 9 . 10½
Long .....do .....do 19 . 3¾

(8.4) Defective girder from Bull bridge.

They found that one of the cast-iron girders had fractured, unusually near to one of the abutments, rather than at the centre of the beam. The track was supported by a pair of identical girders with Barlow rails cut to length laid across the inner flange, with asphalted ballast on top, just below the sleepers. When Captain Tyler examined the fracture surface, he found it rusted over, but the evidence of those who had seen it first showed just what had happened. The girder had broken vertically from an enormous defect in the web and flanges *(8.4)*, where there was a complete gap between the sides. The girder was completely defective here, but why no one had spotted it before the accident remains a mystery. Tyler suggests that it may have grown from an internal void with time, simply because such a defect would surely have been discovered either by the foundry or the builders. The girder had been installed twenty-three years ago in 1837, and should have supported a central load of 90 tons if in good condition. The pair of girders should have supported a total load of 360 tons distributed over all the structure, and Tyler stated that the girder was much bigger than was needed for the job. The engine weighed 31 tons and the tender 18 tons.

The source of the defect remains unknown, but may have been caused initially by a 'cold shut', where the molten metal does not fuse together during casting. It often occurs when two waves of fast cooling iron meet, but why it should have occurred only about 10ft from one end remains unknown. It could have grown with repeated loading from passing traffic, and Tyler thought it lucky that it had failed when a goods train was passing, rather than a passenger train, when casualties would have been inevitable. So fatigue had claimed yet another cast-iron bridge.

Together with the sudden failure of Wootton bridge, there should have been some concern within the railway companies about the number of cast-iron girders used as under-bridges on railway lines. Whether or not such structures were inspected is unknown. Later events seem to negate the possibility.

Harrington Viaduct, 1860

Deterioration could affect the many wooden viaducts everywhere on the network, such as that on the Whitehaven viaduct just to the south of Harrington station. It was inspected by Captain Tyler, who reported on its parlous state in a letter dated 15 December 1860. Local residents had complained that the timber was rotting away at many points in the structure, endangering trains passing over. It was about sixteen years old, was 400ft long and passed over two local roads. Part of the bridge had in fact given way under a train only ten days before, but fortunately without being derailed. The bridge was being restored at the time, by replacing the rotten wood by new timbers, although Captain Tyler felt that more durable materials should be introduced, such as iron or masonry. The railway company made considerable income from the line, and he felt that it should invest in its infrastructure to improve safety. Timber had clearly found widespread application in railway bridges, probably because of the low cost and speed of erection. But there would be problems in the future when the timbers started to rot and crack, especially if it affected the permanent way.

Clayton Tunnel, 1861

In the early days of the railways, many accidents were caused by the problems of tunnels, particularly their restricted visibility, and thus the movement of trains had to be controlled very precisely. This was a time when train movement was controlled by the time interval system, when there was supposed to be an interval of at least five minutes between following trains. It was to be many years before the 'block' system was to be introduced, where trains were separated by space rather than by time. In the meantime, many accidents and disasters occurred on what was a less reliable system than it could have been.

The Clayton tunnel accident of 25 August 1861 is a case in point. Three trains were involved at the tunnel, just north of Brighton where the railway ran under the chalk downs. Each end was protected by a signal box, with a direct telegraphic link between them. The Brighton end was also protected by a signal. The first train passed through without problem, but the following train came up only three minutes behind. The signal failed to return to danger owing to a malfunction, so the second train steamed ahead thinking the line was clear. The signalman (Henry Killick) had not heard from the other box whether the first train had exited the north end of the tunnel, and tried to stop the second train entering by waving a red flag just as the train was entering the tunnel. However, he could not be sure that the driver had seen his signal. He then heard from the north box that a train had come out. The third train then approached, only four minutes behind. Henry Killick thought that the line clear message from the north box referred to the second train, although in fact it was about the first train. He let the third train enter, thinking that all was safe. In the meantime, the second train had seen the red flag, stopped within the tunnel and was reversing back to investigate. The last train collided with the reversing train in the tunnel, the locomotive riding up over the guards van and the last carriage, causing terrible casualties. There were twenty-three deaths and 176 passengers were injured, the worst yet on the national network.

But there had been several previous incidents involving a similar problem, for example at New Street, Birmingham on 10 December 1857. A passenger train entered the north tunnel near the station, and the signalman allowed a single locomotive travelling fast to enter, after apparently receiving the all clear signal from the north signal box that the tunnel was clear. In fact, it was still in the tunnel, and the second locomotive smashed in to the back of it, injuring forty-four passengers. Captain Tyler made a very detailed report, and warned of the problems with the telegraph system then in use. His recommendations for improving communications were accepted, and he checked that they worked at Birmingham by talking to the signalmen concerned. Errors of perception or lapses in memory could cause serious collisions, but Tyler's reports and recommendations were not always acted on by other railway companies.

The Clayton disaster was to be used by Charles Dickens in a ghost story published at Christmas 1866, *The Signalman*. He tells a tale about a lonely signalman who is haunted by a spectre who appears at the entrance to the tunnel just before an accident. He is warned of the spectre's coming by a bell which vibrates, but does not ring, in his cabin. Dickens makes maximum use of the telegraph signal system then in use to create suspense, especially the bell and telegraph needle movements. There are three accidents the author (or narrator) relates: the first is a tunnel collision very similar to the Clayton tunnel accident, which will have been a fresh memory with his readers. The second is the death of a young woman on another train, and the third is his own death. Dickens had been deeply affected by a train crash in which he had been involved as a passenger, that at Staplehurst in Kent on 9 June 1865.

The reports of accidents were published for public consumption as well as the railway companies, and had a wide readership. They are terse and to the point, although sometimes lacking in the technical detail which we nowadays expect of accident reports. Acting according to the example set by Captain Simmons, they arrived at the scene of an accident as fast as possible, so that the surviving evidence could be examined while still fresh. And they covered a multitude of problems, and not necessarily related to the severity of the accident in terms of casualties, but rather to the reasons for an accident or incident. Prior warnings of a specific problem are often more value in preventing further accidents of the same kind, and the Inspectorate were very aware of their public duty in warning the railway companies of problems with equipment, systems or structures.

Tornado Explosion, 1860

The greatest stress in a cylindrical pressure vessel is exerted in the hoop direction (around the circumference of the cylinder), so that cracks grow preferentially along the length of a cylinder rather than longitudinally. The work of William Fairbairn described this phenomenon very precisely in papers read to the Royal Society in 1858, based on experiments on glass cylinders. He had investigated numerous explosions in static steam engines in mills, in the 1830s and 1840s. His work laid the basis for an understanding of the several different causes of boiler explosions, although conditions under which locomotive boilers worked were different to those used in static steam engines. Corrosion was a common cause, when deliberate tampering with the safety valves had been eliminated.

Captain Tyler gives a good example of an accident caused by such corrosion in his report of an explosion on the Exeter line of the South Devon Railway in 1860. The report is fairly typical of the many reports made by the inspectors during this period:

The locomotive Tornado arrived at Totnes station on April 13th, 1860 with 22 goods wagons and a guard van just after midday. The driver left the wagons at the goods shed, and proceeded to the water tank to replenish his supply. The fireman pricked up the fire while he was doing this, causing the pressure to rise with steam issuing from the safety valves. He returned to the station platform to couple up some wagons, and another on a siding, backing the locomotive up against the train. He had no sooner completed this when the boiler exploded suddenly. Both driver and fireman were on the footplate at the time, the driver being blown back onto a van behind the engine, and suffered serious head wounds. He then fell onto the line and was run over by the engine and vans driven forward by the blast. The fireman fell on the engine buffers, and could not be interviewed owing to the severity of his injuries, by Captain Tyler when he arrived to investigate the very next day.

The engine was a standard tank engine with six wheels, weighing 36 tons. Its boiler heated surface was 1,256 sq. ft, 121 of which were in the fire-box and 1,135 in the tubes. It had two safety valves, one in the dome and thus inaccessible to the men, the other a Salters balance set to 120psi. The engine had been built at the Vulcan works near Warrington to a Gooch design in 1854. After 62,136 miles, it was retubed in October 1859, and the stays renewed at the same time. Since then it had run 12,232 miles without repairs, but a longitudinal stay under the boiler had been replaced to stop a leak at the fire-box end the day before the accident.

The explosion unpeeled the outer wrought-iron shell at the rivets, and it fragmented into three large pieces. The first piece, about 4ft 9in long by 13in wide, was blown through the side of the goods shed, knocked in the side of a truck and fell on the rails. A similarly sized piece hit a brick wall 30 yards away, making a large hole, while a slightly larger piece fell on the rails about 15ft away. The safety valves were lost entirely, but the whistle was found 330 yards away, giving an idea of the force generated by the blast.

The clues to the cause of the explosion lay not in the engine remains but rather in the fragments, especially when the broken edges were matched together. The force of the explosion was upwards and to the left. The side and roof of the goods shed had been blown away on the left, and the recoil of the engine had bent the rails under the engine. The piece found inside the shed on the rails, and another of the large pieces, had separated at a rivet line on a seam, and it was likely that the seam was close to the initiation point. The edge of the outer plate had been severely corroded in a line parallel to the edge of the inner plate. The metal had been eaten away to about ³⁄₁₆in of a sheet originally ¼in thick, with very little metal left at all in some places. The same corrosion groove was found on all the seams of the boiler walls, the corrosion being deepest at ledges where water could remain after the overall level had dropped. It was Tyler's first investigation of a boiler explosion, and he attributed some of the corrosion to poor caulking at the lap joint, and mechanical damage from the tools used for caulking (sealing) it. We now know that this is unlikely, because of the frequency of such attacks.

The corrosion in *Tornado* was made that much worse by the brackish or slightly salty water used in her boiler, and Captain Tyler recommended an improved water supply for the locomotives. But that the consequences of such groove corrosion could be much different was shown by the state of a sister engine named *Ixion,* this engine was owned by the same company, but drew passenger trains. It leaked water from an affected seam, the leak proving impossible to seal so the boiler was stripped. The same groove corrosion was found at the seam welds, but it was fortunate that it was discovered in time to prevent a devastating explosion. Tyler noticed that there was an important difference between the design of the two boilers. The boiler of *Ixion* was supported by more stays than *Tornado*, and they gave extra support to the horizontal seams most at risk. This critical difference meant the total loss of the one engine and the death of its driver, while the other could be renewed for further service. By this time, after a decade or more of horrendous boiler explosions, it was becoming very clear that most locomotive explosions were caused by groove cracking. It was a design defect because of the lap joints in the wrought-iron shells of the boilers.

Groove Cracking

One authority, C.H. Hewison, himself a retired railway inspector from British Rail, has shown that it was the major cause of all boiler explosions from the start of locomotive building. But knowing the cause of a problem, and then correcting it, are separate and distinct activities. In the following decade there were thirty-nine such boiler explosions in locomotives, the majority being caused by groove corrosion. So how could they occur if the cause was by then already well known? To discover the cracks at the groove required a complete strip of the boiler and fire box, an expensive and time-consuming exercise that was not undertaken as frequently as the severity of the problem demanded. And there were variations in policy between different companies. While the LNWR had few explosions because of a rigorous boiler maintenance programme, other companies were more tardy in their approach.

The problem could only be eliminated by changes in design practice when constructing the locomotives in the first place. Single lap seams were the root cause, especially horizontal seams subjected to high hoop stress, so using a double joint could prevent crack initiation.

But it took some time before designers changed their practice in new locos and introduced butt seams, where the boiler plates are abutted and then reinforced by external plates at the joint. Boiler explosions from groove cracking would continue for many more years as the rail companies kept old engines working.

There was one particularly important person in this scenario, who perhaps should have been consulted to a greater extent than he was (apart from over the Longsight explosion). He had much experience of examining boiler explosions at fixed locations, such as mills and factories.

Fairbairn and Boilers

William Fairbairn, the eminent engineer who had designed the Britannia and Conwy tubular bridges, had originally helped develop the machine-riveted joint, and researched the strength and longevity of such joints. His work also showed that the pressure inside a cylindrical vessel, such as a boiler, exerted two forces in the wall of the vessel, the hoop stress and the longitudinal stress. Each stress was dependent on the pressure, the wall thickness and the diameter of the vessel, with the hoop stress being twice the size of the longitudinal stress. Failure of a pressure vessel was thus caused primarily by the hoop stress acting on the wall. The stress acts around the circumference of the cylinder, so cracks tend to form along the length. In the case of a riveted boiler, it means that longitudinal welds or riveted joints are the ones most at risk of failure. His work was published in 1858 in the Proceedings of the Royal Society, and he disseminated his experience of boiler design and failures in book form, as well as in papers for learned journals.

He was well aware of the brittle nature of cast iron, as previous chapters have shown on the Dee disaster, but was also keenly interested in the properties of riveted wrought iron, which he himself had championed. He had tested different configurations of rivets and plates to destruction, and determined that riveted butt joints gave a much higher strength than riveted lap joints. The results were also published in the Proceedings of the Royal Society. It is curious then, why butt joints were not immediately adopted by locomotive builders. Lap joints were obviously cheaper, using fewer rivets and plate, but would surely eliminate the inner corner of the lap joint and all the problems which followed from that. Perhaps conservative forces won the day, and it took time for them to change their practices. The problem of stress corrosion cracking from the inner corner of lap joints would continue for some years yet.

The boiler problem is also explicable in modern terms. Since one plate forms a sharp corner with the other at this lap joint, there is a stress concentration which accelerates corrosive attack (a phenomenon now known as SCC, or stress corrosion cracking, where a crack forms and is accelerated by corrosion). Fatigue probably also added to the problem, because boilers were subjected to cyclical pressurisation every time they were steamed up for a working day (stress corrosion fatigue, SCF). Both SCC and SCF are important failure modes in many structures, including bridges. The Silver Bridge collapse in 1987 was caused by SCC in a hanger, and caused the entire structure to fall when the hanger finally cracked after about forty years in service.

Charles Dickens had some ironic comments to make on the problem of exploding boilers, as he said in *Household Words* in 1851:

> *When a boiler bursts, why was it the very best of boilers; and why, when somebody thinks that if the accident were not the boiler's fault it is likely to have been the engineer's, is the engineer then morally certain to have been the steadiest and skillfullest of men?*

Perhaps society regarded boiler explosions as the inevitable price of progress, the dark side of the improvement in material wealth. The Great Exhibition had demonstrated that progress to the world in the same year, but engineers should have known better. And they did try to improve matters, but rather late in the day. In 1859, the Vulcan Insurance Society was founded in Manchester by local businessmen, with William Fairbairn a driving force on the technical aspects of boiler design and operation. By inspecting existing boilers they could refuse insurance cover, and so force manufacturers to improve their boiler designs and the way they were maintained.

Hartley Colliery Disaster

Cast iron found use not just in large beams for bridges and buildings but in oscillating beams for static steam engines, commonly used to dewater mines in the Victorian period and even earlier. In James Watt's day, they had been built of great beams of wood, often of composite construction owing to their great size, and reinforced by wrought-iron straps. But, as casting technology improved, designers turned to the possibilities of cast-iron construction. It would be considerably cheaper, and enable very large beams to be used. Such beams came into widespread use in the 1840s despite their greater weight, and the need for much heavier duty bearings to withstand the greater weight of iron.

If anyone outside the bridge or railway fraternity had bothered to read the results of the Royal Commission, they might have noted the problems of large cast-iron structures. The Commission established the deleterious effects of intermittent dynamic loads from trains crossing cast-iron bridges, with the example of the Dee bridge disaster fresh in their minds. Their conclusions should have rung alarm bells in other industries where very large castings were employed. Not only was cast-iron weak in tension or bending, but it could shatter very suddenly owing to its brittle nature.

The danger in large castings was to become horrifically apparent on 16 January 1862, when just such a gigantic cast-iron beam suddenly shattered, and one half fell into the shaft of Hartley colliery, Northumberland. The 34ft long beam was constructed from several smaller castings, and weighed 42 tons. Its age is unknown, but the lower seams being worked were deep and needed dewatering, so it is likely to have been several years since it was introduced into the pit. Estimates at the time suggest that its maximum load from the rods and buckets was about 55 tons, and it worked at upwards of 4.5 strokes per minute. Failure of a rod had occurred before, but without any apparent damage to the beam itself.

The failure could not have happened at a worse time, because it was a shift change in the underground workings, so the number of miners was much greater than normal. Moreover, the mine was worked by only one shaft, with a brattice dividing it to provide ventilation. The broken beam weighed about 21 tons and destroyed everything in its path as it hurtled down the shaft. The wooden brattice collapsed beneath the weight of moving metal to form an impenetrable blockage about 300ft down the 600ft deep shaft. It effectively entombed 204 men and boys, the two shifts being in the act of changing. Despite heroic rescue attempts to break through the jam in the shaft, it was impossible to rescue the miners in time to prevent their suffocation. There was no other access route into the underground workings. After about a week of frantic digging, the rescue party broke through but found only corpses, making it the worst pit disaster up until that time, bearing comparison with some of the worst pit disasters ever. It was a unique event, because most colliery disasters are caused by gas and coal dust explosions rather than mechanical failure.

So what was the cause of the catastrophe? A contemporary picture of the accident *(8.5)* shows a brittle fracture running through the centre of the beam end left *in situ* at the pithead. All the four separate fractures appear to have occurred in solid metal, and the axle is complete and unharmed. The upper pair of surface fractures appears to be straight when compared with the lower halves. The surface at lower right is distinctly curved, as is the corresponding surface at lower left. It is likely that the fracture started in the upper part of the beam, simply because this is where the greatest bending load will occur. It is also interesting to observe that the upper surfaces show large internal voids or blowholes just where expected: at the centre of the thickest sections of the beams. They were reported and discussed at the time, but thought not to have caused the disaster.

The greatest load is at the very top of the structure, in the two beams. The left-hand section seems to show more features of a slowly growing crack than the right-hand, with lines curved from the inside to the outside edge. They could represent the intermittent growth of a fatigue crack, invisible externally at first, but plain to see in the final stage of propagation. Much depends on the accuracy of the engraving, but they were usually based on photographs taken on the spot, and there is nothing to show that the features of the fracture are imaginary. Other engravings of the same surface are less distinct however, so the exact nature of the failure must remain a mystery unless further evidence emerges.

At the time, the failure was attributed to overload from the pump rod system attached to the end of the beam, causing the beam to crash heavily into the supports. The shock then fractured the beam, but no supporting evidence for the theory was produced by the Mines inspector, who reported to Parliament on the disaster. In any case, other parts of the pump rod system might have been expected to fail first, as had happened before. Although the rods were made of lengths of pine, they were of much smaller size than the massive beam. Whether the makers of the beam were consulted, and whether it had been tested, remains unknown. There will have been many similar beams elsewhere, which may have

(8.5) Brittle fracture of cast-iron beam at Hartley colliery, 1862.

raised alarm at the time, but the consequences for design are also unknown. Although the Mines inspector J. Kenyon Blackwell had condemned the single shaft, he suggested that such cast-iron beams should be reinforced by wrought-iron rods about 3in in diameter. His report does not bear comparison with the rather more thorough reports from the Railway Inspectorate, perhaps because the disaster was outside his normal experience of pit disasters. The inquest jury was much more forthright. They said:

> *The Jury cannot close this painful enquiry without expressing their strong opinion of the imperative necessity that all working collieries should have at least a second shaft or outlet, to afford the workmen the means of escape, should any obstruction take place, as occurred at the New Hartley Pit; and that in future, the beams of colliery engines should be made of malleable iron, instead of cast metal.*

However, the disaster did have an immediate effect on legislators, because the accident highlighted the problem of working a pit from only one shaft. *(8.6)* The public outcry forced the government to legislate in an attempt to reassure the nation. A short, one clause Act was passed quickly to insist that all collieries be worked by two shafts, separated by at least 15 yards. However, unique this disaster was, it re-emphasised the hazards of coal mining, where large scale loss of life was frequent, mainly from methane (firedamp) coupled with coal dust explosions. Despite the widespread use of 'safety' lamps, such disasters continued on an ever increasing scale, such as The Oaks disaster of 1866 near Barnsley, South Yorkshire, which claimed 388 lives after not just one but many successive explosions.

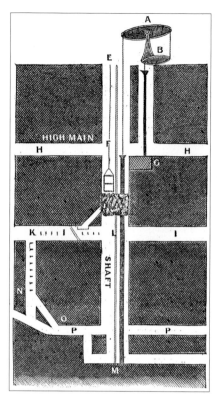

(8.6) Section of Hartley colliery with main shaft blocked by debris.

Bessemer and Steel

If the world was waiting for one key invention, it was a way of mass manufacturing steel, a seemingly magical material which would, in the end, solve the many problems of cast iron, especially its treacherous brittleness. The man who solved the problem was not an engineer at all, but a professional inventor named Henry Bessemer. Early in his long and productive career, he had developed a way of making 'gold' paint, much in demand by artists and architects for display, but containing no precious metal whatsoever. In need of money, he spotted that German manufacturers were the sole source, maintaining a high price through their monopoly. So he analysed a sample, both chemically and under the microscope, and found that they were only using small flakes of brass.

He then developed a new way to comminute cheap brass into tiny flakes using automatic machinery, which was then mixed with linseed oil and other binders, to produce the final product. The raw materials were cheap and the product expensive (but cheap when compared with real gold), which was a successful way of making sellable products with a small capital investment. He did not patent the invention, but rather relied on keeping the secret within a small coterie of relatives and close friends. They were employed to make the paint in his workshop in London as a cottage industry, no single worker knowing the whole formula. This was the traditional way of protecting secret formulae, and was well known to the medieval Guilds of artisans, Renaissance philosophers like Leonardo da Vinci (who used a mirror code in his many inventive drawings) and is still well used today.

The monks of Chartreuse in the French Alps, for example, protect the secret formula for their liqueur by restricting knowledge of the many ingredients to the Abbott himself, who passes the secret on to his successor when his end approaches.

Bessemer describes himself (in his highly readable autobiography) the first success of his new process in the early 1840s:

> *Thus, my new 'gold paint' was brought out, and those who knew how to use it, and what substances it could be successfully used upon, were delighted with it; while the attempts of others were a complete fiasco, and it was by them condemned as a failure, notwithstanding which as many as 80,000 bottles of it have been sold in the course of a year. Among its various uses, a very odd one was due to the cuteness of a Birmingham manufacturer of 'coffin furniture.' Instead of stamping in brass the variety of ornaments used on the sides of coffins, he stamped them in the cheaper metal zinc, and made them beautiful with gold paint; they lasted much longer than was necessary for the purpose, and only turned black after some time.*

But his greatest invention was to come. His work on the paint involved considerable expertise in designing machines to cut brass to the required degree of fineness (using a small steam engine). He became interested in glass making, perhaps being influenced by the success of the Crystal Palace of 1851, and invented a way of making float glass with much improved surface quality. It involved developing a detailed knowledge of furnaces used for melting glass, and he applied it to the thorny problem of manufacturing cheap iron in the late 1850s. He was aware of the problems of cast-iron bridges (like everyone else), but his immediate attention was drawn to the problem of making reliable cannons, that is, cannons which did not explode when fired. The problem was, of course, the very brittle cast iron of which they were made. He describes the problem first:

> *Practically, all objects in iron, except such as were simply castings, were at that time [1854] made from wrought iron manufactured by puddling. The object I set before myself was to produce a metal having characteristics comparable with those of wrought iron or steel, and yet capable of being run into a mould or ingot in a fluid condition. I was aware that Fairbairn and others had sought to improve cast iron by the fusion of some malleable scrap, along with the pig iron, in the cupola furnace. This fusion of scrap-iron, intermixed with a mass of coke, was found to convert the malleable iron into white cast iron, which was at the same time much contaminated with sulphur. Therefore, to a great extent, this system had failed in its object. In my experiments I avoided the difficulties inseparable from Fairbairn's method, by employing a reverberatory furnace in which the pig-iron was fused.*

He then hit on the idea of blowing in air to react with the molten iron in his carefully designed 'converter', so the excess carbon would burn away:

> *All being thus arranged, and a blast of 10 or 15 lb. pressure turned on, about 7 cwt. of molten pig iron was run into the hopper provided on one side of the converter for that purpose. All went on quietly for about ten minutes; sparks such as are commonly seen when tapping a cupola, accompanied by*

hot gases, ascended through the opening on the top of the converter, just as I supposed would be the case. But soon after a rapid change took place; in fact, the silicon had been quietly consumed, and the oxygen, next uniting with the carbon, sent up an ever-increasing stream of sparks and a voluminous white flame. Then followed a succession of mild explosions, throwing molten slags and splashes of metal high up into the air, the apparatus becoming a veritable volcano in a state of active eruption. No one could approach the converter to turn off the blast, and some low, flat, zinc-covered roofs, close at hand were in danger of being set on fire by the shower of red-hot matter falling on them. All this was a revelation to me, as I had in no way anticipated such violent results. However, in ten minutes more the eruption had ceased, the flame died down, and the process was complete. On tapping the converter into a shallow pan or ladle, and forming the metal into an ingot, it was found to be wholly decarburised malleable iron.

So he had found a way of removing the carbon to make wrought iron in far greater quantities than before, a critical step in the advance to making steel by careful control of the burn in his converter *(8.7)*.

The story from then on is somewhat convoluted, because Bessemer had been using very pure ore from Cumberland, and the process did not work with other ores. However, despite many successes and failures, he established a large factory in Sheffield for making steel, and so the city began to give engineers a much better, much tougher material for use in a wide variety of structures. We are still living with the revolution he started.

Stretton 1862

Wooden viaducts needed close monitoring for the deterioration of the timber, as the Harrington bridge of 1860 showed. But accidents could occur when maintenance work was underway owing to the disruption of the track. Special care was needed to ensure that trains were diverted if the track was down, as the accident at Stretton in August 1862 on the LNWR showed. Timber beams on the viaduct six miles north of Rugby station were being replaced by iron girders. One of the two lines over the viaduct was closed, and loop lines with points were inserted at either end of the bridge so that trains could use the single line still open. Signalmen were to be stationed at either end to warn approaching trains, and the works were well advertised to all drivers on the line. Every train was ordered to stop to pick up a signalman to guide the driver over the bridge.

On the night of 13 August 1862, a goods train bound for Preston was approaching the viaduct at about 9 p.m. It picked up the signalman and proceeded to cross the bridge. Meanwhile, another goods train (300 yards long with fifty-one wagons) was travelling down from Scotland on the other side of the bridge. Since the signalman could not turn the southbound train on to the single line for fear of a collision, it continued on the track and crashed through the gap in the bridge, fell 16ft to the ground and killed both the driver and his fireman.

The gap in the track was invisible to the driver, and there was no way he could have seen the gap as he approached. He should have been warned at the previous station

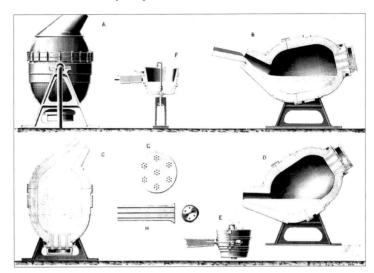

(8.7) Prototype
Bessemer converter.

(Stafford) but the inspector there had been attending to other matters, so he missed the direct warning of the problem. The signalman at the north end of the bridge had warned the approaching train with a detonator on the line, and by flashing his red light at the train, but it was raining heavily at the time, and the driver probably missed this warning too. Captain Tyler recommended that more warning should have been given, for example, by providing fixed signals at either end of the bridge.

Problems of track and structural maintenance at bridges were to continue, however, as the next terrible accident demonstrates. It was an accident with more serious consequences, because a passenger rather than goods train was involved. Moreover, one of those passengers was rather distinguished.

Staplehurst accident, 1865

Failure of a cast-iron bridge led indirectly to a disaster in which Charles Dickens was involved, a survivor when ten other passengers died. It occurred at Staplehurst in Kent on 9 June 1865, and happened like this *(8.8)*. The line from Folkestone to London was owned by the South-Eastern Railway Co., who operated boat trains to meet cross-channel ferries. Work had been proceeding for about three months on a 168ft-wide viaduct crossing the river Beult. The bridge effectively spanned the stream and its flood plain. Timber baulks were being replaced on the structure, and since they were part of the support for the track, the rails had to be removed for access. The repair work was being carried out intermittently between trains, and the work that day would have completed the renovation. Two lengths of rail had been removed to replace the final baulk by the time the train arrived. Captain Rich described the bridge as follows:

> *The Beult viaduct … has eight openings, each 21 feet wide. The railway on the viaduct, is about*
> *10 feet above the bed of the river, which is now a small muddy stream, but covers the whole space*

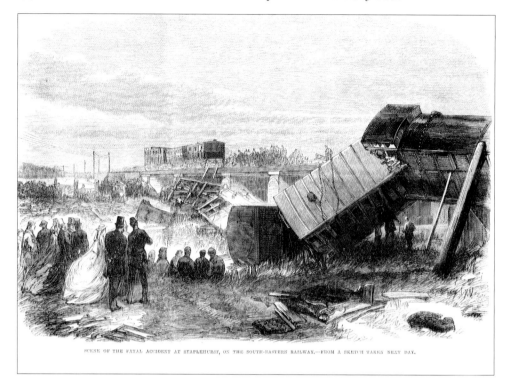

SCENE OF THE FATAL ACCIDENT AT STAPLEHURST, ON THE SOUTH-EASTERN RAILWAY.—FROM A SKETCH TAKEN NEXT DAY.

(8.8) Staplehurst rail crash.

under the viaduct in winter. The piers of the viaduct are brick, 3ft thick, and the rails are carried over each opening on wooden beams, which are laid in cast iron trough girders. The outside girders of the bridge, which carry the platform only, are also cast iron, and the platform outside and between the rails consists of chalk laid on corrugated iron sheeting. In order to remove the last baulk on the Beult viaduct, two lengths of rail, each 21 feet long, had been taken out of the up line, after the up train due at Staplehurst at 2.51 pm had passed on 9th inst. Only 13 feet of the baulk had been removed. This piece carried the rail on that part of the bank, next to the viaduct. The remainder of the baulk, from which the second length of rail had been removed, was still in the trough girder when the tidal train arrived.

The strength of the platform for the rails was thus provided by the cast-iron troughs. There was no wall on the sides, thus no protection against wagons tipping sideways from the viaduct, and no guard rail was fitted to the permanent way *(8.8)*.

The boat trains always arrived at a different time owing to the changing tides, and the foreman had been given the timetable for the period. However, he mistook the time. He read the time as being for 10 June rather than the ninth, at 5.30 p.m. rather than 3.15 p.m., a difference of over two hours. So he thought he had much more time to finish the repair than was actually available. He was required to place a lookout with a red flag 1,000 yards ahead of the line, or over half a mile away, so as to warn any approaching trains. The same signalman should also have placed detonators on the line at regular intervals. In fact, the lookout was only just over 500 yards away at the time the boat train approached, and no detonators were put on the line at all.

The boat train was travelling at about 50mph, and saw the warning of the lookout, immediately the brakes were applied and the engine reversed. However, its momentum carried it over the viaduct at about 30mph by the time it reached the spot where the rails had been removed. The heavy engine fell from the end of the free rail, ploughed across the baulk, and the cast-iron girder below fractured, but in time to allow the engine to remain upright. The tender, however, twisted around across the track, and the following wagon tipped over the edge of the viaduct at a precarious angle. The rear of the first-class coach behind fell from the side of the bridge, but the coupling held, so it was left leaning at a steep angle against the viaduct. On examination by Captain Rich, several other girders were found to be cracked:

The whole of the near side rails of the up line on the viaduct, were torn away, and from the end of the viaduct to where the engine stopped, they were bent and the chairs broken. The off side rails were bulged where the engine first dropped, in consequence of the two rails having been taken out. The next two lengths of rail were all right. All of the others, up to the place where the engine had stopped were torn up. The cast iron trough girders carrying the rails consisted of two beams bolted together. The outside beam of the first girder, where the rail had been taken out, had pieces broken off at both ends. It was broken in two at the centre, and had fallen into the bed of the river. It appears to have been broken by the tender striking it heavily. The second and third outside girders were also broken, and the sixth and the eighth were cracked. The corrugated iron sheeting between the girders, which was covered by chalk, was broken through in several places. The eastern abutment of the viaduct, and the first three brick piers, were damaged by the falling carriages. The fourth pier was slightly grazed.

Although the root cause of the accident was a mistake by the foreman, it revealed yet again the weakness of cast-iron girders in railway structures. If the girders had withstood the overload from the impact, the carriages may have stayed upright, and the high number of casualties limited.

Charles Dickens was in the first-class carriage left dangling behind the engine, but several carriages were almost completely destroyed, leaving ten passengers dead and many more injured. He extricated himself and gave help to the dying and injured, but was deeply affected by the experience. Train journeys after that were a severe trial for him, and indeed, he wrote to *The Times* on 26 January 1867 about one such journey, from Leicester to London, which he was forced to abandon at Bedford:

As it is better to prevent a horrible accident by a timely caution than sagaciously to observe after its occurrence that any one acquainted with the circumstances out of which it arose could have easily foreseen it, I beg most earnestly to warn the public through your columns against the morning express train on the Midland railway between Leicester and Bedford. I took that train this morning, leaving Leicester at 9.35. The reckless fury of the driving and the violent rocking of the carriages obliged me to leave it at Bedford rather than come on to London with my through ticket. When we stopped at Market Harborough general alarm was expressed by the passengers, and strong remonstrances were urged on the officials, also, at Bedford. I am an experienced railway traveller at home and abroad; I was in the Staplehurst accident; I have been in trains under most conceivable conditions, but I have never been so shaken and flung about as in this train, and have never been in such obvious danger.

He died exactly five years after the Staplehurst accident on 9 June 1870. His descriptions of railways cannot be bettered, as shown by this rather gloomy extract from *Mugby Junction*, a short story written in 1866:

A place replete with shadowy shapes, this Mugby Junction in the black hours of the four-and-twenty. Mysterious goods trains, covered with palls and gliding on like vast weird funerals, conveying themselves guiltily away from the presence of the few lighted lamps, as if their freight had come to a secret and unlawful end. Half-miles of coal pursuing in a Detective manner, following when they lead, stopping when they stop, backing when they back. Red-hot embers showering out upon the ground, down this dark avenue, and down the other, as if torturing fires were being raked clear; concurrently, shrieks and groans and grinds invading the ear, as if the tortured were at the height of their suffering. Iron-barred cages full of cattle jangling by midway, the drooping beasts with horns entangled, eyes frozen with terror, and mouths too: at least they have long icicles (or what seem so) hanging from their lips. Unknown languages in the air, conspiring in red, green, and white characters. An earthquake, accompanied with thunder and lightning, going up express to London. Now, all quiet, all rusty, wind and rain in possession, lamps extinguished, Mugby Junction dead and indistinct, with its robe drawn over its head, like Caesar.

His description was apparently based on Rugby station on the LNWR line built by Robert Stephenson, but could have applied equally to any major junction on the network. Perhaps the fearful allusions in the text reflect his own experience at Staplehurst, a vision of untamed and uncontrollable technology.

The accident which so affected the famous story-teller was directly caused by mistakes by the foreman and his staff, but this still cannot conceal the fact that the accident became a disaster because the cast-iron girders fractured catastrophically when impacted by the moving train.

Somerset House Incident

The widespread use of cast-iron girders in buildings could also give rise to catastrophic failure. Benjamin Baker reported a dramatic failure of several girders at King's College in the winter of 1869, in a wide ranging discussion of the problem of fatigue in his book on long span railway bridges published in a revised edition of 1873. The beams supported the terrace above the main dining room at King's in Somerset House just off the Strand, causing great damage, but fortunately without loss of life. The floor consisted of the girder and brick infill arches and there were no dynamic loads to consider. However, it supported a dead load of 21 tons at the centre, compared with its strength of 33 tons. Since the dead load was $\frac{2}{3}$ of the strength, Baker thought it unsurprising that failure occurred, but does not say when it was installed and whether or not any of the girders contained casting flaws.

The cause of the failure could have been overload from an unknown source, fatigue, or a problem known as 'static fatigue'. The phenomenon is found in products loaded near to their ultimate breaking strength for some time, when failure occurs suddenly. A crack grows very slowly from the most serious stress concentration until it reaches a critical size, and then grows uncontrollably. We do not know if there was an inquiry, who designed the building, or who paid for the damage caused by the collapse. It will remain something of a mystery until further research unearths more details.

The Cholera

The experience of the Inspectorate was widely known because of their many reports on railway accidents following the expansion of the network in the 1840s and 50s. Their investigative skills could be used to tackle other problems.

With the growth in towns and cities as the century progressed, the spectre of infectious disease rose. Sanitation for the growing urban population had been neglected, and was given political prominence by the cholera outbreaks of 1831–32, 1848–49, 1853–54 and 1866 in London. The extent of pollution of the river Thames was a scandal which came home to Parliament itself, when it was forced to close in 1859 during the 'Great Stink'. Something had to be done. A grand new project was initiated to build an entirely new sewage system for the capital, engineered by Bazalgette. He would also construct a new embankment for the centre of the city, to prevent flooding from the Thames. But the system took time to build, and many parts of London were still exposed to pollution from raw sewage.

The problem was highlighted by the final major outbreak of cholera in 1866. It is a terrible disease. Its victims could fall ill in the morning and be dead by nightfall. Much had been learnt during the previous epidemics. It was thought for many years that the disease was spread through the air by some virulent organism, hence the obsession with the smell from raw sewage in the rivers. This view was prevalent in the first three great epidemics, but was not based on clear arguments. Dr John Snow practiced medicine in Soho, London, and was an early pioneer of anaesthetics such as ether and chloroform. But he was also interested in infectious diseases, which were a major cause of death in mid-Victorian Britain. He had published a pamphlet in 1849 in which he suggested that the virulence was present in the drinking water, and not the atmosphere. He presented epidemiological evidence of poor water supplies in certain parts of the city (the East and South of London), and linked it to a high incidence of the disease. He especially discussed the poor state of the river Lea, heavily contaminated by raw sewage, from which drinking water was taken for supply to East London.

He made further critical observations in the next outbreak in 1854. He noticed a high mortality in residents of Broad Street Soho, who used a common water supply at a nearby pump. Victims even included some people who lived away from the district, but who had drunk the very same well water. He persuaded the parish to remove the pump-handle to stifle consumption, and the disease diminished in intensity. He also noted that the well was very shallow and that a sewer passed within a few feet. He published his results in medical journals, noting other correlations at Deptford.

He was met by a wall of silence. The mindset of the time suppressed rational debate of the problem. In 1857 he published a comparative study of mortality rates in Lambeth and Southwark, again drawing attention to the connection between contaminated drinking water and outbreaks of the cholera. Matters came to head in the final epidemic of 1866, despite Bazalgette's new sewage system under most of the city. However, this time the outbreak was more isolated, being confined to areas supplied by the East London Water Co. They had a large reservoir almost directly adjacent to the still-polluted river Lea, and it was suspected that seepage from the river had contaminated the reservoir. Captain Tyler was asked by the Board of Trade to investigate.

Tyler, as usual, conducted a very thorough investigation, one of the most intensive and wide-ranging in his career. He included extensive evidence from the official mortality statistics, but above all, a direct examination of the possible source of the contamination. Here are his observations, after he asked for the reservoirs to be emptied:

> *I devoted three hours on the Sunday afternoon to wading about in the water, and thus making the best examination which the circumstances would permit. I found a spurt of water issuing from the brickwork across an old sluice through which water had been formerly admitted to the reservoirs from the river, and I saw water issuing from more than one of the piers by which the arched covering was supported. I observed also a considerable amount of soakage into the reservoir from the slopes of brickwork at its side ... There was much discolouration in different places, where the water entered, which appeared to indicate a want of purity ... It was less agreeable to the taste than the Company's filtered water.*

He took samples and they were analysed. All the samples had a green or yellow green colour, and all possessed organic matter in suspension (up to over 1 per cent). He concluded that the reservoirs were seriously contaminated and that here was the source of the cholera which had, by that time, killed many people. It was a brave act to taste this water.

In spite of the different environment to those with which he was familiar, Captain Tyler had excelled in producing a definitive report which helped bring the crisis to an end. It was to change medical opinion at long last, and so improve the health of the population, not just in the cities, but in the country at large, where well supplies had all too often been contaminated in just the same way.

9

Hubris

With increased prosperity among all classes as a direct result of many productive new industries, pressure once again grew for political reform, especially extending the vote to all adult males. The 1832 Reform Act had only enfranchised a relatively small section of the population, ratepayers of a certain standing. It was still open to widespread corruption, with many seats in the House of Commons in the ownership of wealthy or aristocratic individuals. The difference was now that the new rich could indulge an interest, such as George Hudson, the Railway King. But the aristocracy also played a major role, just as before 1832. Parliament had been radicalised, however, thanks to the likes of Grey, Brougham, Pitt and Russell in the early governments. A new class of politicians were inspired to carry further reforms of the system through, especially Gladstone and Disraeli, who would alternate regularly as Prime Minister (and often Chancellor as well). Disraeli's efforts resulted in the second Reform Act of 1869, which extended the franchise to the whole adult male population, and thereby introduced a more populist element into politics. Public opinion was of greater importance than before, or at least opinion as judged by the press and popular illustrated weeklies, such as *Punch*, the *Illustrated London News* and the *Globe*.

The railways had matured, and relatively few new lines were built in the 1860s and 1870s, often for reasons of geography. Those that were built included links in Scotland, especially the east coast route to link Edinburgh with Dundee and Aberdeen, where the route faced almost insuperable obstacles in the form of the Forth and Tay estuaries. Railway accidents remained high throughout the period, and some of the worst ever disasters occurred in the period between 1870 and 1880, including Newark, Oxford, Abbots Ripton, Norwich and, finally, the Tay bridge disaster. Many were triggered by mechanical failure, and exacerbated by failure to invest in technology which had been available for some time, such as pneumatic braking systems. Yet others were bedevilled by poor design practices, bad management and cost restrictions.

Prince of Wales

Some incidents involving bridges would never be exposed to the glare of publicity, if a defect was found during regular maintenance for example, and quietly rectified. However, it would be much more difficult to conceal unusual events to trains themselves because passengers might have been aware of what had happened, and complain to those in authority or the press. And if one of those passengers was a celebrity, then publicity was assured. Just that happened to a train crossing the Drumlithie viaduct south of Aberdeen on 6 October 1869, when it derailed. Aboard was the Prince of Wales, riding in a saloon carriage. He was the future King Edward VII, eventually succeeding his mother Queen Victoria in 1901. He was aged twenty-seven at the time of the accident.

The driver suddenly heard a wheel grinding against its cover, turned round and saw dust rising in front of the loco. His left leading wheel had dropped from the inside of the rail. He whistled the guard, applied the brakes and reversed the engine to bring it to a halt. The brakeman and driver went to investigate, and found nothing wrong with the engine. Having sent a police inspector back to warn following trains of the problem, he then cautiously started forward and the engine remounted the rail.

Captain Tyler investigated the incident a few days later, and found the permanent way on the viaduct the worse for wear, largely owing to the poor state of the timber sleepers. The viaduct had been built in 1859, and was 282 yards long and 50ft above the valley at its highest point. It was made of timber-framed arched ribs mounted on masonry piers in eleven spans of 60ft each. The permanent way had been renewed just six years before the incident. It was mounted on longitudinal beams, which had decayed and cracked, allowing movement of the rail itself. The movement of these timbers had allowed the rail to move sideways by 2.75in (the width of the wheel), so derailing the one wheel of the loco. The damage had been accumulating for some time, and it was lucky that the other wheels had remained on track. He concluded in his report to the Caledonian Railway that:

> This accident was caused by the defective condition of a portion of the longitudinal timbers carrying the chairs and rails on the Drumlithie viaduct, and His Royal Highness, and the other passengers by the train, had an almost miraculous escape from the most serious consequences. I recommend that the permanent way be immediately renewed, and that, pending the completion of this work, the speed of the trains passing over it be reduced to 10 miles an hour.

Deterioration of another local bridge would not, however, be caught in time to prevent a major tragedy, and worldwide attention. It was owned by a rival company, the North British Railway, at Dundee, much further south.

Wheel and Axle Fractures

Other safety-critical components of locomotives were the wheels, or their tyres. They were the cause of many terrible railway accidents, and they can still cause mayhem, especially on fast trains, as the 1999 disaster at Eschede showed, with 101 victims killed when the derailed train hit a motorway bridge, which then collapsed on the train. They were a continual cause of accidents on the Victorian railways, owing to a combination of factors. They were obviously highly loaded parts of a train, especially so in the case of engine wheels, bearing the weight of increasingly heavy engines. Extra attention was needed to their design to ensure longevity. They were also visible to inspection, so faulty parts could be removed when found, unless hidden flaws were growing insidiously within the metal, or were hidden by the wheel bearings. Failure of the wheels themselves

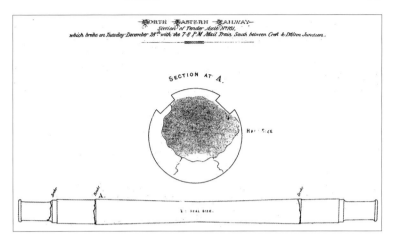

(9.1) Broken axle from Night Mail (Dalton Junction, 1869).

could also cause terrible accidents. Axles too were a frequent cause of serious accidents, especially as their loss deprived the vehicle of two wheels rather than just one.

Cold weather increased the likelihood of fracture, as Fairbairn had shown before the Royal Commission, as the following series of accidents shows quite vividly. The first occurred to the Night Mail train travelling south at Dalton Junction on the North-East Railway on 28 December 1869. The train consisted of an engine and tender, five carriages, two post offices and two brake vans. It left Darlington at 8.25 p.m., and after about four miles, and moving at 40mph towards Dalton Road bridge, the driver felt a sudden shock at the back of the engine. On looking around, he saw fire flying from the tender, and shut off the steam. The fireman couldn't apply the tender brake since the step to the brake had broken in the incident. The driver whistled for the guard's brakes, but did not reverse the engine for fear of damage to the carriages behind. The engine came to a dead stop in 220 yards from the point of alarm, and both guards and firemen went to the nearest stations to alert any oncoming trains of the blockage to the line. The engine was fine, but the tender had lost both leading wheels, an axle and axle-boxes, it stood upright with the other four wheels intact, but was off the rails. Most of the following vehicles were similarly damaged and off the track, damage being mainly confined to the wheel assemblies, but injuries were minimal, with only one passenger complaining. Six post office clerks were 'considerably shaken'. The tender axle was eventually found in four separate pieces, having fractured across the shaft ((9.1) lower) and the rails were severely damaged as well.

The axle was made of best Lowmoor wrought iron, and had run about 220,000 miles during its seven years' service (normal life was ten years or 300,000 miles). The fracture surface of the principal break at A in the figure, showed what is now called a slow growth region on the outer part of the diameter, with a fast growth section at the centre ((9.1) centre). Although Captain Tyler did not recognise the problem as fatigue he had seen many similar fracture surfaces in his career and attributed the break to the two key holes machined into the outer surface of the axle. He was quite right. The fatigue cracks probably grew from one or more of the sharp corners of the keyways, extending slowly around the circumference until the axle could no longer support its load, and the crack (or cracks) grew catastrophically. The load on an axle is complex, but involves both bending from the load in the vehicle above, and torsion from the rotation of the axle. He suggested that the four keyways rather than two be used, effectively spreading the load. Nowadays, the sharpness of the corners would also be reduced, so lessening the stress concentration. Thickening the shaft was done after this accident, and would have helped to lower stresses in the axle.

Newark Disaster, 1870

Axle failure could occur under any conditions, however, and could have devastating consequences for other trains too, if they happened to be passing at the wrong moment. This is just what happened on 21 June 1870, when an axle on a goods train broke suddenly, and a long excursion train ran into the debris, killing eighteen passengers, and injuring forty others of the up to 381 who had been travelling that night in the train's twenty-three carriages. The goods train was running south from Doncaster at midnight to London, and had just passed under Clay Lane bridge, when the driver felt a sudden jerk. The engine sprang away from the thirty-vehicle train behind him, so he closed the regulator and stepped down to find out what had happened. Just about the same time, he saw a passenger train with white headlights approaching at speed on the opposite line, and tried to warn the driver of a problem by waving his arms, but all to no avail. Apparently, he saw or heard nothing further, but having lost his train of wagons, brought the engine to a halt about 760 yards from the Clay Lane bridge. He descended the locomotive and returned along the line, finding the lead wagons 300 yards from his stopped engine (which he had now directed the fireman to follow slowly with the engine). He started coupling the wagons to the tender, but at that moment, a guard ran up and told him that a terrible accident had occurred further back on the line. The passenger train had smashed into some wagons, which had fouled the other line, creating an awful disaster.

So what had happened? The rear guard said that he had felt a sudden stoppage as he was passing under the bridge, being thrown forward by the jerk. When he went to investigate, he found seven wagons had derailed, with the end of one blocking the adjacent line. In the words of Captain Tyler:

> *… he had not gone ten yards. … before he saw the excursion train coming towards him, and heard the engine driver … whistling … either for the Newark signals or the Midland level crossing. He showed a red light to the engine-driver … and he saw the engine … strike the wagon … on the line. This wagon was on its side … with its wheels pointing southwards, and was forced back by … the collision against the other six wagons … it appears to have become jammed against [them and] grazed all the passenger carriages in succession as they passed … and caused some of the injury to the passengers. But the principal injuries were … received in the third, fourth and fifth vehicles next behind the tender … which, having run in between the three first on the off-side, and the engine on the near-side, were almost destroyed on the slope of the cutting west of the line.*

Tyler attempted to reconstruct what the excursion driver would have seen just before impact:

The night was dark, and the engine-driver of the excursion train, who can no longer speak for himself, would have seen no indication of danger until he was close upon the wagons which partly obstructed the down line. The engine which he met on the up line would have presented to him only the usual head lamps, consisting of two green lights. He would have seen nothing in the goods van but a white light from the front of the side-light on that van; and the red light from the hand-lamp of the goods guard would have been visible to him for a moment only before the collision occurred.

Further details emerged during his investigation of the remains. He gave a very precise description of the damage to the permanent way, saying that the section where the accident had happened had been relaid the previous year with new 21ft steel rails held by cast-iron chairs spiked into Baltic red timber. With no blame to anyone on the excursion train, the primary cause of the accident was due to the derailment of wagon No.3,238, which had been carrying 5 tons of potatoes. The leading axle had fractured, fell between the lines and derailed the following wagons, one of which blocked the down line. The excursion engine had hit the wagon, was forced off the line, and then hit the bridge, damaging the arch with its funnel in the process. The following carriages derailed and fell on one another in the cutting by the bridge.

The axle showed an extensive flaw, which 'had grown by degrees during the running of the axle'. The sound portion measured $2\frac{5}{8}$ to 3in across the fractures section, compared with the full diameter of $3\frac{7}{8}$in. Presumably Tyler meant that the fatigued area was at the outer edge, and the fast growth region to the centre he called 'sound', but which was of course incapable of supporting the imposed load of potatoes. There were no records for the axle (it was considered impracticable by the railway company, the Great Northern Railway), despite an earlier plea by Tyler after the Tilbury accident for a register to be kept for all axles. No doubt they would argue that the register should only apply to locomotive axles. There was thus no way of knowing its age or history. The axle had been examined by wagon inspectors and the greasers at Doncaster and Retford, but their tapping had shown the axles and wheels to be running cool, with nothing apparently untoward in the way of visible defects. He recommended that the thicker axles of $4\frac{1}{2}$in diameter, in use elsewhere, replace all the older and thinner axles. He did not recommend, however, that any kind of quality control measures be adopted by the manufacturer, the Patent Shaft and Axle Co., or any measures to identify their products by date of manufacture, or by batch number. The axle, in today's terminology, was untraceable. Neither did he ask for the company to re-evaluate the design to eliminate any stress raisers along the surface. Fatigue cracks usually started at the slight ridges in the shaft at the edge of the wheel journals, exacerbated by any tiny defects on the ridges. Yet again, fatigue had caused mayhem in what should have been a happy return journey for the excursion revellers.

Such terrible accidents caused by axle fractures, which had occurred since the opening of the railways, led a German engineer, August Wohler, to conduct very detailed research into the problem, leading to design guidance for axles. He built machines which could test axles under bending and rotation, to simulate real use, and he also produced maps of the fracture surfaces to show how fatigue cracks grew with time.

Hatfield and Oxford

Problems occurred with similar frequency on the wheels themselves, and especially so during cold weather when the toughness of the wrought iron diminished.

Just such a tyre fracture occurred on Boxing Day 1870 at Hatfield on the Great North line. The driver of the 4.25 p.m. train from Kings Cross to Peterborough felt a series of oscillations when passing over a level crossing at Marshmoor, and, looking back, saw that he had lost his train. The tyre of the left-hand leading wheel on the vehicle behind the engine had fractured, and the wheel disintegrated, together with the coupling to the engine. The leading vehicle and two following carriages derailed, and ran into the road, killing the mother and sister of a railwayman standing there. Six passengers in the two carriages were also killed. The tyre had been riveted to the wheel, and the inspector recommended the use of Mansell wooden composite wheels.

One of the most horrific accidents occurred at Oxford on the afternoon of Christmas Eve 1874, when a packed passenger train derailed just north of Kidlington, killing thirty-four and injuring sixty-nine passengers. The event was undoubtedly made more difficult by the cold and snow present on the ground at the time. It was the worst accident to happen on the Great Western Railway to date (after the collision at Shrivenham in 1848, when six died), and occurred because a wheel cracked and disintegrated on an old third-class carriage (No.845) while the train was moving at a speed of about 40mph. The subsequent investigation, however, showed that the small four-wheeler carriage just behind the main locomotive, was held upright for a considerable time on its three remaining wheels by the couplings with the other carriages. The Railway Inspector, Colonel Yolland, was able to trace the course of the damaged wheel by the debris left on the track for a distance of 370 yards, before the *dénouement*.

What happened was this: the long train of fifteen vehicles (180 yards) was moving along the straight towards a small bridge over the Oxford Canal under power from two engines, when both drivers realised simultaneously that something was wrong. One driver (Richardson) saw the communication cord shake, and snow and dirt being thrown up on the right-hand side of the train, while the fireman of the pilot engine saw a man leaning from the carriage window on the left-hand side seeking his attention by shouting 'Whoa, Whoa'. Richardson shut off the steam, reversed the engine and whistled for the brakes to the guards van. The other driver did the same, and both firemen applied the brakes on their tenders. The coupling with carriage 845 fractured, and both engines raced ahead leaving the rest of the train behind them. All the carriages and vans were derailed, the unfortunate carriage 845 being completely demolished, almost without trace, according to Colonel Yolland.

The remains were scattered along the track and beside the embankment above the flood plain of the river Cherwell, near the small village of Shipton, close to the wooden bridge over the canal *(9.2)*. The bridge was severely damaged by the impact from some of the carriages, but fortunately remained intact. It was very similar in design to the Wootton bridge, but presumably without cast-iron girders supporting the floor. If it had failed, the casualty list might have been even greater. After the accident, the guard and some surviving passengers went back to Woodstock Road station to warn the oncoming cheap train of the disaster, and prevent it from crashing into the wrecks. The pilot engine went forward to the next station to issue a similar warning. There was some delay in

(9.2) Shipton
disaster: wreck of
the train at the
Oxford Canal.

rescuing survivors owing to the bad weather and the destruction of the telegraph line next to the track, but workers from the local paper mill sheltered them, and others were taken to Hampton Gay manor house close to the track. Lord Randolph Churchill and several ladies from Blenheim Palace (near Woodstock) assisted the survivors with food and cordials. Most of the passengers were travelling for Christmas, and included a number of students from nearby Oxford University (some of whom died).

Careful inspection of the track after the accident revealed the cause: the broken tyre from carriage 845 *(9.3)*. The tyre had in fact broken in two places on the rim. One piece was about 3ft, and the other about 8ft long, having been stripped from the wheel rim. Both were transverse or radial fractures, one near the letter 'R' in the 'LOWMOOR' stamp on the side of the tyre (it had been supplied by the Lowmoor Iron Co. in 1865, and fitted in 1868), partly in a weld. The tyre had been attached to the rim by four rivets, countersunk on the tread, and three had broken in the accident. The other fracture occurred in the solid, but no fracture surfaces were supplied with the official report, or any close-up pictures of the breaks. This would have been useful since the report mentions small flaws found in the metal.

Colonel Yolland was so concerned about the number of such tyre failures that he summarised previous reports from the Inspectorate. There had been twenty-six accidents between 1847 and 1857 caused by broken tyres, and fifty-four accidents since 1857. Most of them involved riveted tyres, and they had called for better designs to be used in several of their reports. In an accident on 28 January 1861 on the Shrewsbury line, a very similar derailment had occurred, with two deaths and four injured passengers. They quoted the following passage:

It is certainly unquestionable … that the tyres of wheels on locomotive engines, carriages, and wagons are particularly liable to break during severe frost; and the cold of the present winter has caused a very large number of these fractures, and the accumulation of a large quantity of broken and disabled carriages and wagons at many of the principal stations. Experience has also established the fact that these fractures almost invariably take place either at the holes through which the tyres are bolted or riveted on to the

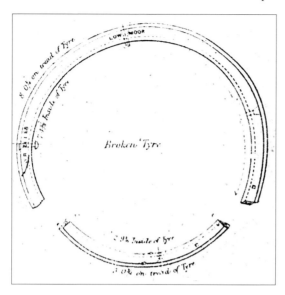

(9.3) Remains of the broken tyre from carriage 845.

inner rim of the wheel, at the weld where that is in any way defective, or at some part of the tyre where there may have been some flaw…

The statement reflects the way fatigue cracks usually start at stress raisers such as holes, or flaws, which raise the local stress above the breaking strength of the metal. As Fairbairn had shown at the Royal Commission of 1849, iron lost strength at low temperatures, and enough to embrittle normally tough wrought iron. They advised railway companies to change their practices, and use the many types of wheel which were not riveted through the rim, and which if they did fail, did not result in loss of the tyre. Their advice had not just been ignored, but actually reversed by the GWR. After an earlier tyre accident, they had replaced riveted tyres, but then started using them again. GWR responded by blaming another railway company they had taken over, who had brought a stock of old carriages into their system. Such a lack of a uniform policy across the many railway companies was clearly working against public safety.

The absence of a continuous braking system was another feature of the accident to which they drew attention. Again they listed a series of serious accidents where poor braking was involved. At Shipton, derailment was caused not so much by the broken tyre but by the reactions of the drivers to the alarm. Because they braked hard, coach 845 had been totally destroyed by the momentum of the following train, and had effectively derailed the rest of the carriages, creating mayhem. The GWR had removed a rule from their regulation book stipulating that trains should not be allowed to proceed without efficient brakes. Continuous air brakes had been fitted by other large companies, such as the LNWR (the successor to the L&BR), and once again, lack of investment in the technology had turned what would have been a minor incident into a major disaster.

The final criticism made by Yolland concerned the poor communications between the engine driver and the rest of the train. The cord had failed to ring the gong in the engine cab, probably due to faulty adjustment; a broken pulley found in one carriage had not been at fault, since the driver had seen the cord shake. The system was unsatisfactory, and the Inspectorate had previously recommended a telegraph system for all trains. The LNWR, for example, maintained such a system on the Royal Train, and it had proved successful. The system then in place on most railways provided an external mechanical connection between the vehicles, and in the future it would bring the cord inside, making it more accessible to all passengers in an emergency; a link to the continuous air brakes would also make it much more reliable in stopping a train.

Colonel Yolland concluded that the drivers could not be blamed for the disaster, but rather the fault lay in the poorly equipped train, and the use of an old carriage carrying passengers just behind the engine. Earlier reports from them had recommended that an empty carriage be put behind the engine, an opinion which went back to the Sonning disaster of Christmas Eve 1841. The immediate cause of the accident was a broken tyre on an old wheel of a type which had caused many previous accidents. Their circular to the railway companies prompted by the Shipwell accident had revealed that many companies had replaced such riveted wheels by wooden composite wheels, such as the Mansell wheel. It was more reliable, and stood up better to damage like the loss of the tyre. The accident at Shipwell had turned into a major disaster because of the lack of continuous brakes, and poor communications between the drivers and the rest of the train, both problems being solvable with existing technology.

The brake problem was to lead to a new Royal Commission later in the decade, and the railways would ultimately adopt the Westinghouse pneumatic system, which relied on a pressure supply of air to all vehicles, so that the brakes were kept free. If the pressure dropped for any reason, the brakes were applied automatically and continuously, bringing the train to a smooth halt.

The *Illustrated London News* report of the disaster lamented the fate of the victims, when it quoted the words of their artist, who had been sent to the scene to sketch the remains. His words do more than anything else to remind us of the personal consequences of such horrific accidents:

> *Leaving the carriage and retracing my steps along the line, I went down a path of slush and mire to a range of low buildings, where the most painful part of my duty was to be accomplished. Passing the policeman at the door, I entered … a low, bare, whitewashed cellar with deep-set windows of small squares of glass, through which the dim light struggled, adding a gloom to the awful spectacle of twenty-six mutilated corpses lying in grim array on their beds of straw, awaiting identification for the inquest before their removal. There are times in every man's life when all the fortitude of his nature must be subdued by the will; yet with all the determination I could command to overcome the effects of the scene, I found myself weak to struggle against the emotions that awoke within me as I looked on the silent forms of husband, wife, brother and sister stretched before me, crushed and battered out of existence, without a moment's notice, and in the full tide of expectant joy.*

There would be similar scenes at Abbots Ripton in January 1876, when critical signals were stuck in the 'line clear' position by snow and ice, culminating in the worst ever tragedy, at the bridge over the Tay near Dundee, when there were over seventy-five victims. Unlike the earlier disasters, however, many of the bodies of the Tay victims would never be found at all.

The Tay Bridge

The Tay bridge had been long planned by Thomas Bouch, a railway engineer of great experience. It would eliminate at a stroke the lengthy detour for train passengers to Dundee from Edinburgh caused by the estuary of the river Tay. The Firth of Forth was another obstacle to be tackled, but that would be taken on after the Tay had been bridged.

The bridge was beset by problems from the start. Contractors went broke, and the foundations were found to be less than adequate to support the brick piers planned for the viaduct. Since the bridge needed to span more than two miles of estuary, this was a very serious setback for the whole project. Bouch responded by replacing the heavy brick and stone piers needed for the high route (over 80ft above the waters of the estuary) with a cast-iron pipe spaceframe. He had already built just such a bridge across a deep valley in the Pennines at Belah in 1862, and the technology was proven and tested, ever since the magnificent Crumlin viaduct had been built in South Wales in 1857 by Thomas Kennard. The design had also been used by Gustav Eiffel in the Massif Central in France, for a single track railway. He had built several such pipe bridges to cross deep valleys. All such bridges were braced together by wrought-iron tie bars in specially made joints with the brittle cast-iron columns.

So it seemed a reasonable design change to make at the time. It would save costs and time since such structures could be erected quickly by fitters. There would also be a substantial saving in material, but the consequences of the change would in the end be catastrophic. In the first place, the piers of the centre section (high girders section) were to be 257ft apart to support massive wrought-iron girders weighing over 300 tons each span. Each pier in the new design would now weigh just over 100 tons, so a simple calculation should have revealed that the towering structures were very top heavy, and even more so with a heavy train travelling over the bridge.

There was another problem, again not recognised as such at the time. The cast-iron pipe towers were braced by tough wrought-iron bars connected to the base and top of each individual column. Best practice from the previous experience of such viaducts dictated that the connections be separate from the column itself, such as a wrought-iron strap around the circumference of the column, a separate cast-iron collar, or by a joint well below the flange. Someone, however, decided to further economise by integrating the joint into the column itself. So the joint at the column was formed from cast iron, well known as a very brittle material. Whether Bouch approved of the new design remains to this day unknown. The straps were tested by David Kirkaldy using his 300-ton hydraulic test machine at Southwark, and approved. The straps proved very strong, but the critical joints were not tested at all, until well after the disaster.

Bridge in Action

The bridge was finished in September 1878, tested in February by General Hutchinson of the Inspectorate, and approved for public use. It was opened for public traffic in June of that year, and proved a tremendous success. It became a tourist attraction in its own right owing to its great length (over two miles end-to-end) and the vistas it offered. All the usual politicians and worthies visited to admire the structure, but worrying signs of deterioration had begun to be noticed that autumn. The man in charge of maintenance was Henry Noble, previously employed by Bazalgette on the London sewage works.

While visiting the many piers to check their foundations, he heard the tie bars 'chattering'. The tie bars were fitted with joints along their length by which they could be put into tension. It was achieved by hammering wrought-iron pins (called cotters) into a space cut into the bar itself and two short bars connecting to the column joint. Normally the space would be small due to overlap of the bars, but hammering in the wedges caused the space to become bigger, so tensioning the joint. If they were rattling in the joint, they had become loose and were therefore no longer acting correctly. Noble reacted by inserting shims of thin metal to stop the rattling (bought at his own expense), which of course effectively froze the joints into an untensioned state. They could no longer brace the columns, so they were free to move if stimulated by other forces. Noble failed to notify Bouch, a negligent action since he was contracted to report any problem directly to the engineer of the bridge.

Next summer, the bridge was repainted from end to end, and further concerns were raised, although again apparently not transmitted to Bouch. Train travellers noticed that when trains were crossing from south to north, they frequently exceeded the 25mph limit imposed by the BoT. Speeds of up to 40mph were measured by some passengers. It induced lateral sway and other unexpected movements in the carriages. Meanwhile, the painters experienced lateral movements of the high girder piers, on the highest towers of the entire bridge. Often by as much as several inches, the movements occurred as trains approached, and the painters had to hang on by any possible means to prevent being thrown from the towers into the estuary below. Queen Victoria crossed the bridge that summer on her return from Balmoral *(9.4)*.

The structure of the high girders at the centre of the bridge was becoming unstable, mainly because the joints had worked their way loose under repeated vibrations from the traffic overhead. The worst damage was probably done by the northbound trains, speeding on the straight before braking hard on the bend, and steep incline into Tay Bridge station. Bouch was knighted that summer together with Henry Bessemer, an ironic pairing of eminent engineers, particularly in view of subsequent events.

A storm had been building from the west on Sunday 28 December 1879, and it reached a crescendo as the express train from Edinburgh arrived at the south end of the bridge, near to 7 p.m. The previous train across had been a local service, and had suffered severe buffeting from the westerly wind blowing down the estuary. Sparks were seen coming from the wheels, either meeting the guard rail as they heeled over, or by something much more sinister. If the high girders had become loose, then it is likely that they were swaying again both by the action of the wind and the train crossing through them. The train was given approval to proceed over the bridge, an amazing decision given the strength of the storm. This was the last to be seen of the train for many months.

Disaster Strikes!

The centre section collapsed completely as the train was passing through the high girders *(9.5)*. Although the wind was strong that night, the Official Inquiry found that it was not a hurricane as some authors have tried to suggest. All aboard the train were lost: over seventy-five souls including all passengers and the crew. There were several witnesses, but their testimony was contradictory, hardly surprising given that it was night and a storm was raging down the estuary.

The Inquiry was established in a week, chaired by Henry Rothery (commissioner for Wrecks) with Colonel Yolland representing the Inspectorate, and William H. Barlow the Institution of Civil Engineers. They inspected the piers from which most of the towers had collapsed, visiting them by boat. There were two partly intact tiers which gave a clue to how the collapse had occurred. They were strewn with broken cast-iron lugs which had attached the east–west or lateral tie bars to the columns, and had broken in the initial stages of the disaster. With loss of this bracing, the towers were completely destabilised and split into two parts, which then fell into the estuary. The exact sequence of the fall, whether the towers fell from the north or the south, could not be established. Latent defects were exposed in the fractured lugs: the bolt holes were tapered, so all the bracing load fell at the edge of the hole, increasing the local stress, and hence the chance of failure. The lugs should have been drilled to give a straight hole, and so spread the applied load. Recent examination of the debris piles on the piers shows that all lugs were tapered, the only drill holes being those through the flanges of the narrower columns. David Kirkaldy tested intact parts from the standing tiers, and confirmed the low strength of the lower lugs: they were just a third of the strength they should have been. We now know that a

(9.4) Queen Victoria crossing the Tay bridge, June 1879.

(9.5) The fallen Tay bridge, with the entire centre section collapsed.

circular hole produces a stress concentration factor of three. The strength was also very variable, due to the presence of blowholes and other defects of the cast iron. Recent analysis of the debris, performed by enlarging the high-quality photographs taken at the time by Valentines of Dundee for the Inquiry, show features that can be explained by a fatigue mechanism. The visible evidence of the remains taken just about a week after the disaster, indicates that the entire high girder section was oscillating from side to side as a result of wind pressure on the train as it entered the section during the storm. The oscillations were most violent at the north end, so it may have fallen first. The train was trapped between the fourth and fifth piers and fell almost intact vertically down within the wrought-iron girders of the span.

No bodies were found in the train, but a number were collected from the waters of the estuary as time went by. Many bodies were never recovered. After six months' deliberation, the Inquiry concluded that the disaster was caused by a bridge which had been:

> … *badly designed, badly built and badly maintained…*

The recently knighted Sir Thomas Bouch was blamed by name, and he died a few months later.

The Inspectorate did not get off lightly, however. General Hutchinson had approved the bridge for public use, but was saved by several key points in his report. It was he who had imposed a speed limit on trains on the bridge, which had been violated by the North British drivers. He had also commented that he would want to see the effect of a side wind on the structure, but had not been able to do so before the bridge fell. President of the BoT, Joseph Chamberlain, was forced to defend the Inspectorate in the House of Commons.

A new bridge was planned to replace the original, and was built a short distance away by W.H. Barlow and his son Crawford Barlow *(9.5)*. The original piers were left in place to act as breakwaters for the new piers, which were built using steel and wrought iron. It opened for two-way traffic in 1880, and it assumed the title of 'longest bridge in the world'. Bouch had been planning a suspension bridge to cross the Firth of Forth, but it was abandoned after the Inquiry report was produced. A quite different design was chosen: a cantilever bridge using riveted steel tubes. It was designed by Benjamin Baker and John Fowler, and has become an icon of engineering skill and achievement.

All of Bouch's many bridges were inspected and some strengthened where necessary. Another would be demolished entirely. A Royal Commission on Wind Pressure was announced and it reported in 1881, making a call for further research on the problem. Designers would have to evaluate wind pressure as an extra design parameter for large structures.

Kinzua, 2003

Some interesting new evidence on iron viaducts has emerged. An old viaduct at Kinzua, Pennsylvania, collapsed on 21 July 2003 when it was struck by a tornado *(9.6)*. Originally built of wrought iron in 1882, it was rebuilt in steel in 1902, and supported a 2,054ft-long single railway track in the Pennsylvanian Allegeny hills for the Erie railroad. There were twenty high towers in the structure, rising to over 300ft above the valley floor. It closed to freight traffic in 1957, and was being renovated at the time the storm struck the bridge. The tie bars and columns of the viaduct were badly rusted, so needed restoration.

The bridge was struck at about 3.15 p.m. by an F1 tornado. It was established by the investigation held after the event that the structure swayed several times from side to side. The investigators estimated that a 94mph wind acted to produce a force of 39 tons on the top of the highest tower, but that the wind speed was probably much higher. Unlike the Tay bridge disaster, however, eleven of the central towers fell almost intact, having sheared from their rusted base bolts. The joints in the towers remained largely unaffected, although many were destroyed by impact with the valley floor. Most of the original base joints had been retained for the 1900 viaduct, and a majority showed old fatigue cracks of the collars holding the bolts. The rest had failed in a ductile fashion by overload after the collapse had started. Renovation work had not attempted to replace the base bolts before the accident, but fortunately there were no casualties.

So, high winds can bring large structures down, and catastrophic failure is most likely if the structure has been badly designed, or has deteriorated from corrosion and fatigue of critical joints. The Kinzua viaduct was well designed originally, and the towers were braced against lateral wind action by a broad base tapering up to the narrow railroad track. However, it could not withstand the huge forces unleashed by tornado action, a quite unexpected event for this quiet area of a northern US state.

Montrose Bridge

Bouch had been building a smaller version of the Tay bridge to cross the estuary of the river Esk at Montrose further north on the main line to Aberdeen. It was 1,400ft long, comprising thirty spans of 47ft, built on cast-iron columns just like the Tay bridge. The piers were much lower, however, being at the most only four tiers high, carrying a single

(9.6) Remains of the Kinzua railroad viaduct, Pennsylvania.

line track a maximum of 48ft above the river. It was inspected by Colonel Yolland, and he presented his report in November 1880. Most of the piers consisted of four columns, two vertical and two raking, attached at their tops just under the wrought-iron girder spans, similar to the northern end of the Tay bridge as it approached Dundee station. There were three larger piers formed from four vertical and four raking columns at the highest point of the viaduct.

The piers were built on cast-iron piles screwed into the river bed. The columns were braced with wrought-iron tie bars attached to the same design of lug as had been used on the Tay bridge. The viaduct had been finished in October 1879, just before the fall of the larger structure. Bouch had ordered that all the cast-iron lugs be drilled after the disaster, and larger bolts used to give a more even purchase. Additional bracing had also been inserted into the piers. With an eye for detail and the revelations of the defects of the parent structure, Yolland found further problems in the Montrose bridge. The columns did not fit one another at all well. Although there was a spigot on the end of a column which would fit into the hollow of another, there was an area of metal above the level of the joint so that flanges did not fit tightly to one another. However, the general state of the cast iron appeared good, but he could obviously not comment on the inner structure of the metal.

The foundations of the bridge were faulty. After some use by trains, it was found that the girders did not rest uniformly on the piers. Some of the piers had sunk into the bed of the river, leaving gaps between the pier tops and the lower edge of the spans. Yolland observed that although the track was a straight line, the piles were not straight or fixed at right angles to the line. He noticed, for example, that one pile was not in line with the column above, so that the metal parts of the flanged joint were not parallel. Yolland made the general comment about the bridge:

> *One obvious defect of the structure as erected is the insecurity of the foundations, but that in my opinion is of far less importance than its general design and the nature of the material (cast iron) with which the piers have been constructed. The evidence brought before the Court of Inquiry that investigated the causes*

that produced the fall of the Tay bridge, fully proved that cast iron in columns of small diameter could not be relied on … The Court of Inquiry were unable to state positively what was the actual cause of that accident, or to say for a certainty that it was not caused by fracture of one of the vertical columns in one of the piers which fell; and so in this viaduct, the fracture of one of the vertical columns, in anyone of the piers, might possibly cause the viaduct to fall, and on that ground, I am of the opinion, that piers constructed of cast iron columns should not in future be sanctioned by the Board of Trade.

This is an interesting comment by one of the commissioners of the Tay Inquiry, suggesting that column failure in the high girders could have caused the disaster. A few cracked columns had been found in other parts of the structure, but this new theory did not receive support from his colleagues on the panel. Since the bulk of the high girder piers now lay at the bottom of the Tay, they had not been examined. In any case, how would it be possible to distinguish between original cracks and those formed in the accident?

He went on to mention that a new project for an overhead railway line in Liverpool had proposed a six-mile viaduct of cast-iron columns about 20ft in height. Yolland had objected, and the engineer had at once redesigned the structure in wrought iron. Like the Tay bridge, there was no protection at the side of the track to prevent a derailed train from falling over the side, and Yolland wanted something substantial here. Even the use of a second, or check rail came under his scrutiny. There had been a recent accident at Southall when wagons had been derailed by a chain caught in the gap between the two rails.

The bridge would, on his recommendation, have to be completely demolished and a better structure put in its place. The shadow cast by the Tay disaster was long indeed.

Solway Viaduct Collapse

There were other cast-iron column viaducts on the national rail network. One of the longest crossed the Solway firth, and had been built near Annan in 1868 and opened for single line traffic in 1870. It was also to suffer the forces of Nature, but in a quite different and totally unexpected way.

It was over a mile long at 1,940 yards, and comprised 181 single piers and twelve double piers. Each single pier was made of five 12ft columns, three inside vertical and the outer two raked so as to buttress the pier against lateral loads. The columns were braced together with wrought iron connected to the struts, with no cast-iron lugs. The double piers were simply two single piers braced together.

Major Marindin reported on the events of January 1881, when ice floes coming down the river destroyed key parts of the bridge. He and General Hutchinson would inspect together every stage of the construction of the Forth bridge to be built by Baker, Fowler and Arrol. But again there had been indications of problems in the bridge before its eventual collapse, the first serious damage having occurred in the winter of 1875−76. No less than thirty-three columns were found cracked, probably by thawing of the ice within the columns. Ice has a maximum volume at about 4°C, so that ice at 0°C, will expand as the temperature rises. If constrained by solid walls, then the internal force exerted can easily crack many containment materials, as many house owners know when they discover plumbing leaks after a heavy frost. Remedial measures of the time included replacing the vertical columns and hooping the raking columns affected since the cracks ran up the length of a column. Holes were bored to allow water to escape.

The severe weather of late January 1881, however, caused much greater problems. The country was struck by the worst winter weather for many years. In London, the Thames was frozen over (exploited by skaters when the weather had subsided), and one of the highest tides ever recorded had flooded parts of the capital. Many piers and jetties were destroyed by the ice, and several ships sunk in the docks. The storm had produced severe blizzards throughout the country, wrecking 131 ships, and many sailors lost their lives. The severe weather undoubtedly contributed to the damage to the Solway bridge.

Two columns and thirteen braces were found to be cracked on 19 January, and they were all repaired. But only six days later, a thaw started, and ice floes started floating into the estuary. This time, the cracks were lateral rather than longitudinal, and impossible to hoop. By 29 January, large blocks from 6 to 18ft thick were knocking against the piers on a tide running at 10mph. By late afternoon, the blows of the ice could be felt on the superstructure, and the noise could be heard a mile away. Damage was not as severe as anticipated, however, and a few passenger trains were allowed across. But the following day, workmen in a hut on the bridge heard piers collapsing. In the words of one of them:

> I remained on duty all night with three other men, ready to commence repairing the damages as soon as the tide went down. We were in a hut over No 68 pier (a double pier). Between 3 and 5 am upon Sunday I heard the piers cracking. I said to the men 'It's time to be off; every man for himself', and we went to the shore. When it was light we found some piers had fallen but no girders. We had felt the ice bumping in the night, but I had not any fear about the hut coming down.

Four piers had, in fact, fallen totally, leaving the track suspended in mid-air. The situation could only deteriorate as the tides ebbed and flowed with the ever larger floes. One beached floe was actually measured at 27 yards in area, by 6ft thick! At noon on 1 February, fourteen piers collapsed in a powerful spring tide. Soon after a large part of the centre of the viaduct fell, leaving a large gap in the centre of the bridge. The bridge was a wreck. Marindin commented on the cause of the slow-motion collapse:

> This disaster furnishes a very convincing proof of the unreliability of small cast iron columns when used for the piers of viaducts in positions where they are likely to be subjected to any blow or sudden shock; and, as it was proved with the fate of the Tay Bridge that they are equally unreliable in cases where they are exposed to heavy transverse strains from wind pressure, it must be evident that, whether for high viaducts exposed to wind, or for viaducts across estuaries in this climate, where they are subjected to sudden changes in temperature and to blows from floating ice, it would be far better in future to avoid any such mode of construction.

It was an unusually severe winter in 1881; locals said that they had never experienced similar conditions, others that it was the worst since 1814. Exceptional weather scuppered

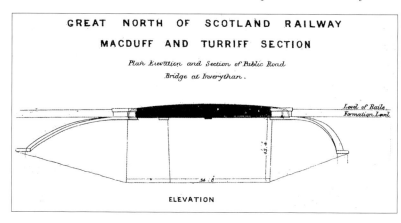

(9.7)
Inverythan
cast-iron girder
bridge.

the viaduct, and reinforced the message from the Tay. Cast iron was a poor material for bridges. The bridge was abandoned, and the line closed for ever. It must have been a great disappointment for the engineer, James Brunlees, who had appeared as an expert witness at the Tay Inquiry the previous year. In his defence of the design, he pointed out that he had built two similar but shorter viaducts across parts of Morecambe Bay without such problems. But then they hadn't experienced such problems with floating ice as the Solway Firth.

The bridge took a year to rebuild, and finally closed in the 1920s. Some of the cast-iron columns still remain on the coast, a forlorn reminder of its former glory.

Inverythan Collapse, 1882

There was more to come after the collapse of the Tay and Solway bridges by a combination of natural forces and poor design along with the demolition of the bridge at Montrose. Numerous small viaducts had been installed on the Highland line covering parts of north-eastern Scotland when it was built in 1857. Many were made from cast-iron girders, rather than wrought iron (which was available for bridges at the time thanks to Fairbairn's research). They were of relatively low cost, being made from a few large castings or girders, and sometimes braced with wrought-iron straps.

On 27 November 1882, a train was approaching just such a skew viaduct near Inverythan on the track from Aberdeen to Banff. The bridge was about 39ft long and about 15ft high over a road. It was a single line track, so the bridge was only about 10ft wide (section at (9.7), plan at (9.8)). The track was supported by wooden beams laid on the lower flanges of the massive castings used to form the main structure. Each of the two main spans were made from two castings bolted together at the centre of the bridge. Each casting was curved upwards towards the centre, so as to counteract the greatest load there, and the central joint was reinforced underneath by a wrought-iron boss. It was a mixed freight and passenger train, with five loaded wagons and four carriages. As the locomotive passed over, one of the girders suddenly collapsed into the road below. Although the engine reached the far side safely, most of the train fell into the gap, instantly killing four

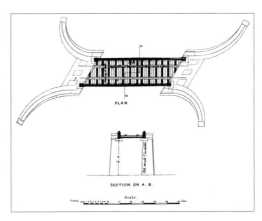

(9.8) Plan of Inverythan bridge.

passengers *(9.9)*. Another passenger died soon afterwards, and fourteen others were badly injured. Major Marindin conducted the investigation, a most thorough one as it turned out. A new attitude was evident among the Inspectorate after the Tay bridge disaster.

The casting had broken not at the centre joint but rather just by the side of it, as shown in *(9.10)*. It was a simple vertical crack running up from the bottom flange to the top of the girder, and inspection showed a very large, but hidden, blowhole at the thickest part of the section, where the flanges met the web. It was also clear that this defect had cracked some time before, judging by old rust marks on the face of the crack. This region could easily be distinguished from the fresh fracture surface caused at the moment of the accident. Samples were cut from the broken girder for testing by David Kirkaldy in Southwark, who had previously tested the many samples from the Tay Bridge for the Official Inquiry in Dundee. While cores were being taken by drilling holes in the sample, it suddenly fractured along the line of holes, showing that there was a considerable level of 'residual stress' *(9.11)*. This is commonly encountered in many products, and is usually caused by manufacturing methods. Some parts of the product will be in a dangerous tensile state, balanced by other parts in compression. In this case, with the cast-iron girder, it was probably produced by uneven shrinkage in the original casting as it cooled from the melt, and will have lowered the failure stress by a considerable margin, over and above the stress-raising effects of the blowhole and its slowly growing brittle crack. Kirkaldy's tests showed a wide variation in tensile strength, the lowest of about 4.5 tsi from a sample taken near the fractured flange, the mean being 7.5 tsi.

So much for the causes, but what about the effects? A survey of bridges on the Great North of Scotland lines showed some 331 cast-iron bridges in operation, but of variable length and structure. Only eight were actually of similar double structure, and no doubt they were inspected and replaced as quickly as possible. There must have been considerable disruption to traffic while they were being replaced, perhaps similar to the disruptions which occurred after the Hatfield crash of 2000, although more restricted in scale. On the other hand, did other companies read and take action on the many other cast-iron bridges on their networks? Was north-east Scotland too remote for the accident to be ignored and then forgotten? No one could blame the Inspectorate this time for having done a rushed or skimped enquiry. On the contrary, it was detailed and pointed.

(9.9) The accident at Inverythan.

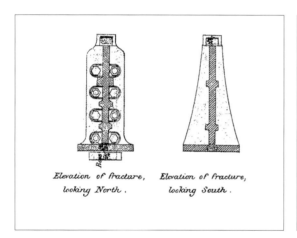 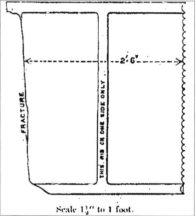

Above left: (9.10) The broken cast-iron girder at Inverythan.

Above right: (9.11) Sample of girder taken for testing which broke during drilling.

(9.12) Norwood Junction accident, 1891.

The examination of the broken parts was scrupulous, and made good use of Kirkaldy and his test apparatus. Earlier reports done on mechanical failures often omitted critical details of the fracture surfaces, which is perhaps why the mystery of the exploding boilers remained unsolved for so long before the penny dropped.

The Board of Trade refused to approve any new cast-iron bridges under the tracks (apart from the well tried and tested arch bridges) with effect from August 1883. They also circulated all railway companies in 1885, about the dangers of cast iron, and asked what steps were being made to ensure the safety of existing bridges. The response is unknown, but it is clear from one later development, that the circular had been ignored by at least one company.

Norwood Junction, 1891

The world found out how companies had reacted when another cast-iron under-bridge collapsed under a train on the Southern network near London. Fortunately, no one was killed or injured, and the accident had a salutary effect on complacent railway companies to examine their cast-iron structures, and replace them.

It happened on 1 May 1891, as a Brighton express train was approaching the bridge over the Portland Road at Norwood Junction on the London, Brighton & South Coast Railway. It was moving at about 40mph as it arrived over the cast-iron under-bridge at about 8.45 a.m. It was an all-first-class train. The locomotive *The Hayling* was an 0-4-2 type and the train was known as *The City Ltd*, which was presumably a reference to its first-class clientele. As soon as the driver sensed something amiss, he applied the Westinghouse brakes, and brought the engine to a halt. *(9.12)* It was derailed but still upright and had crossed the bridge safely, as had most of the carriages with their precious cargo. However, the brake van ran back into the hole created by the fracture, ending up in a vertical position, suspended from the last carriage and held in the festoon created by the sagging rails. There were no serious casualties, apart from one passenger's dislocated ankle; everyone on board was very shaken by their near-miss, however. There was some dramatic testimony from one of the signalmen (James Sawyers) in the box nearby:

> *The train approached the bridge at about 9.41 am, and was approaching at its usual speed with signals off, quite 40 miles per hour, when I heard a loud report like a cannon exploding. I was near the south end of the cabin at the time, but not looking southward, until I heard the report, and then on looking down I saw that there was a hole in the bridge on the west side, from which the woodwork had all gone, and I heard from the noise of scrunching and grinding that the train was off the rails.*

The investigation was conducted by the redoubtable General Hutchinson, by now familiar with cast iron and all its foibles. The cause was similar to that at Inverythan: a large blowhole at the junction of the web and lower flange of the girder. It was completely hidden from external view, which would otherwise have prevented its use. The Horsley foundry of Tipton, which made the girder, would later apologise for supplying it. There had been many changes in the bridge here, all of them variants in cast iron *(9.13)*.

(9.13) The broken cast-iron girder bridge at Norwood.

The first bridge was built in the late 1830s when the line was introduced here by the London & Croydon Railway Co. There were two cast-iron girders spanning 20ft over the road. It was enlarged in 1852 for another track, the span remaining the same. Then, in 1859, it was rebuilt when the station was constructed, the span widened to 25ft and expanded to no less than seven lines. Each line was supported by two main girders across the gap, and then by cross girders every 3ft along their length. The cross girders were formed from two lengths of rail bolted together, but separated by a baulk between them, and were 9.75ft long. They rested on the lower flanges of the main girders, into specially designed sockets cast into them. The main girders were 30ft long, with ten such sockets on the inner flange. The flanges were asymmetrical, the inner being 13.25in wide, the outer 5in wide, with a web of 1.5 to 1.75in. The girders were 27in deep and their flanges varied in thickness from 1.5in at the outside to 1.75in at the web.

The failed girder was on the west side of the up main line, and it had broken into three pieces as a result of the fracture. The primary fracture occurred 1.75ft from the centre of the girder, forming two large fragments 13.75 and 11.75ft long. They fell into the road below. The third piece about 4.5ft long was left hanging from the north abutment. The central fracture was nearly vertical (just like that at Inverythan) and close to the inside of one of the cast-in sockets.

The fracture surface exposed a very large blowhole within the girder. Although no picture is provided in the report, the description shows just how large it was. It was shaped like the letter L extending up 7in in the web from 0.5in at the base, and extending into the inner flange by 5in. The hole was about an inch in width and 0.5in deep, although it was 3in deep at one point. The flaw met the surface of the web, but was hidden from view by a thin sheet of wrought iron placed over it during casting. The iron sheet was placed there to support that part of the mould between gussets, and remained there when supplied to the railway company in 1860.

PUNCH, OR THE LONDON CHARIVARI.—August 1, 1891.

ON THE BRIDGE!

(9.14) Punch cartoon
of the cracked bridge
problem.

Two other similar cast-iron girders in another part of the bridge had fractured in 1876, when an engine had run onto the flooring from a siding. There were no rails in position at the time of the previous incident, and the broken girders had been replaced. It was yet another example of the known weakness of cast-iron girders on rail under-bridges, and one wonders what other incidents there were which went unreported to the Inspectorate. It seemed similar to the fracture of the underbridge at Staplehurst in 1865, when the boat train left the rails, and derailed passenger carriages. As events on the Dee bridge showed, cracks could occur without major loading, for example by fitment loads.

Hutchinson then went on to analyse the strength of the girder, and the effect of the major flaw near the centre. As the Inverythan accident showed, this was the worst possible place for a serious defect, simply because the greatest tensile load from passing trains occurred here, at the centre of the beam.

What Happened to Cast-iron Under-bridges?

A second BoT circular was issued shortly after the Norwood accident, asking all railway companies for the number and type of bridges on their lines. After the Inverythan accident, little had been done to inspect and replace old cast-iron girder under-bridges, perhaps because it was far away, on an obscure line with apparently little relevance to the bulk of the railways. How wrong they were. Because the Norwood accident happened on a fast commuter line into London with a rich and vocal clientele, close to the workings of government, the BoT were chivvied into action very rapidly. Even *Punch* raised the problem of weak bridges in a cartoon from their August 1891 issue *(9.14)*.

The response was very slow and the final table of returns not made public until 1895. The final results are, to put it mildly, quite astonishing. There were many hundreds of cast-iron bridges on the national network, and little had apparently been done since the Inverythan accident. The returns form a snapshot of the state of rail bridges at that time, and it is clear that cast iron was the major material used in their structure, together with timber and lesser amounts of wrought iron. There was relatively little steel, despite approval of the material by the BoT as early as 1878. W.H. Barlow, Colonel Yolland and James Hazledine had recommended it for use in railway bridges owing to its demonstrably greater strength than wrought iron and it was, of course, far superior to cast iron. Cost was presumably the main hurdle to its wider application, although steel rails were commonplace by now.

The returns indicate that plans were being made to replace many of the cast-iron girders with wrought iron or steel, but there will have been much disruption to the network as this work went ahead at an inevitably slow pace. The cost will have been enormous, simply because so many bridges were involved. Most structures had been inspected as requested by the BoT, but detecting defects or hairline cracks was not particularly easy. Inner defects like blowholes will have been invisible, and hairline cracks only seen when the bridge was heavily loaded, so that cracks opened up. X-rays had only just been discovered, and an application to use this inspection method on large structures was many years away. And above all, girders were often buried within structures, and thus difficult to access.

BoT Returns

The Welsh lines appeared on paper to have more wrought-iron under-bridges than cast iron. Thus Cambrian Railways disclosed 301 timber, eighty wrought-iron but only six cast-iron under-bridges. The latter had been renewed, but with cast-iron girders again. One hopes that they were tested to a greater breaking load so as to give the required safety factor of six. The Great Eastern Railway had 373 wrought-iron, 207 timber and 185 flat cast-iron girder bridges on their network. It appeared from the return that many cast-iron structures had been replaced by wrought iron or steel, although the same table shows that thirty-five cast-iron bridges were said to be in a 'good' state, and presumably were left as they were. Nine of these bridges dated from the 1840s. The Great Northern Railway had 164 cast-iron girders, sixty-two timber, 294 wrought-iron and 47 steel bridges. The Great Western Railway had 1,307 wrought-iron, 170 flat cast-iron, 416 timber, but only sixteen steel bridges, although many of the cast-iron and timber bridges were being renewed by wrought iron. The only distinction made in the archive is between arch and flat cast-iron bridges, so the emerging total included both shaped girders with curved flanges and upper surfaces (but flat lower surfaces), as well as plain flat girders.

The Lancashire & Yorkshire Railway, perhaps because of its history, had 245 flat cast-iron girder but 410 wrought-iron and 103 timber viaducts. The London & North Western Railway had 120 cast-iron with the same number of wrought-iron bridges, but only three timber and six steel bridges. The separate Crewe and Holyhead line, on which the Dee bridge was situated, had fifty-five cast-iron bridges with a smaller number of wrought-iron structures (thirty-one), five steel and only one timber under-bridge. Some of the cast-iron bridges still survive, such as that at the old Wolverton station. The main line now bypasses the spot and the bridge survives intact, still spanning a 26ft gap over the Grand Union Canal.

The London & South Western Railway also had a large number of cast-iron bridges, with 234 flat girders being recorded in the BoT return, compared with 293 wrought-iron structures. Some were very old and dated to the construction of its lines in 1837 with spans up to 30ft, about the same as the bridge at Inverythan, and greater than the Norwood Junction bridge. The companies were asked about the condition of every bridge, and in this case some were reported as 'fair' rather than 'good', whatever those terms might mean.

The London, Brighton & South Coast Railway stated it had 135 cast-iron flat girders, fourteen timber and just one wrought-iron bridge, but explained that since 1885, 114 bridges had either been renewed or strengthened. The statement must refer to the earlier accident on the Macduff Railway, when all companies had been circulated about the dangers of cast iron. The line over the Portland road appears in this entry, where it is stated as 'now being reconstructed'. Not surprisingly, the entries are more detailed than for the other companies. It is also interesting to observe that under the heading 'Date of last inspection', the company stated that all its bridges are 'Constantly under supervision', where other companies are content with a single date. Many of its bridges were built in 1849, when the line was first constructed, others from 1861, when it was expanded. By contrast with the preponderance of cast-iron bridges on the Brighton lines, the London, Chatham & Dover Railway Co. had only fifty-eight flat cast-iron girders compared with 146 wrought-iron structures. The entries are also very detailed, however, with girder sections to show specific dimensions of the girders in their bridges. The Staplehurst bridge is not mentioned, so must have been rebuilt in wrought iron after that particular accident, when the cast-iron girders fractured under the weight of Charles Dickens' train.

Northern Railways

Other companies appear to have responded to the earlier circular of 1885. Thus the Manchester, Sheffield & Lincolnshire Railway had only forty-seven cast-iron bridges left on its network, compared with 138 wrought-iron, sixteen timber and one steel bridge. It also said that thirty wrought-iron bridges had been built since 1885. Of the London underground companies, the Metropolitan and District lines also appear from the record to have been busy replacing cast-iron bridges, claiming 200 reconstructed since 1885, with forty-five in the course of rebuilding. They are shown to have 110 flat girder bridges made from cast iron, compared with 938 wrought-iron structures. The Midland Railway Co. gave details of their bridges line by line. They describe 138 flat cast-iron girder bridges and a larger number of wrought-iron structures. The North-Eastern Railway had 298 flat cast-iron bridges in the Southern sector, and 156 in the Northern sector, the largest single total of 454 was for the NE network, again reflecting their historic role in the development of the first railways at Stockton and Darlington. There was a total of 198 wrought-iron bridges, but no steel (surprising, given the growing importance of the industry to the region) and only twelve timber viaducts. Even more surprisingly, their table reveals the existence of two composite cast-iron bridges, one of which at Sherburn and Leamside is described as being made from 'composite trussed girders'.

It was built in 1844, when trussing was in its heyday, in a very long bridge of 55ft span. Why it survived for so long after the Dee bridge tragedy remains unexplained, as well as when it was demolished, or replaced, or even conserved. At least one was reused as the balustrade of a brick arched railway bridge, a rare survivor of a past long gone, at Halifax railway station *(9.15)*. The cast-iron girder is very large, and was originally a three-piece structure. The slot for the wrought-iron truss is visible on the left in *(9.16)*, and why it was kept is a mystery: most will simply have been sold for scrap and melted down. Its size suggests that it was first used somewhere very close by, perhaps in the same position as it is now. It is an intriguing fossil from the first days of the railways.

Work-in-progress

So, the returns to the BoT circular show that there were an enormous number of flat cast-iron under-bridges throughout the network. There were about 1,880 flat cast-iron girder bridges of very variable span. Such a large number of potentially dangerous structures needed continuous inspection and monitoring to prevent further disasters or accidents. The ones in most urgent need of replacing would be those with the greatest span, or those composed of two or more separate castings to achieve that span. The plans for acting fell into two camps: first, to bite the bullet, dismantle and replace, or second strengthen with extra supports under the girders involved. As at the Dee bridge, it could only be a temporary expedient, and the more costly option would inevitably face the railway companies. The replacement programme would take many years, cause great disruption to travellers, and cost a great deal to correct.

But why had it come to this? When the companies were building the first railways, it was one of the cheapest options to simply sling a few girders across a stream, a road or

Opposite: (9.15) Cast-iron balustrade at Halifax station.

Right: (9.16) Close-up showing joint between castings and truss connection.

any other gap in the line. Masonry or brick was expensive and slow. Timber was also very cheap, but rotted within. By contrast, cast iron was cheap, cheaper than wrought iron, and relatively easy to erect in a few simple steps, and was resistant to corrosion. There were several reasons for its cheapness. Molten iron could be poured directly from the furnace into sand moulds, while wrought iron required further processing stages: 'puddling' to reduce the carbon content, and forging to shape the product. Then girders needed to be built up by riveting, and the larger the girder needed, the more labour was required. Cast-iron girders seemed to be the answer to low-cost construction, and even possessed some advantages in terms of longevity, being more resistant to corrosion than wrought iron or timber, for example. Its Achilles heel was its brittleness, its tendency to fail suddenly under load. That in turn was encouraged by casting defects, especially blowholes buried within the solid, and often invisible to the eye. Repeated loads could encourage brittle cracks to grow from such defects, with only one possible outcome: catastrophic failure.

There seemed to be only one way of limiting their presence: testing the cast product. This route was expensive if the casting failed, and the girder would have to be recast (although it could be recycled easily). Telford had pioneered testing components, and so produced much more efficient designs than the Ironbridge. Arch bridges were a much better solution to the problem than flat girders, but did need extra work in designing spandrels to resist the load from the road, and abutments to resist the thrust of the arch.

But there was one big difference now. Steel was available in the quantity needed, and at a reasonable price. The gigantic Forth Rail bridge had clearly demonstrated that the material was wholly capable of meeting the demanding role in highly stressed structures, although the corrosion problem still remained. The solution involved painting with red lead, a solution adopted by many other bridge engineers both here and abroad, such as at the Golden Gate bridge in San Francisco. The Water Street bridge, for example, was replaced in 1904 using steel, and most other cast-iron girder under-bridges suffered the same fate. Girder bridges of smaller span do survive, however, as the Stephenson bridge at Wolverton station demonstrates. It carries no trains at all, after diversion of the main line some years ago.

Railway Overbridges

Many other cast-iron girders, however, survive as railway over-bridges, where the imposed loads are lower, usually from passing road traffic. For example, the East London line, now part of the London underground system, was opened in the 1860s, and Surrey Quays station in 1884. It possesses a cast-iron girder roof to its platforms, so cast-iron girders were still being used until the late Victorian period. The space between the girders is filled by cross girders and jack arches, a technique of great age, going back to its first use in warehouses towards the end of the eighteenth century. It supports the road and street above.

Other over-bridges are widespread across the country, and include many small countryside roads which cross the railways. They are usually restricted by a weight limit, which can be as low as 1 ton, but are often higher. If examined below, many can be seen to be built with jack arches across the lower flanges of cast-iron girders, and others are wrought-iron riveted girders suffering badly from rust. The last tests were performed during the Second World War, and afterwards by the Building Research Station. Their examination was initially prompted in 1944 by the needs of the D-Day convoys transporting heavy equipment like tanks to the offloading points in the South of England, Portsmouth and Southampton.

Modern Problems

The problem of fatigue is still one of the most intractable problems facing modern engineers, especially when combined with other forms of material attack, such as corrosion. A review of fatigue on the railway systems worldwide by R.A. Smith gives an overview of the current problems, and highlights recent tragedies caused as a direct result of metal fatigue. Eschede is one of the worst in terms of the sheer number of deaths and serious injuries, a disaster which occurred on 3 June 1998 to a high-speed Deutsche Bahn Intercity Express (ICE) running north from Munich to Hamburg. Sudden fracture of a single carriage wheel initiated a sequence of events which ended with the deaths of 101 passengers on the train. The wheel had fatigue cracked from within the wheel, itself a new design involving a rubber core in the tread. The rubber was meant to absorb wheel vibrations at high speed, vibrations which were disturbing travellers in the coaches above, and had been developed on low-speed trams. Monobloc wheels were normally used on trains, that is wheels made from a single piece of metal, but the new design was not tested to destruction before being introduced into service. The fatigue crack grew from the edge of the cavity enclosing the rubber damper, so was completely hidden from external view, and thus impossible to detect visually. The affected carriage remained upright until it hit a set of points at high speed and derailed, some of the carriages hitting a motorway over-bridge, which collapsed onto the derailed carriages, increasing the casualty rate yet further.

A less severe rail disaster in terms of casualties occurred at Hatfield on 17 October 2000, when an express train going north hit a badly cracked set of rails, and derailed. Although only four passengers died, the accident had severe repercussions on British railways, as R.A. Smith puts it:

... an examination of the UK network led to the discovery of more than 2,000 sites containing potentially dangerous cracks. Severe speed restrictions were imposed whilst repair and replacement of track took place over a period of many months. In the long history of Britain's railways, no previous accident had caused such widespread public anger, managerial panic, disruption and eventual political crisis.

The privatisation of the rail system between 1996 and 1998 splintered the network into many different companies, who had different commercial priorities and objectives, with safety falling behind punctuality and profit. At least the national system created by nationalisation, initially during the world wars and more formally in the late 1940s, had created a centralised system where safety was of the highest concern. In the Victorian period, the Inspectorate fought many long battles with the Railway Companies over essential safety measures (such as the block system, and brakes), which were only introduced on a piecemeal basis, and hence endangered public safety on conservative parts of the network.

Another problem on railways involves ballast movement, which, where localised at the tips of the stones (promoted by fatigue cracking) allows settlement and puts the rail itself under extra loading. New carriages made from aluminium have suffered fatigue cracks, requiring expensive repairs, and air-tight carriages for high-speed trains also need regular inspection for fatigue cracks from stress concentrations at rivet holes. Infrastructure problems can occur with overhead wires, and other electrical components where thermal fatigue can be worrisome. Rod Smith says that there remain surprising gaps in current knowledge of the dynamic stresses to which modern equipment is subjected in service, a reminder of the long history of dynamic problems on the railways.

Fatigue is a common problem in most branches of engineering: wherever there is an intermittent mechanical load, there is a chance of fatigue. Any material can be at risk, although since metals and alloys are the most commonly used, then they tend to show the greatest number of fatigue failures. It is, for example, found in all moving motor vehicle components, such as axles, crankshafts, pistons, and many other components (such as fuel lines) besides.

Modern Methods of Study

There are now a host of methods available to engineers to study the phenomenon of fatigue cracking, especially in the laboratory, where fracture surfaces can be examined in great detail. Microscopy (sometimes called metallography) enables the features of such cracks to be mapped and analysed. There are often lines on the slow growth crack region, which may represent each load cycle, so simply counting the lines can give an estimate of how many loading cycles occurred relative to the failure. Such striations, or beach marks, are often extremely closely spaced, so very high power microscopes are needed even to see them at all. Electron microscopes are essential for their study. The same method also allows the detection of the different elements present on the fracture surface and distinguishes them from the wavelength of X-rays emitted by electron bombardment. So if fatigue has been enhanced by the presence of certain aggressive chemicals, for instance, they can usually be found somewhere on the surface. So, although the attacking chemical has long since disappeared, its attack can be inferred from the presence of elements peculiar to that chemical. Chlorine, for example, attacks a wide range of materials, even at very low concentrations, so if chlorine is unexpectedly found on a fracture surface for no reason, then it can be deduced that it may have been involved in the cracking.

Test and inspection methods are now highly sophisticated, especially for components in the aerospace industry, where sudden failure of a safety-critical component can be catastrophic. Gas turbine blades, for example, have ruptured and caused airplane disasters, as have other parts of the jet engines. The terrible fire at Manchester Airport in 1985, which caused fifty-five deaths, was caused by explosion of the combustion chamber by growth of a fatigue crack in another problem known as thermal fatigue. Fuselages of modern aircraft are liable to fatigue because they are pressurised when flying at high altitudes, this was the direct cause of the Comet disasters in the 1950s. The aluminum skin of the Comet was too thin, and there were many stress raisers at rivets used to join the sheets of metal together, as well as windows and other ports with sharp corners. In addition to those design defects, brittle cracks had been formed in the sheets by poor fabrication methods, and from which fatigue cracks grew. The several Comets which suddenly disintegrated when climbing under internal cabin pressure, failed at less than 1,000 pressurisation cycles, much lower than their predicted design lives.

The multiplicity of different materials now available to design engineers presents a serious obstacle to reducing fatigue failures, since new materials are often introduced before in-depth fatigue testing. New materials with attractive physical properties may have hidden and unsuspected defects, which could be deadly. Titanium alloys, for example, are used widely in safety-critical jet engines owing to their high strength and low density. It is an expensive and difficult metal to process, however, and sudden fracture of a turbine fan disc in mid-flight created a life-threatening crisis on 29 July 1989 in the USA. Shrapnel from the fractured hub destroyed vital hydraulic lines, and it was only great skill by the pilots that enabled it to crash land at Sioux City, Iowa. The landing destroyed the aircraft however, and 111 passengers died in the resulting inferno, although 194 miraculously survived. The critical fatigue crack was caused by a tiny hard particle left within the metal, which was not picked up by quality control. The investigation traced the critical fragments of the disc, a Herculean task given the area over which they had fallen from the aircraft, and other discs from the same batch were also traced. They also showed signs of fatigue cracking, and happily were found, and removed from service.

Composite plastic materials have very high resistance to fatigue crack growth, which is why, for example, they are used in all helicopter rotor blades. Several crashes were caused by fatigue cracking of the metal blades, leading to the development of composite blades. Such materials have been introduced into the airframes of many commercial airlines, especially the airbuses, not just for their fatigue resistance but also for their very low densities. However, design using composites must resist all possible stresses they will encounter in service. In other applications, composites have failed by fatigue, although the crack mechanism is quite different than in metals. For example, a large 100-ton capacity tank failed suddenly after about two years in service, releasing a wave of near boiling water at the chemical plant where it had recently been installed. The tank had been built of fibreglass, but of a type unfit to be exposed to high temperatures. The walls of the tank were subjected to high stresses at the base when the tank was filled, and it was filled and emptied with increasing frequency towards the latter stages of its short life. The high cyclic loads and thermal cycling led to fatigue cracking at the weakest point in the base, a circular pipe joint designed to drain the hot contents. The thermal cycling led to delamination of the wall, followed by catastrophic rupture. Fortunately there were no workers in the immediate vicinity, so there were no casualties. The tank had been under-designed using the wrong materials, so short-term failure was inevitable.

Plastics and rubbers fail by fatigue in a not dissimilar way to metals, especially if under-designed for their function. A driver suffered severe injuries when her car skidded, and she ran head-on into a lorry on the opposite side of the road. She skidded on a patch of diesel fuel in the road and the police tracked the leak to a faulty fuel pipe on a garage breakdown van. The van driver seemed to be unaware of the problem, which was easily fixed. A plastic fuel return pipe had a transverse break, which the local forensic science service deemed to have been caused by vandalism. Not so. The pipe was well-hidden within the engine compartment, and would have been unaffected by knife damage. Detailed examination using scanning electron microscopy showed that the 'cut' was actually a fracture showing striations indicative of fatigue. It had started when a small leak of sulphuric acid from the battery above had attacked the edge of the nylon pipe, and formed tiny brittle cracks in the edge. One such crack had grown to form a small leak, which then became progressively deeper with vibration loads from the engine, the leak worsening every time the engine was started. The van driver should have noticed the leak, and rectified the problem. The crack finally severed the pipe, and diesel fuel pumped out onto the road surface, where it caused the car following to crash uncontrollably.

Plastic tanks have also failed suddenly, and without prior warning, leading to severe damage to surrounding equipment, if no casualties. A 30-ton polypropylene tank failed in such a way in a factory near Warrington, releasing a large quantity of concentrated caustic soda. The tank had been designed wrongly, with a thin wall near the base. It failed after just four complete fills of the chemical, by fatigue from a small defect in the thin wall, the crack surface showing the four beach marks before failure. It is a good example of very low cycle fatigue, showing why under-design for the expected loads is so dangerous.

Endword

Modern analysis of product failure, often now known as forensic engineering, owes a great debt to pioneers like William Fairbairn, but especially the many individual railway inspectors, who became highly professional in their task of investigating railway accidents, and other problems, such as the last cholera outbreak in Britain. They approached their task in a neutral, disinterested way, so as to arrive at the precise cause or causes of accidents, not always succeeding, but usually giving the correct advice in how to eliminate or minimise a particular problem. The fact that their reports were published and available in the public domain put pressure on the railway companies to clean up their act and give a safer service to the travelling public. Although the companies did not always act on their advice, the fault for this cannot be laid at their door, but rather on timid politicians, afraid to legislate on important issues such as the time-interval system of controlling trains, or the lack of efficient braking systems.

One of their first crises was at the fall of the Dee bridge, mainly because General Pasley, one of the first railway inspectors, had approved its public use. However, Captain Simmons's investigation was thorough and wide-ranging. It showed that the bridge had been under-designed for the loads it was intended to carry. The very principle at the heart of trussed cast-iron girder bridges was faulty, because the wrought-iron trusses deformed when the girder deformed, so could not reinforce the structure. However, the wrought iron was much tougher than the cast iron, so probably delayed the fall of the girder enough to allow the locomotive and tender to reach the bank. However, the carriages fell back into the river, and the fireman was killed when he was thrown out of the tender. In all, five people died in the accident. Most similar bridges were reinforced immediately prior to demolition and replacement.

Robert Stephenson denied that the principle of the trussed bridge was faulty, both in the original inquest and afterwards at the Royal Commission on the use of Iron in Railway Structures. Willam Fairbairn had warned him of the danger in the design of the bridge over the Dee in a lecture at the Civil Engineers, but was ignored. He also offered a design in riveted wrought-iron sheet, but was rebuffed, despite Fairbairn's pioneering work on the Conwy and Britannia bridge prototypes. He strengthened the Dee bridge not by demolition and rebuilding in wrought iron, but rather by imposing yet more cast-iron girders on top of the existing ones. Yet more girders broke, and he still did not get the message, despite the great success and integrity of the new wrought-iron tubular bridges further up the new line to Holyhead. Much later, he admitted that the whole concept was flawed, accepting the consensus of his fellow engineers (which had been expressed by his closest friends, even as early as the Chester inquest).

So ended the saga of the trussed girder bridge. But problems remained in the larger number of simple cast-iron girders. They had been installed on much of the new system in the 1830s and 1840s without much thought, or careful design, and some would fail unexpectedly a few years later, such as at Wootton and Bull bridges. Internal defects stimulated fatigue cracks, which became critical. Boiler explosions had been among the earliest kinds of failure of high-pressure steam engines, sometimes from faulty or deliberately manipulated safety valves, but more commonly, from corrosion within. Fatigue cracks could easily be initiated at corrosion pits, especially near lap joints, where there was an existing stress raiser. Heavily loaded moving parts were also increasingly at risk from fatigue, especially axles and wheels, as the Newark and Oxford disasters showed. The inspectorate investigated all the major accidents involving loss of life or injury, as well as many smaller incidents, such as near misses, simply because they could expose a new problem before major accidents occurred; their recommendations could thus prevent future tragedies, rather than always having to report yet further disasters. They also introduced ideas which are commonplace today, such as the concept of traceability, so that faulty products could be traced back to their origin, and if generic, others from the same source detected and eliminated.

Fatigue is a real and present danger in many vehicles and products which are loaded. Advances in understanding the problem have eliminated many possible sources, but others remain, especially in new and often untested materials or design. Constant vigilance, intensive testing before introduction into service, and rigorous and searching inspection for hairline cracks can catch the vast majority, although there will always be something totally unexpected that will take the user unaware.

Early Industrial Chronology

Revolutionary War with American colonies starts	**1775**
Ironbridge erected in Coalbrookdale	1779
Ironbridge opened	1781
Storming of the Bastille	**1789**
Floods on Severn and tributaries	1795
Buildwas bridge erected by Telford	1795
Pontcysyllte aqueduct started	1795
Longdon-on-Tern cast-iron trough aqueduct finished	1796
Sunderland bridge opened	August 1796
Chirk aqueduct opened	1801
Pen-y-Darren locomotive tested in Merthyr Tydfil	1803
Pontcycsyllte aqueduct opened	1805
Felling mine disaster	1812
Blenkinsop locomotive	1812
Battle of Waterloo	**18 June 1815**
Coalport bridge reconstructed in cast iron	1818
Peterloo massacre in Manchester	**16 August 1819**
Stockton & Darlington Railway opened	1826
Rainhill trials	1829
Liverpool & Manchester Railway opened	1830
First Reform Act passed	**1832**
London & Birmingham Railway partly opened	1835

Dee Bridge Chronology

Dee bridge completed by Stephenson	September 1846
Inspection and approval by Maj.-Gen. Pasley	4 October 1846
Dee bridge opened for traffic	4 November 1846
Painting of bridge	April–May 1847
Six trains pass over bridge safely	morning of 24 May 1847
Stephenson orders ballast laid on timer baulks	afternoon of 24 May 1847
Local train crashes through final girder	**around 6.15 p.m. 24 May 1847**
Captain Simmons inspects fallen bridge	27 May 1847
Simmons examines broken parts and conducts tests	28 May 1847
Stephenson writes to Directors of Chester & Holyhead Railway suggesting that train derailed and caused crash	31 May 1847
Inquest at Chester Town Hall opens	4 June 1847
Publication of Simmons and Walker investigation	15 June 1847
Jury gives final verdict	**18 June 1847**
Commissioners of Railways minute to HMG requesting Royal Commission	29 June 1847
Royal Commission on Iron in Railway appointed	August 1847
Conwy bridge opened	April 1848
Royal Commission on Iron in Railway reports	26 July 1849
Britannia bridge opened	1850
Great Exhibition at Crystal Palace, Hyde Park	1851
Crumlin viaduct opened	1856

Later Chronology

Wootton bridge (Warwickshire) collapses under freight train	12 June 1860
Bull bridge, Ambergate, failure	26 September 1860
Hartley colliery (Northumberland) disaster	16 January 1862
Stretton viaduct accident	13 August 1862
Staplehurst (Kent) rail accident	**9 June 1865**
Newark rail accident	21 June 1870
Shipton-on-Cherwell (Oxford) rail disaster	24 December 1874
Tay bridge disaster	**28 December 1879**
Montrose bridge inspected, demolished	1880
Solway bridge destroyed by ice floes	28 January 1881
Inverythan disaster	27 November 1882
BoT circular on cast-iron bridges	1883
Norwood Junction rail accident	1 May 1891
BoT circular on cast-iron bridges	1892

Bibliography

As in all subjects, the internet has revolutionised our sources of information. The resource is still developing very rapidly, and it has been of immense value in preparing this book. There are many key sources, especially:

http://en.wikipedia.org for a general resource for railways, accidents, disasters and personalities.
http://www.railwaysarchive.co.uk for a excellent source of UK railway accident reports, and Acts of Parliament.
http://structurae.de for a worldwide listing of bridges.
http://bridgemeister.com for a suspension bridge listing, mainly, but not exclusively US.
http://parlipapers.chadwyck.co.uk for a British parliamentary reports, including railway accidents, accessible through libraries.
http://www.hdowns.co.uk for detailed discussion of a half scale reconstruction of Ironbridge.
http://www.dcnr.state.pa.us for the report of the Kinzua viaduct failure.

Many out-of-copyright books are available online through many websites, especially:

http://www.gutenberg.org: for free downloadable texts of *The Signal-man* and *Mugby Junction*. The site is supported by Carnegie-Mellon University in Pittsburgh, and is based in Illinois, USA.
http://www.history.rochester.edu/: for their online version of the autobiography of Sir Henry Bessemer.

A dramatic new entrant to the field in November 2006 is http://www.google.co.uk/books, a search engine which gives access to references to specific topics in many old engineering journals, such as *The Civil Engineers and Architects Journal*, which provided the issue dealing with the Dee bridge disaster in the July 1847 issue (free to download). Other early works available for free download include many of Thomas Tredgold's and several of William Fairbairn's books, being US editions of their works. Specialist reports are also provided, including Robert Stephenson's report on the Atmospheric Railway for the C&HR, and James Walker's report comparing fixed engines and locomotives for the L&MR. No doubt many more early engineering texts will follow. It follows the success of their earlier search facility which accesses academic journals, at http://scholar.google.com/.

There are also many smaller and specialist websites which focus on particular aspects of failure mechanisms, including http://materials.open.ac.uk/mem/index.html, which provides case studies of failed products, some involving fatigue. Copies of papers on the Tay and Dee bridge disasters are available here for free download. Other specialist websites include http://www.warwickshir-erailways.com, which kindly supplied tiff files of the Wooton bridge collapse. A local website gives details of the Sankey viaduct incident, including a full extract from the *Mechanics Magazine*, at http://www.n-le-w.co.uk/.

Most of the information on the Dee disaster is buried in official reports, but is commonly mentioned by many secondary sources. The following is a selection of the most important sources I have used in writing this book, including the early history of cast iron, and later events:

Andrew, J.; Stein, J.; Tann, J.; and Macleod, C., *The transition from timber to cast iron working beams for steam engines*, Trans Newcomen Soc., 70, 197-220 (1989)

Anon, 'The late railway accident at Chester', *Illustrated London News*, 12 June, 380 (1847)

Anon, 'The Norwood Junction Accident of 1891', *The Railway Magazine*, (March 1936)

Acworth, W.M., *The Railways of England*, 5th ed., John Murray, London (1900) (Ian Allen reprint of 1964)

Baker, B., *Long Span Railway Bridges*, 2nd ed. (1873)

Baughan, P.E., *The Chester & Holyhead Railway, Volume 1: The Main Line up to 1880*, David & Charles (1972)

Beaumont, R., *The Railway King: a biography of George Hudson*, Headline Books (2003)

Berridge, P.S.A., *The Girder Bridge after Brunel and others*, Robert Maxwell Publisher (1969)

Braithwaite, F., *On the Fatigue and consequent Fracture of Metals*, Proc Inst of Civil Eng, XIII, 463-475 (1854)

Booth, H., *An Account of the Liverpool and Manchester Railway*, Frank Cass Reprints (1969)

Bourne, J.C. and Britton, J., *Bourne's London and Birmingham Railway*, David & Charles reprints (1970)

Chaloner, C.H., *Vulcan: The History of 100 Years of Engineering and Insurance*, Vulcan Boiler and General Insurance Co. Ltd (1959)

Chettoe, C.S.; Davey, N.; and Mitchell, *The Strength of Cast-Iron Girder Bridges*, Proc Inst Civil Engnrs, **22**, 243-292 (1944)

Chrimes, M.; and Thomas, R., *Iron Railway Bridges*, in *Robert Stephenson: The Eminent Engineer* (ed. Bailey, M.), Abingdon Ashgate (2003)

Conder, F.R., *The Men who built Railways*, Thomas Telford Ltd, London (1983)

Conner, J.E., *Stepney's Own Railway: a History of the London and Blackwall System*, Conner (1984)

Cossons, N.; and Trinder, B., *The Iron Bridge: symbol of the Industrial Revolution*, Philimore & Co Ltd (2002)

Cragg, Roger (ed.), *Civil Engineering Heritage: Wales and West Central England*, 2nd ed., Inst Civil Engineers (1997)

Day, T., *The Failure of Inverythan Bridge, 1882*, J. Railway and Canal Historical Society, 33 (107), 404-415 (2000)

De Haan, D., *The Rolt Memorial Lecture 2003: The Iron Bridge – New Research in the Ironbridge Gorge*, Industrial Archaeology Review **XXVI**, 1-18 (2004)

Den Hartog, J.P., *Mechanical Vibrations*, Dover Publications, New York (1985)

Drysdale Dempsey, G. *Tubular Bridges*, Kingsmead Reprints (1970)

Duckham, Helen; and Baron, *Great Pit Disasters: Great Britain 1700 to the present day*, David & Charles (1973)

Dunn, J.M., *The Chester and Holyhead Railway*, Oakwood Press (1948)

Fairbairn, W. and Bellhouse, *Report on the cause of the falling of Messrs Radcliffe's Mill at Oldham*, Thomas Baines, Liverpool (1846)

Fairbairn, W., *On some defects in the principle and construction of Fireproof Buildings,* Proc Inst Civ Engs, vii, 213ff. (1847)

Fairbairn, W., *An Account of the Construction of the Britannia and Conway tubular bridges*, Longman (1849)

Fairbairn, W., *On Tubular Girder Bridges*, Proc Inst Civ Engrs, ix, 233 ff (1850). Free download available at Google Books.

Fairbairn, W., *An experimental enquiry into the strength of wrought iron plates and their riveted joints*, Phil Trans Roy Soc, **140**, 677 (1850)

Fairbairn, W., *On the Application of Cast and Wrought Iron for Building Purposes*, New York, John Wiley (1854)

Fairbairn, W., *Useful Information for Engineers*, Longmans, London (1856). Free download of 1860 edition available at Google Books.

Fairbairn, W., *On the Resistance of tubes to collapse*, Phil Trans Roy Soc, **150**, 389-413 (1858)

Fairbairn, W., *VIII Experiments to determine the effect of Impact, Vibratory Action, and long-continued Changes of Load on Wrought-Iron Girders*, Phil Trans Roy Soc, **154**, 311-325 (1864)

Fairbairn, W., *The Life of Sir William Fairbairn* (ed. W. Pole) David & Charles reprint (1877, 1970)

Faulkner, A.H., *The Grand Junction Canal*, David & Charles (1972)

Fernyhough, F., *Liverpool & Manchester Railway 1830-1980*, Book Club Associates (1980)

Fitzgerald, R.S., *Liverpool Road Station, Manchester, An historical and architectural survey*, RCHM/Manchester Council (1980)

Garfield, S., *The Last journey of William Huskisson*, Faber and Faber (2002)

Hall, S., *Railway Detectives: 150 years of the Railway Inspectorate*, Ian Allen (1990)

Halliday, S., *The Great Stink of London: Sir Joseph Bazalgette and the Cleansing of the Victorian Metropolis*, Sutton Publishing (1999)

Head, F.B., *Stokers and Pokers, or The London and North-Western Railway, The Electric Telegraph and The Railway Clearing House*, David & Charles reprints (1968)

Hewison, C.H., *Locomotive Boiler Explosions*, David & Charles (1983)

Hills, R.L., *Power from Steam: a history of the stationary steam engine*, Cambridge UP (1993)

Hobsbawm, E.J. and Rude, G., *Captain Swing*, Pimlico (1993)

Humber, W., *A Practical Treatise of cast and Wrought Iron Bridges and Girders*, Alburgh Archival Facsimiles (1987), first published by Spon (1857)

Kirkaldy, W.G., *Results of tests made by Mr Kirkaldy on portions of the Tay bridge*, Parliamentary Papers, **XXIX**, 704-709 (1880)

Labrum, E.A., *Civil Engineering Heritage, Eastern and Central England*, Thomas Telford (1994)

Levy, M. and Salvador, M., *Why Buildings fall down: How structures fail*, W.W. Norton & Co. (1987)

Lewin, H.G., *Early British Railways, 1801-1844*, Locomotive Publishing Co. Ltd (1925)

Lewin, H.G., *The Railway Mania and its Aftermath*, 1845-1852, David & Charles reprints (1968)

Lewis, P.R., *Premature Fracture of a composite Nylon Radiator*, Engineering Failure Analysis, **6**, 181-195 (1999)

Lewis, P.R. and Weidmann, G.W., *Catastrophic Failure of a Polypropylene Tank Part I Primary Investigation*, Eng Fail Analysis, **6**, 197-214 (1999)

Lewis, P.R. and Reynolds, K., *Forensic Engineering: a Reappraisal of the Tay Bridge Disaster*, 1879, Interdisciplinary Science Reviews, 27(4), 287-298 (2002)

Lewis, Peter R., *Beautiful Railway Bridge of Silvery Tay: reinvestigating the Tay Bridge Disaster 1879*, Tempus (2004)

Lewis, Peter Rhys; Reynolds, Ken; and Gagg, Colin, *Forensic Materials Engineering*: Case Studies, CRC Press (2004)

Lewis, P.R.; and Gagg, C., *Aesthetics vs Function: the fall of the Dee Bridge, 1847*, Interdisciplinary Science Reviews, 29(2), 177-191 (2004)

Lewis, P.R. and Hansworth, S.V., *Stress Corrosion Cracking of a Nylon Fuel Pipe*, Eng Fail Analysis, **6**, 197-214 (2005)

Gloag, J. and Bridgwater, D., *A History of Cast Iron in Architecture*, George Allen and Unwin Ltd (1948)

Macdonald, P., *Hotheads and Heroes: the Bristol Riots of 1831*, Petmac Publications (1995)

McCutcheon, J., *The Hartley Colliery Disaster*, 1862, E. McCutcheon, Durham (1963)

McEvily, A.J., *Metal Failures: Mechanism, Analysis, Prevention*, John Wiley (2002)

McGowan, C., *The Rainhill Trials*, Little, Brown (2004)

Mechanics Magazine No.373 – Saturday 2 October (1830)

Mitchell, G.R., *Dynamic Stresses in Cast Iron Girder Bridges*, National Building Studies Research Papers No.17, HMSO (1954)

Morton, G.R.; and Moseley, A.F., *An Examination of Fractures in the First Iron Bridge at Coalbrookdale*, Journal of West Midlands Studies, **2** (1970)

Nock, O.S., *The Railways of Britain, Past and Present*, Batsford (1949)

Nock, O.S., *Historic Railway Disasters*, 2nd ed., Ian Allen (1969)

Nock, O.S., *The South Eastern and Chatham Railway*, Ian Allen (1971)

Parris, H., *Government and the Railways in Nineteenth Century Britain*, Routledge & Kegan Paul (1965)

Pearce, E., *Reform! The fight for the 1832 Reform Act*, Pimlico (2004)

Petroski, H., *To Engineer is Human: the Role of Failure in Successful Design*, St Martins Press (1982)

Petroski, H., *Design Paradigms: Case Histories of Error and Judgment in Engineering*, CUP (1994)

Pilkey, W.D., *Peterson's Stress Concentration Factors*, 2nd ed., Wiley (1997)

Raistrick, A., *Dynasty of Iron Founders: The Darbys and Coalbrookdale*, Sessions/Ironbridge Gorge Trust (1989)

Rankin, W.J.M., *On the causes of the unexpected breakage of the journals of railway axles*, Proc Inst Civil Engnrs, **ii**, 105-8 (1842)

Ransome, E. (ed.), *The Terrific Kemble: a Victorian self-portrait from the writings of Fanny Kemble*, Hamish Hamilton (1978)

Rennison, R.W. (ed.), *Civil Engineering Heritage: Northern England*, 2nd ed., Inst Civil Engineers (1996)

Rennison, R.W., *The Influence of William Fairbairn on Robert Stephenson's Designs: four bridges in north-east England*, Industrial Archaeology Review, **XX**, 37-48 (1998)

Rolt, L.T.C., *George and Robert Stephenson: The Railway Revolution*, Penguin Books (1984)

Rolt, L.T.C., *Red for Danger, the Classic History of British Railway Disasters,* Sutton Publishing (1998)

Rolt, L.T.C., *Thomas Telford*, Penguin Books (1985)

Rolt, L.T.C., *Victorian Engineering: A fascinating story of Invention and Achievement*, Penguin Books (1988)

Sibley, P., *The Prediction of Structural Failure*, PhD thesis, University of London (1977)

Sibley, P.; and Walker, A.C., *Structural Accidents and their Causes*, Proc Inst Civil Engineers, 62, 191-208 (1977)

Simmons, J.; and Biddle, G., *The Oxford Companion to British Railway History*, Oxford University Press (1999)

Simmons, J.L.A.; and Walker, J., *Report to the Commissioner of Railways on the falling of the bridge at the river Dee of May 24ᵗʰ, 1847*, Parliamentary Papers, **LXIII** (1847), Appendix.

Smiles, S., *The Lives of George and Robert Stephenson*, Folio Society (1975)

Smith, D., *Structural Model Testing of Railway Bridges in the Nineteenth Century*, Trans Newcomen Soc., March (1977)

Smith, R.A., *The Versailles railway accident of 1842 and the first research into metal fatigue*, Fatigue 90 (Conference Proceedings), IV, 2033-2041

Smith, R.A., *Railway fatigue failures: an overview of a long standing problem*, Mat-wiss. u. Werkstoffen, **36** (11), 697-705 (2005)

Tilly, G. (Gifford and Partners), *Conservation of Bridges*, Spon Press (2002)

Trevelyan, G.M., *Lord Grey of the Reform Bill*, Longmans (1920)

Turner-Thomas, R.J., *Pontcysyllte Aqueduct Restoration: Winter 2003-Spring 2004,* Pensoft (2005)

Walker, Peter (ed.); Lewis, P.R.; Reynolds, K.; Braithwaite, N.; and Weidmann, G.W., *Chambers Dictionary of Materials Technology*, Chambers-Harrap, Edinburgh (1994)

Warren, J.G.H., *A Century of Locomotive Building by Robert Stephenson & Co*, Andrew Reid & Co. (1923)

Wermiel, S., *The Fireproof Building*, John Hopkins University Press, Baltimore (2000)

Winship, I.R., *The Decline in Locomotive Boiler Explosions in Britain 1850-1900*, Trans Newcomen Soc., Feb (1989)

Wrottesley, J.; Willis, R.; James, H.; Renne, G.; Cubitt; and Hodkinson, E., *Report of the Commissioners appointed to inquire into the application of iron to railway structures*, Parliamentary Papers, **LXV** (1849)

Woodham-Smith, C., *The Great Hunger, Ireland 1845-1849*, Penguin Books (1991)

Index

If you are interested in purchasing other books published by Tempus,
or in case you have difficulty finding any Tempus books in your local bookshop,
you can also place orders directly through our website

www.tempus-publishing.com